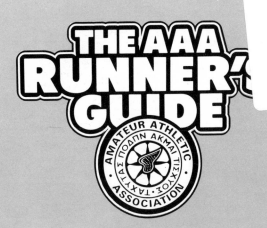

THE AAA RUNNER'S GUIDE

Foreword by
Steve Ovett M.B.E.

COLLINS

Picture credits
All-Sport Photographic: cover and pages 81, 103
Anne Brown: page 153
Jack Fitzgerald: page 77
Ian Fox: pages 34, 35, 36, 37, 38, 39, 40, 41, 42
Popperfoto: page 4
Al Rockall: page 79
Running Magazine: pages 11, 15
Mark Shearman: pages 2, 4, 13, 17, 31, 47, 49, 50, 54,
57, 59, 60, 64, 65, 73, 75, 82, 84, 101, 111, 127, 139, 164,
176, 179, 182
Joyce Smith: page 126

First published in 1983
by William Collins Sons & Co Ltd
London · Glasgow · Sydney
Auckland · Johannesburg

© Sackville Design Group Ltd 1983

Designed and produced by Sackville Design Group Ltd
32-34 Great Titchfield Street, London W1P 7AD
from an idea by Al Rockall

Editor: Heather Thomas
Art director: Al Rockall
Illustrators: Lyn Brooks, Phil Evans, Roy Woodard
Typeset in Times roman by Sackville Design Group Ltd

ISBN 0 00 411753 0

Printed in Italy by Arti Grafiche Vincenzo Bona, in
association with Keats Printing Ltd

How do I start?

How far do I have to train to be good?

What should I eat?

When should I train?

There seems to be only one thing greater than ambition in sport, and that is ignorance. The spectacular growth of athletics as a sport and, in particular, running over the last decade has produced a massive running populace who have very little positive information available, which is either easily understood or relevant to the specific problems we may all encounter as we progress or just jog along.

Running is simplicity itself, or so it seems until something goes wrong ... that little niggling pain at the back of your leg ... stomach cramps ... over-tiredness. These are all physical problems that you may well experience and wonder first, "why?" and then, "what do I do?"

Physical problems either clear up and eventually disappear or sometimes they just refuse to go. It's a black and white question with a black and white answer. But what about the grey areas of uncertainty? For example, how do I increase my training without causing problems? How do I peak for an important race? Should I vary the terrain and speeds of my training runs at my age?

Well, I think that you can see that there are a fair number of minor and major obstacles in every runner's path which can either be tackled sensibly with a little information or crashed into with blissful ignorance.

This book will not be the answer to all the questions in our sport — but it may answer some of yours and, looking at the contributors and contents, it may answer a few of mine as well.

However, the hallmark of any good book is when it can be picked up and enjoyed and referred to long after its initial reading. I hope that this book falls into that category and that it will be as useful in years to come as it is now.

Best of luck.

Steve Ovett.

Roger Bannister

Ian Thompson

Seb Coe

Brendan Foster

Some of the landmarks in modern athletics were produced by these outstanding athletes. Roger Bannister cleared the way with his record-breaking four-minute mile in 1954. Since then Ian Thompson has set a UK record of 2:09:12 for the marathon; Brendan Foster has excelled at 10,000 and 5,000m; and Seb Coe has delighted spectators with his record-shattering performances at 800m, and one mile.

Contents

CHAPTER ONE

The history of the AAA

by Mike Farrell

Athletics as we know it today has been in existence for a little over 100 years, but in fact the sport can trace its origins back for nearly a thousand years in this country.

Young Londoners were leaping, throwing and running during the reign of Edward II, and apparently Edward III became so worried about the falling attendances at archery practice, due to the new passion for hammer throwing, that he actually passed a statute forbidding it. Even so, Henry VIII enjoyed throwing the hammer at 'revels' a few hundred years later. Athletics continued through the centuries at country fairs and church festivals, although the Puritans put a stop to the latter during Cromwell's time. The events remained fairly constant, with trials of strength such as putting the stone, tossing the axle (of a cart) and throwing the sledge (hammer), leaping (the forms varied) and running.

By the sixteenth century, opinion was divided as to whether these rustic sports were 'genteel' or not, but the common people, quite untroubled by such considerations, continued their sport with unabated enthusiasm. One manuscript records that a football match at Chester around 1600 was cancelled because of rowdyism, and a foot race was run instead. Little has been written about the early beginnings of athletics as a sport, probably because it was largely the preserve of the common people who did not feature often in written records. However, history does give some detail about the Cotswold games. A Captain Robert Dover, attorney of Barton on the Heath, was for 45 years director of these pastimes, for which he had obtained permission from James I. These 'rustic sports', as they came to be called, continued well into the nineteenth century, when they more or less died out with the decline of the country fairs as more people moved into the towns.

Alongside these 'holiday' athletics, a class of professional pedestrians was developing, first of all from the footmen employed by the nobility to travel with their carriages in order to run ahead to deliver messages and make sure that the accommodation was ready at the next inn. Sporting gentlemen attached great importance to the fleetness of their footmen, often wagering large sums of money on contests between their own and rival runners. As the sport became increasingly popular with masters and servants alike, a class of professional athletes· began to emerge. They were drawn from all walks of life but all made their living, and often a very good one, by running or walking — sometimes over very long distances. For instance, one Foster Powell (a lawyer's clerk) ran from London to York in under six days, and he was in his fifties when he did it. He even broke his own record two years later at the age of 59 with a time of 5 days 15 hours. Sadly he died soon after and lies buried in a corner of St Paul's Churchyard.

Training methods and diet were typical of their age, but now seem bizarre to say the very least. Recommended foods included beef, mutton, stale bread, strong beer and Glauber salts. Foods we would regard as healthy, especially fish, vegetables, cheese and eggs, were forbidden. The exercise consisted of constant morning walking and sweating: 'The patient should be purged with constant medicines, sweated by walking under a load of clothes and by lying between feather-beds'. A later training manual recommended some even stranger treatment called simply 'rubbing'. Basically it was a massage but with some odd variations, such as 'the rubber fills his mouth with water from a glass, blows it in a fine rain over a portion of the victim, and then proceeds to polish that portion, first with a towel and then with his hand'.

Footracing continued to attract large crowds until about 1825, and then interest waned for about 25 years, although the sport by no means died out. The 1850s saw some very important and far-reaching developments, the first of which was a 'College foot grind' organised by some undergraduates of Exeter College, Oxford, in the winter of 1850. They had apparently become tired of hacking cross-country on horseback and felt that it would be more fun on foot. The meeting was a success and the idea spread rapidly to other colleges in Oxford and Cambridge and also to the schools, thus developing a closer-knit and somewhat more organised amateur athletic fraternity. The professionals meanwhile continued to thrive — *Bells Sporting Life* carried notices of as many as 50 athletic meetings in a week for the professional 'peds'. During this period, many amateurs were matching themselves against the professionals, but as yet the impetus was still lacking to form a true athletic club and a governing body for the fast developing new sport.

The first 'amateurs only' meeting was a handicap cup which took place on 26th July 1862 at Hackney Wick, but it was not considered a success as it did not attract sufficient betting. However, the London amateurs made a further effort the next year to form themselves into a club, which became known as the Mincing Lane Athletic Club (soon to be renamed the London Athletic Club). At the beginning of 1866, a rival club was formed by ex-university and London athletes calling itself the 'Amateur Athletic Club', which held the first ever championships in the spring of the same year (1866) before the University Boat Race. For fourteen years, the two clubs vied for position as to who was to run athletics in England. Strangely enough, the Amateur Athletic Club had a hand in other sports as well. One of their founder members wrote the rules of boxing competition when the Marquis of Queensberry donated a set of Challenge cups for the first ever amateur boxing tournament, and the Queensberry Rules are with us today, in more or less their original form.

Athletics was developing rapidly and so were the

divisions and problems. In the north, where most of the participants were artisans, mechanics and labourers, they were accepted as amateurs in their own meetings, but at Lillie Bridge, the home of the A.A.C. Spring Championships, they were not accorded amateur status. A further problem arose as to the timing of the championships. For a few years after 1866 when the first championships were held, most of the top runners came from either the universities of Oxford or Cambridge or were gentlemen of private means who could afford to spend time training during the winter months. However, the London clerks and business men who made up the London Athletic Club, together with their northern colleagues, had to train after work, and therefore in the dark during winter if they wished to be in form for the Spring Championships held by the Amateur Athletic Club.

This argument, not only about the date of the Championships, but also which body should run athletics in England, continued to rage, the elitist A.A.C. hoping that they would become the MCC of athletics, but this was not to be. In 1879, the Waddell brothers, now the managers of the London Athletic Club, decided to boycott the Spring Championships and hold their own summer championships at their Stamford Bridge ground. In the same year, the Northern Counties had formed their own association, maintaining that a championship should be open to all, regardless of social class, provided that the competitors had not run for money. The L.A.C. summer championships were not a success, and the following year notices appeared again advertising the Spring Championships. However, London runners were urged not to attend. Fortunately reason at last began to prevail and three young men from the Oxford University Athletic Club, Clement Jackson, Bernhard Wise and Montague Shearman, managed to convene a meeting on 24th April 1880 at the Randolph Hotel, Oxford, with delegates representing the nine clubs from the Midland

Association, 16 clubs from the Northern Association and fifteen others. On this momentous day was born the Amateur Athletic Association, its three main aims being:

(1) to improve the management of athletic meetings and to promote uniformity of rules for the guidance of local committees.

(2) to deal repressively with any abuses of athletic sports.

(3) to hold an annual championship meeting.

However, life for the new association was far from easy: there were arguments with the Cyclists Association over which sports body should organise meetings at which both cycling and athletic events were featured. There were also difficulties in defining amateur status and problems of dealing with the numerous abuses of the system, particularly with regard to handicapping. Nonetheless, the AAA survived and continued to be an influence for order and good sense. It gained the confidence of the clubs and provided a set of rules of competition, 16 in all (there are now well over 100 rules), which were enforced at athletic meetings throughout the country. In 1908, the AAA staged the fourth Olympic Games of the modern era, in the new stadium at White City, London. At this event, the rather odd distance for the modern marathon was set, being the distance from Windsor Castle, where it was started by Queen

Alexandra, to the finishing line in front of the Royal Box at the stadium, 26 miles 385 yards away (the distance used previously was 40 kilometres). The athletic events in the 1908 Olympics were basically the events we have today, although the techniques in some of the jumping events were somewhat different.

The International Amateur Athletic Federation was formed in 1912 and the AAA joined this organisation in 1914 to represent the whole of Britain in the international field. During these years, athletics grew increasingly popular at a participant level, possibly more so than they are today. In 1922, attempts were made to include women in the AAA, but after two years of wrangling and indecision with more than a touch of male chauvinism, the women decided to form their own association, which is still with us today.

The late 1920s saw a rise to even greater popularity of the Olympic movement, and athletics generally became much more organised throughout the world. At this time, the AAA were still representing Scotland internationally, but the Scots, taking exception to this, attempted to join the IAAF separately. Unfortunately, their application was refused on the grounds that they were not a political entity. As a compromise, the British Amateur Athletic Board was formed in 1932 to represent the four home countries, England, Northern Ireland, Wales and Scotland, at international level. It was basically a sub-committee of the AAA.

The sport was now developing steadily, with many new clubs being formed all over the world. Indoor athletics were started and the first AAA Indoor Championships were held at the Empire Pool, Wembley, in 1935. Coaching was also developing along more scientific lines.

World War II put a stop to the championships and most other athletic competition for the next few years, although H.M.Services continued to hold various regimental sporting events. After the war,

Britain was asked to stage the 1948 Olympic Games, giving the AAA just 18 months to organise this international event. In spite of rationing, quotas and a bomb-damaged city, the seemingly impossible task was achieved, and the first post-war Olympics were opened at Wembley Stadium. Although the event was an outstanding organisational feat, there was disappointment that Britain won no gold metals. Sadly, since that time no major international championships have been held in this country.

And so on to the golden years of the 1950s, with Bannister's record-breaking four-minute mile, and the world records of Christopher Chattaway, Derek Ibbotson and Gordon Pirie. Not only were there record performances, but record crowds came to the White City to watch them as athletics grew in popularity again. However, this euphoria was short-lived and, by and large, athletics were in the doldrums during the 1960s, with only Dave Bedford and his new 10,000m world record, and David Hemery with his Olympic gold in the 400 metres hurdles, enlivening an otherwise dismal scene. But the pendulum soon began to swing up again, and with the advent of Brendan Foster and Alan Pascoe, the crowds began to return to watch their heroes.

Now, one hundred years after it all started, the AAA are fortunate to have a galaxy of ascending stars in Steve Ovett, Steve Cram, Sebastian Coe, Keith Connor and Dave Moorcroft, to name but a few. The explosion of popular marathon running in the last few years has probably involved more people in distance running than at any other time in history. This is all the more interesting since it has sprung not from the athletic clubs, but more or less spontaneously from the man in the street who has discovered the joys of putting one foot in front of the other, first of all as a means to health and later for the sheer pleasure of running. What of the future? Success brings its own problems, none of which are insoluble given men of goodwill and good sense, and the AAA intends to stay the course.

Running gear in 1910 bore little resemblance to that of today. These young men are waiting on the starting line ready to race around the streets of Falmouth, a small Cornish seaside town.

CHAPTER TWO

Getting started

by Al Rockall

A running revolution has been sweeping across Britain in the last few years and, far from being a fashionable craze or a passing phenomenon, running is growing as one of this country's most popular sports and is here to stay. The ever-growing popularity of running is borne out by the response of runners to the 1982 Gillette London Marathon, which had a field of 18,000 starters and had to turn away another 60,000 hopefuls. Wherever you go, in city streets and parks, on country roads and fields, on riverbanks or along the beach, you will see people of all ages running.

Why do they run? Well, there are many reasons: to lose weight; to stay physically fit; to keep youthful; to reduce the risk of developing heart disease; or simply because they enjoy it. For running is the ideal form of exercise: it's cheap — your only expense is kitting yourself out with a good pair of running shoes and a tracksuit; it's easy to master as you get fitter and train more frequently, as you need no special athletic ability; and it can be done anywhere at any time. You do not have to book a squash court, wait for your local swimming pool to open or find a partner to play tennis. You can run in any weather in any place at any time of day that suits you. You just get changed into your running gear, perform a few stretching exercises to stretch out tight muscles and then set out along the road into the local park or across fields and country tracks, wherever your fancy takes you. You can run all the year round and there is no better way to explore your neighbourhood or see the countryside.

There are some books on the market guaranteeing fitness in just 30 minutes a week. Don't believe it. To get really fit, you will have to work hard at your training and make a definite commitment to running. You cannot expect to excel at running immediately and it will take at least two months before you begin to feel like a fit and competent runner. During this time you can gradually build up your endurance and stamina as you build greater challenges into your personal fitness programme. To test how fit you are, try walking briskly for 20 minutes without stopping. If you are short of breath, dizzy or your legs ache, then you are very unfit indeed, and it might be a good idea to try walking before you start running and gradually build short bouts of running into your walking programme.

Some controversial views about the beneficial and detrimental effects of running on health have been expressed by doctors in the press recently. Generally, it is the people who are non-runners who claim that running may be harmful in certain circumstances. Most doctors agree that regular running can bring about a low resting heart rate, a drop in blood pressure, a greater capacity to take in oxygen and more efficient heart and lung action. This is because running is a truly aerobic form of exercise which helps strengthen the cardiovascular system (heart, lungs and the circulatory system) and makes your body process oxygen in a more efficient manner. This is referred to as the 'aerobic training effect'. Scientific studies carried out in the United States have found that runners are less likely than non-runners to suffer from heart disease, and they have a higher stress-toleration threshold.

As a regular runner, your fitness will increase, your health will probably improve and you will reduce the risk of developing heart disease. Now even some postcardiac patients start running as part of their convalescent therapy. So running can be an all-round conditioner and play an important part in preventive medicine. It may help to reduce stress, worry and nervous tension as it has a pleasantly tranquillizing effect and is astonishingly therapeutic. When you run, you can escape from the pressures of everyday, modern life and enjoy a wonderful sense of freedom and relief from tension. You may arrive home in the evening feeling tired after a hard day's work. You want to sit down in the warm and have a nap in an armchair in front of the television, but you know you cannot miss your daily training run. After a short run, you will feel restored and exhilarated and less tired than you imagine. For running relaxes you and while you are out pounding the roads and grass you will find that you can banish all worries and unpleasant thoughts from your mind. If you are lucky, you may even give yourself up to the sheer pleasure of running and experience the so-called 'runner's high', a feeling of euphoria and of entering a higher plane, which can set in while you are out running.

Running is also an excellent form of weight control and regular training will make you slimmer as you can burn up to 1,000 calories per hour on a hard run. You can half-starve yourself on some trendy diet to lose weight quickly but the lost pounds will soon return if you do not continue to control your weight. Running is far more effective as you lose weight, whether you change your diet or not. When you run, you burn up unwanted surplus calories which the body otherwise converts into fat. Exercise can increase your metabolic rate so that you burn up calories faster.

Some people find that running actually depresses their appetite so that they feel less hungry and eat less. In any case, in your first year of running you can expect to lose about 10 pounds in weight. You will probably notice a large weight loss in the first few weeks but this will slow down steadily and eventually your weight will stabilise at what is best for you. This will depend on your weekly mileage total and your calorie intake. If you stop training regularly and burn up less calories, then you may find that you put on lost weight, and carrying extra weight will make a difference to your general performance and running times when you start training again.

Another great thing about running is that you are never too old to enjoy it, unlike many competitive contact sports such as football and rugby. Many committed runners continue running well into their sixties and seventies. They often look more youthful

People of all ages and occupations are taking up running for their health and enjoyment. The ideal sport, you can run almost anywhere at any time in the city or in the countryside.

than non-runners a decade younger than themselves, and stay fit and agile. Children, too, can enjoy running, and some families like to go out training together. Running is natural to children but lack of conditioning sometimes makes it difficult for adults and at first you may have to persevere until it comes naturally again. Follow our training programme for beginners (see page 20) and you will be thrilled at the progress you make.

Some people secretly wish to take up running but they are afraid to do so for fear of looking foolish or being laughed at by their family, neighbours or friends — this is particularly true in the case of overweight people, who take up running to get slim. If you are shy or self-conscious, then avoid running in crowded streets and busy roads but instead run early in the morning while the streets are still deserted, or after dark. Alternatively, find a running route through some uninhabited countryside where your only spectators will be cows and sheep. However, a better way to overcome your shyness and increase your self-confidence is to invest in a flattering, fashionable tracksuit and shoes so that you look and feel like a real runner and train in a local park where you can mingle with the other runners and pass unnoticed into their midst. As your running improves and you become fitter and trimmer, your self-confidence will increase and you will feel proud of your new body.

Another boost to your confidence and a good training method is to find a friend who wants to take up the sport and run together, providing eachother with moral support. In this way, you can share the experience of running and motivate eachother to succeed as a spirit of friendly rivalry develops and you give eachother mutual encouragement. Some people find running on their own boring and prefer to run in company so that they can chat as they run along. Running regularly with friends increases the pressure on you not to miss a run whereas you might sometimes cry off if you always run by yourself.

At all levels, right from the beginning, running can be as individual or as competitive as you want it to be. You can compete against yourself, setting yourself new targets and goals, like getting fit and into shape or running five miles without stopping — it's entirely up to you. Only you can determine how to run, how far and how fast — unlike team sports, there are no set rules to govern your performance, which is under your own control. If you are naturally competitive, you may wish to join a club and compete against other runners as your running improves, either on the track, the road or cross-country. You just have to find your own level of competition. When you start out, you should follow a running programme which is tailored to your own level of fitness and will fit into your lifestyle and daily pattern. Take care that the programme is not over-ambitious or you may not last the course. Follow our suggested training programmes and make a definite commitment to getting into shape. In order to do this, you must initially set aside one hour for exercise on at least three days every week. You will not run for the duration of the hour. You will spend 10-15 minutes warming up and stretching (see Chapter 4) to ease out tense muscles and prevent post-run stiffness, about 15-20 minutes running (and walking at the beginning) and the remaining time, cooling down and stretching and taking a bath or shower to take the sting out of tired muscles. As the weeks pass and your training programme progresses the stiffness and laboured breathing will pass as a new fitness gradually sets in and your body responds more efficiently and feels lighter and more supple.

Once you have survived the first few difficult weeks it is easy to sit back and congratulate yourself on your new level of fitness but do not let the challenge of running fade away. By now, you are probably enjoying the sport as the aches and pains become fewer and it requires less effort to follow your usual running route. Now you really know that running is paying off. Your friends and family may even comment on how well and healthy you look, and you know that you are getting into shape. You may find that running has transformed your life and become a habit that is impossible to break. You have to set yourself new goals such as competing for your local running club or even training for a marathon — the ultimate challenge to many runners.

So, having decided that you want to start running, for whatever reason, how do you go about it? First, you must take a good, long look at yourself and assess your physical condition. If you are heavily overweight (outside the limits given on our weight charts on page 147), or haven't exercised on a regular basis for a very long time, then it might even be a good idea to see your doctor and have a physical check-up before you start running. This is particularly necessary if you smoke or drink heavily and have a family background of heart disease. Your doctor might tell you, of course, that you are mad to even want to run — this is a common reaction among non-running doctors, and if this happens to you, then seek a second opinion from a doctor who does

Running in a group with friends and neighbours can be fun when you are starting out. The whole family can join in and you can offer each other mutual encouragement in the difficult early stages before you get really fit.

run. You must also consult the doctor if you experience chest pains or dizziness when you start running — there is probably a simple explanation but it is always just as well to check it out. Do not be put off or dismayed by all this — most people are capable of starting a running programme and getting fit and there are very few who must not run for medical reasons. However, it is always wise to take precautions and seek advice if you have any doubts about your health.

When should you run?

Well, this depends entirely on your daily schedule. A lot has been written about the best time of the day and how it governs athletic performance. The only hard and fast rule is never to run immediately after eating. Always allow at least two to three hours before running after eating solid foods. It is also wise not to run in very hot or humid weather which could lead to heat stroke.

Try and choose a time of day which you can keep free for running and will enable you to establish a regular routine. Unless you run regularly (at least three times a week) you will not derive any benefits from it and fitness will remain both elusive and undiscovered. So right from the start, set aside an hour at a time which is convenient to you, and if you can stick to that time every day, then running will soon become an enjoyable habit which is hard to break. You may say that you haven't got the time to run, your life is so busy that you could not possibly fit it in. Well, the answer to that is make the time. If you are a naturally early-riser, then get up a little earlier than usual and fit your run in before you leave for work. If you are a night-bird, then run in the evenings and feel the stress and strains of the day slipping away as you run. If you run after dark, stay on the pavements or footpaths and do make sure that you wear clothing that will be visible in car headlights — a white vest or tracksuit with reflective strips, or even a special reflective jacket.

Many people like to run at lunchtime from a local gym or a sports centre which has changing and showering facilities. However, if you often have business lunches or tend to do the shopping in your lunch hour, then choose another more convenient time of day. Always allocate enough time to change, warm-up and stretch, go for your run, cool down and shower or bathe afterwards. Never rush your running — it should always be relaxed and enjoyable. Just make sure that you choose a time that is virtually impossible for you to miss. A good idea is to make a regular appointment to run with friends — this will motivate you not to miss your regular training run.

Where should you run?

You can run anywhere — across the countryside, around your housing estate, a local park, along city pavements or even on the beach. Never start out by running on a local athletics track — not only is the special surface hard on your legs but lapping the same old track can be incredibly boring after a while and your new-found enthusiasm for running will soon fade away.

To combat possible boredom, make sure that you choose several running routes which are interesting and present a variety of scenery for you to enjoy as you run along. Switch the routes around frequently so that you have new things to look at which will help distract you from any small muscular aches and pains that you may feel during the first few weeks.

Mix up your surfaces so that although you include a little road running in your training programme, you run on grass most of the time. Springy grass is less jarring to legs, feet and back muscles than hard road surfaces and helps to cushion you against injury. Avoid running on ground that is uneven and riddled with potholes and hard tussocks of grass which could trip you up or throw you off stride. If the grass is very wet and slippery or the ground is soft and muddy, then wear running shoes with a special studded sole for gripping (see Chapter 3). Running excessively on hard surfaces, roads and pavements is a possible cause of Achilles tendinitis, although the jarring effects can be reduced by wearing good, supportive shoes with special inserts.

How often should you run?

You ought to run at least three times a week to make any progress and build up your level of physical fitness. Do not run on consecutive days in the early stages but have a day's rest in between running days if possible. At first your body may feel stiff as you put it through unfamiliar exercises and ask it to perform new tasks. However, the stiffness should last for only a day and should be no more than a feeling of discomfort. If it is really painful and continues for several days then admit that you have been overdoing it and have run too far or too fast. Next time you train, decrease the distance and run more slowly.

Running is hard at the beginning until you start to feel more supple and relaxed and the first signs of fitness appear. Try to fit your run in regularly and do not look for excuses for missing training, especially when it is cold or wet outside. You can only build up fitness gradually through regular training, and until your body becomes really conditioned and running is an essential part of your life, it is easy to risk forfeiting the progress you have made and put your training back a week or two by missing a few days. Of course, this cannot be helped if you are ill — running with a heavy cold, flu or a virus infection is not recommended although many committed runners frequently do this, insisting that a run 'will make them feel better'. Also, do not run if you are injured and in pain. If the injury persists for more than one week, seek medical advice.

Try not to miss two days on the trot. As you become fitter, running will get easier and as your enjoyment increases there is less likelihood of missing a day's training. You may even feel guilty and miserable if you don't go out!

How far and how fast should you run?

This will depend on your level of fitness and how inactive you used to be. The important thing is to build up distance gradually, starting with maybe only 100 yards or so and increasing the distance slowly as your running improves. If you start to feel tired or your breathing becomes laboured, then stop running and walk for a while until you feel better. You will soon be able to run further and walk less without feeling tired, and then you can think about increasing the distance, and extending your route.

Within a couple of months of regular training you should be able to run two or three miles without stopping and will feel exhilarated and a marvellous

Running on soft ground, grass and footpaths is less taxing on your legs than pounding along the roads on a hard surface. So you are less likely to get injured.

sense of achievement at what you have accomplished. Never rush your training — this can lead to injury if you over-strain muscles that are more used to a sedentary existence. Be patient and build up your running time and distance gradually as your endurance and stamina increase. You do not have to punish yourself to get fit — running must be enjoyable, not a painful chore. So run at a pace that is comfortable to you and get into a regular running rhythm. Initially, this will be just fractionally above a brisk walking pace, but as you get more proficient and the effort required to run decreases you will certainly run faster.

To discover whether you are running at the right speed, you can try the talk test. If you cannot hold a conversation with a friend without feeling winded and short of breath, then you are running too fast and should slow down. For most beginners, this means covering one mile in 10-12 minutes against six minutes for a more experienced athlete. You will find that your speed running is affected by many factors — the time of day, your physical condition, the weather, the level of the ground and whether you are running uphill, downhill or on the flat.

As your running improves you will take less time to cover your usual route and you will have to increase the distance to make up your usual allotted running time. The American cardiologist and running authority Dr George Sheehan claims that just 30 minutes' running a day four times a week will enable you to get fit and increase your cardio-pulmonary endurance, lower your blood pressure and slow the pulse rate.

Taking your pulse rate is a good method of checking up on how your body is responding during a run. Most adults have a resting pulse rate of 60-80 beats a minute but this increases when you run as your heart beats faster to pump the blood around the body. Take your pulse rate by pressing your wrist on the thumb side before you set out for your run, during the run and afterwards. An easy way is to count for 15 seconds and then multiply by four to determine the rate per minute. Your pulse rate when you run, should fall somewhere between your personal maximum and minimum permissible levels. To work out your maximum level deduct your age from 200; and to find the minimum level, subtract your age from 170. Therefore if you are 40 years old, your pulse rate should lie in the 130-160 region. If it is less then you are running too slowly. If it exceeds 160, then you are running too fast and should slow down. You will soon establish a pace that is right for you as you get more experienced as a runner, and after several months you may find that your pulse resting rate decreases as your heart grows stronger and more efficient.

Most runners find that the first few minutes of a run are the most difficult, especially if they have not bothered to warm up and stretch first, but gradually their breathing becomes easier, they feel less tired and they start to fly along as they find their 'second wind'. They feel stronger and more powerful and start to really enjoy the run. This will happen to you, too, so keep going through that laboured, early stage of your run until you find your second wind.

Always respect your body and respond to its warnings when you are overdoing it before you exhaust or injure yourself. Remember that old running maxim: 'train, don't strain' and you can't go wrong. Training should be enjoyable and planned to fit in with your personal timetable and preferences so choose a programme, a distance, a speed and a time that suit you and be flexible in adapting it to fit your lifestyle and schedule.

Running style

It is important to develop a relaxed, flowing running style to make running more enjoyable and reduce the risk of injury. Running should come naturally and easily — do not run stiffly, pounding along with gritted teeth, tense shoulders, your arms punching the air as many new runners mistakenly do. Try to relax and let your body feel loose and easy when you

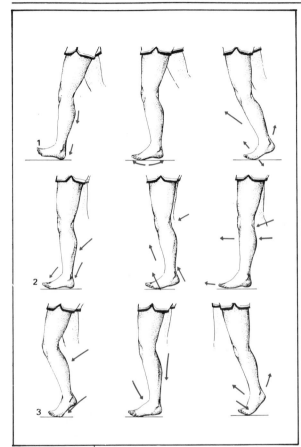

Developing an easy, flowing running style with good foot-strike is important in avoiding injury. Three common styles of foot-strike are illustrated above.
1 Heel-to-toe technique: the heel strikes the ground first, then you roll forwards onto the ball of the foot and take off again from the toes — a good technique.
2 Flat-footed technique: in this action the whole foot hits the ground at the same time and then pushes off.
3 Toe-running technique: the ball of the foot strikes the ground first and then the runner rolls back onto the heel and pushes off in a springy motion.

run. Run erect and tall, not leaning forwards as this can cause back pain and put strain on leg muscles.

Your arms and shoulders give you balance and the rhythm that keeps you going. So relax your shoulders and carry your arms low, moving in rhythm with your body. Your right arm balances the action of your left leg and vice versa. Never clench your fists as this increases tension and body strain. Keep your hands loose and relaxed.

Another aspect of running style is footstrike which should always be light and rocking. There are basically three ways of contact between the foot and the ground. Most long-distance runners use the heel-to-toe technique, landing on the heel and then rocking forwards to the ball of the foot and pushing off from the toes. This is a good style to develop as it spreads out the pressure of the body and cushions your weight as you land.

A few runners are flat-footed and land on the whole foot. This obviously has a cushioning effect also but it can be tiring if carried out over long distances. The third technique, which is common among many women runners who wear high heels regularly, is to land on the ball of the foot and then roll back onto the heel for the push-off. This method often produces sore and aching muscles as it puts a lot of strain on the legs.

You can check your foot alignment and decide which category you fit into by running in wet sand or mud and then analysing your footmarks. You can correct poor footstrike to some extent by using arch supports or special shoe inserts. These act as shock-absorbers when your foot hits the ground and may stop you pronating. Finding the right running shoes will also improve footstrike and help to prevent any injury (see Chapter 3). Always go to a sports shop staffed by runners who can give you expert advice.

When you run, take good strides and not dainty little steps. The most efficient stride is long and smooth and uses less effort than a short, uneven stride. Never over-stride by reaching out too far with your feet — they should be in line with the knee at the point they touch the ground.

It is quite permissible to breathe through your mouth and take great gulps of air when you are out running. Breathing daintily through your nose will not take in enough air to satisfy your body's oxygen needs. Breathe in a relaxed way, expanding your abdomen fully as you breathe in and flattening it as you exhale. In this way, you use your lungs more effeciently, inflating them to their limits. Let your breathing be in tune with the movement of your body and establish a rhythm for your running, so that your whole body moves in harmony.

A last word on running style and technique: many runners try so hard to relax that paradoxically they become self-conscious and tense in the process. The key to natural, easy running is to keep your body loose and fluid and as you run more frequently and your body becomes more supple and firm and your self-confidence increases, your running will naturally become more flowing.

Keeping a running diary

When you start your running programme, it's a good idea to keep a daily log of your progress. So buy yourself a diary or a notebook and jot down the details of your runs — the distance covered, the time taken to complete it, your physical state, running route, the weather and how you felt about the run. If you introduce new running techniques such as strides or interval training, these can be noted down too along with details of your weight and resting and training pulse rates. In this way, you can monitor your progress and create a degree of consistency in your running. This may motivate you to set yourself new running goals and challenges, especially when you are a more advanced runner and ready to compete against other runners. You can also keep a permanent record of any interesting or amusing running experiences to chuckle over when you become more experienced. A diary of this kind is especially useful if

you are embarking on a long period of training for a big event such as a marathon. There may be times, maybe lasting a few days or even a week, when you feel that you are not making any progress at all. On such occasions, you can look back in your diary and chart your progress over the weeks since you started running. This will encourage you to go out and train and maintain your new level of fitness.

So you are now all set to start running. However, before you follow the training schedule outlined by John Hanscomb below, make sure that you look at Chapters 3 and 4 to ensure that you get the right equipment and stretching exercises. So read on and take the first steps down the road to fitness.

Running programme for beginners

by John Hanscomb

Many beginners find it easier to follow a specially designed running programme than to find the time and the self-discipline to devise their own schedule. This programme was formulated for beginner runners who wanted to start running with the target of competing in the London Marathon events of 1981 and 1982. These running 'guinea pigs' volunteered for the training programme and their progress was reported in the *The Observer* newspaper over the weeks leading up to the marathon day from their first faltering steps along the road to ultimate fitness. They were a mixed bunch of people of all ages and occupations, ranging from working mothers and housewives to doctors and musicians, but what they all had in common was the ambition to get fit and run a marathon.

Your first aim, if you have not run before, is to be able to run for 15 minutes three times a week. You will probably find that you cannot run non-stop for 15 minutes and will have to run and walk alternately until gradually you will find that you are running more and walking less. Distance is immaterial, but the run should always be of 15 minutes' duration, even if you have to walk every hundred yards or so. Try to run on soft ground in your local park or common, but if this is not practical then ignore your neighbours and simply open the front door and run and walk for 7½ minutes before turning back for home.

Over the first three or four weeks of following this programme, the amount of walking will gradually diminish and by the fifth week you will probably be able to run without stopping for the prescribed 15 minutes. If you find that you need an extra week or two to reach this goal, do not worry; patience and persistence are part of the build-up programme.

When you have overcome the first hurdle, lengthen your runs to 20 minutes three times a week, and at the weekends extend an outing to 30 minutes. Do not worry if you find that you have to walk occasionally, especially during the longer weekend run — this is quite acceptable. Just keep going out four times a week until you are able to finish all of your runs without walking, no matter how slowly you seem to be going. After a further three or four weeks you should have reached this goal.

You are now ready for the next stage of the programme. You should be feeling much fitter and enjoying your running, which by now is an established part of your weekly routine. Now is the time to build up your running time and the distance covered, and possibly to join up with other runners on some occasions and run together. You will be surprised how much easier long runs become when you can share them with company. Soon you will be running five, and later six, days a week until you are feeling really fit. At the end of this 12 weeks' beginner programme, you may be ready to enjoy running at club-level in cross-country and road events if you have a competitive streak, or you may prefer to go on running alone or with friends just for the fun and level of fitness it gives you. You may even feel, like *The Observer* runners who tried out this training programme and came through it, that you want to start training for a marathon, the ultimate challenge in the running calendar.

The choice is yours but whatever your decision you can feel proud that you have achieved a standard of fitness by your own effort which has enabled you to enrich your life.

Training programme

Weeks 1,2,3,4
Run/walk for 15 minutes, 3 times a week until you can run 15 minutes non-stop

Weeks 5,6,7,8
Weekdays: run/walk for 20 minutes, 3 times a week
Weekends: run/walk for 30 minutes on Saturday *or* Sunday
Keep this up until you can run non-stop for the times given above.

Weeks 9,10
Sunday: very slow run for 45 minutes, perhaps with occasional walk
Monday: steady run for 20 minutes
Tuesday: steady run for 30 minutes
Wednesday: rest
Thursday: run for 15-20 minutes at a brisk pace
Friday: steady run for 20 minutes
Saturday: rest

Weeks 11,12
Sunday: slow run for 45 minutes without walking
Monday: steady run for 20 minutes
Tuesday: steady run for 30 minutes
Wednesday: steady run for 20 minutes
Thursday: run hard for 15-20 minutes
Friday: rest
Saturday: steady run for 20-25 minutes

CHAPTER THREE

Running equipment guide
by Alison Turnbull

Since 1980 many new specialist running shops have opened all over the UK. Shops like these are your best choice when buying shoes or clothing for running as they are usually staffed by experienced runners who will give advice (for which you should not be afraid to ask).

Even in a shop covering only one sport, however, you will be amazed at the variety of equipment, and you may find choosing difficult and bewildering. This chapter sets out to make that choice simple. It starts at the soles of the feet and works upwards, beginning with shoes for all purposes and building up to socks, underwear, vests, shorts, tracksuits, weathersuits and winter gear, safety gear and other equipment. Price is not always an indicator of quality or suitability and it is worth shopping around for bargains. Running shops often offer discounts for members of local clubs, so remember to ask.

Shoes

Running shoes are the most important item in a runner's wardrobe, for they each take the shock of approximately 800 footfalls per mile — the equivalent of 60 tons per foot per mile for a 10 stone runner. Plimsolls, cheap trainers and tennis shoes are not built to take this strain and sooner, rather than later, you should think about purchasing a shoe specially designed for running.

But which shoe? In 1982 there were 120 shoes on the UK market from 24 manufacturers, and this sort of competition inevitably means an awful lot of gimmicks and advertising jargon. Therefore, when choosing a pair of shoes it is important to know the difference between the essential features and the superfluous trimmings.

Basically, a running shoe serves two purposes — comfort and support — which added together mean freedom from injury. Let's look first at the anatomy of a typical road training shoe. Later we will look at shoes for specialist purposes.

The sole, or outsole, of the shoe is the layer of rubber on the base of the shoe that makes contact with the ground. Solid rubber is longer-lasting, whereas 'blown' rubber — where air is bubbled into the rubber — is lighter and bouncier underfoot, but tends to wear out more quickly. Waffle and studded soles give good grip on uneven surfaces and the studs act as shock absorbers, whereas a flat, wavy profile (eg. Vibram) gives good traction on roads and pavements but can be slippery on grass and footpaths. Some shoes have a reinforced area under the heel (heel plug), which does not wear as quickly.

There are endless variations of sole pattern, some combining studs with a flat profile to give maximum grip and wear in the rearfoot and maximum flexibility in the forefoot. For example, some recent innovations are the cantilever sole, flared at the edges and concave in the middle, said to improve shock absorption; and a sole that looks and acts like part of a tractor tyre.

The most important and highy researched area of shock-absorption is the midsole, the area between the upper and the sole, which is usually thicker at the heel. The most commonly used midsole material is Ethylene Vinyl Acetate (EVA), a polymer into which bubbles of air are pressed in varying amounts — the more bubbles, the lighter and more springy the midsole. The midsole may be all one density or

Forefoot	Midfoot	Rearfoot	

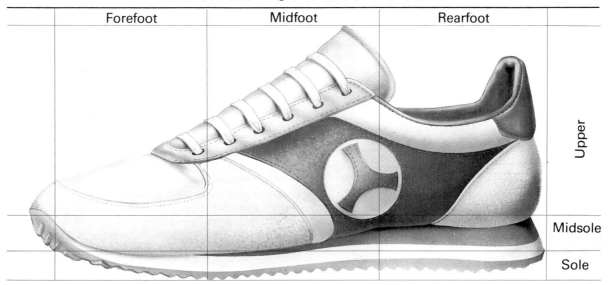

Upper

Midsole

Sole

have a denser wedge (i.e. fewer bubbles) to give firmer support under the heel and flexibility under the ball of the foot. However, take care when choosing — there should still be enough midsole to protect the forefoot.

Manufacturers are still searching for the ultimate in midsole technology — a material that combines lightness, shock absorption and also the ability to withstand several hundred miles of hard pounding without becoming flattened and useless. One way of making a midsole light is to fill it with air by trapping channels or columns of gas within it.

There are countless bits and pieces that can be inserted into the midsoles, or between the midsole and the upper. These fall into two categories: extra shock absorption; and anti-pronation devices.

Extra shock absorption: the 'web' on the Adidas Oregon stretches over the midsole and works like a trampoline every time the foot hits the ground, dissipating shock outwards, so it is claimed, rather than up the legs. Another Adidas shoe, the LA

It is a good idea when buying running shoes to analyse whether the individual features of a particular shoe meet your requirements. It often helps to think of the shoe in sections as illustrated above: the midsole and sole below; and the forefoot, midfoot and rearfoot above.

Trainer, has three rods inserted into the midsole, which can be altered by the runner according to weight, style and running surface. Do not rule these out as gimmicks if the shoe is right for you (see Buying Tips, page 26).

Anti-pronation devices: most runners' feet turn inwards, or *pronate*, as they touch the ground. Where this movement is exaggerated (over-pronation), injuries to shins and knees can result. Several shoes incorporate anti-pronation devices that support the foot in a neutral plane and prevent the roll inwards. But pronation is not something you should diagnose for yourself — if you are injured you should seek the advice of a doctor or physiotherapist before buying a pair of shoes with a corrective device, as your pain may have entirely different roots. The same goes for the wedges, heel cushions and arch supports that you can buy separately to put inside your shoes. Experiment with these, but if your problem persists, seek specialist help.

Rearfoot

The heel counter is a piece of board or plastic stiffening material which supports the heel and stops it moving around inside the shoe. Never buy a shoe with a flabby heel counter. Some shoes incorporate lacing around the back of the heel counter to hold the heel even more snugly. The heel is 'flared' if the midsole and outsole are wider than the heel counter. Up to a point, this makes a more stable shoe.

The heel tab, that part of the shoe above the heel counter which is padded and usually bears the maker's name, is a bone — or rather tendon — of contention. Like the human appendix, it is not really necessary and may require surgery if it gives trouble. It's often called the Achilles tendon protector but in fact high, stiff heel tabs can irritate and in some cases severely damage the Achilles tendon. The golden rule is the lower and softer the heel tab the better.

There are many different ways of lacing running shoes. Some have a choice of eyelets, and hence a choice of width, others D-rings which keep the tension of the laces constant. Worry less about the actual lacing system and more about the cushioning of the tongue under the laces, and the padding of the collar.

In the forefoot, the toe box is a firm material, usually covered with suede, which protects the toes. On some shoes there is extra big toe protection, but beware — it may not correspond with the position of

The three most common sole patterns are shown below. The wavy, flat sole is ideal for training on roads but slips on grass. A studded waffle sole grips well on rough ground, whereas the new cantilever sole helps increase shock absorption and reduces the risk of injury.

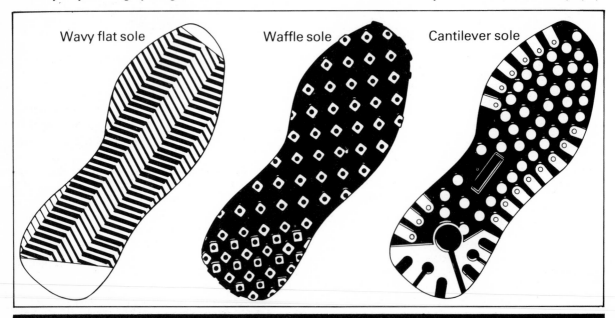

Wavy flat sole Waffle sole Cantilever sole

your big toe. Some runners have second toes as long, or longer, than their big toes (a condition known as Morton's foot) and this can be very restricted and uncomfortable in a reinforced toe box.

Some shoes have 'swaybars' or 'vertical stabilisers' (a good example, incidentally, of how jargon meaning the same thing is used by different manufacturers!). These run from the eyestay to the toebox to support the widest part of the foot. Again, this may not be the widest part of *your* foot, and you may find the swaybars too constricting.

Inside the shoe, the insock comes between the foot and the flat bed of the shoe and serves as an additional shock absorber. It should also absorb moisture (and so keep blisters at bay). The most popular type of insock is that which moulds to the shape of the foot after a few miles. Most insocks are covered with absorbent towelling or sponge and knitted material. Many are now removable so that they can be dried or replaced.

One material coming into wider use for shoe inserts is Sorbothane, a highly shock-absorbent polymer which has been found to absorb about 95 per cent of shock compared with EVA. But Sorbothane is quite heavy and as yet has not been built into a shoe, manufacturers preferring instead to make removable heel pads and inserts.

Running shoes can be constructed in different ways. In conventional or board lasting ones, the upper is stretched over the last and glued to a fibre board. Slip lasting, or moccasin construction, is where the uppers meet under the sole and are stitched together. If the shoe has a removable insock you can see the difference.

There are disadvantages to both lasting techniques. Board-lasted shoes do not bend at the ball of the

Many modern shoe designs are combination-lasted combining the features of board-lasting and slip-lasting. In this technique, they are glued under the heel and then stitched under the forefoot as shown (right).

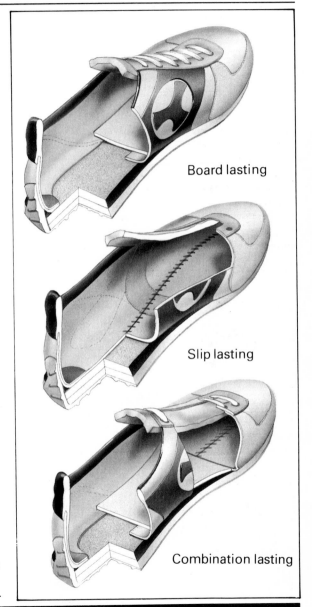

Board lasting

Slip lasting

Combination lasting

foot when your foot leaves the ground, whereas slip-lasted shoes are less supportive at the rear of the foot. As a result, many newer shoes are combination-lasted, ie. board-lasted under the heel and slip-lasted under the forefoot. So look out for a flexible, but well padded, forefoot.

Women's shoes

More and more women's versions of standard running shoes are becoming available in the UK. Many women can run quite happily in standard running shoes, if their size is available, but differences exist between women's and men's feet. Women's feet tend to be narrower at the heel and instep, although pro-portionally the same width at the forefoot; so a shoe that fits you around the toes may not be supportive enough around the heel. You can test this easily for yourself by trying on a standard and a women's shoe of the same size. Women's shoes are usually available in smaller sizes — and of course there is nothing to stop a small-footed man wearing a woman's shoe if it fits. The colours of women's shoes tend to be more 'feminine' and fashionable, but if this is your only criterion for choice remember that there is nothing feminine about mud!

Buying tips

If you buy a musical instrument, you expect specialist help from a musician, and you expect to be able to play the instrument in the shop. So it should be with running shoes. So, rule one: avoid the sort of shop where the shoes on display have shoe trees in them and a 'look don't touch' air about them. Go to a specialist shop where the staff are runners and know what they are talking about. Ask them what shoes *they* wear, and why.

Don't go shopping with fixed ideas about the shoe you want. Allow some time to try on different models and different sizes in the shop — some shops will even trust you on a test drive in the street, which is a better policy than just letting you try one on while you are sitting down.

In length you may well need a shoe a half or whole size larger than your normal walking shoe. Allow ½ inch between the big toe and the toe box area. As a guide to width, the sole of your shoe should take the width of your foot comfortably, that is to say, your foot should not hang over the midsole and bulge into the upper. Some brands have a choice of width fittings. Curiously, the 'average' American foot is narrower than the 'average' European foot, so expect width variations in the shoes you try on, according to where they are made.

Generally, your feet will be more swollen in the afternoon, which is the best time to go shoe-shopping. Wear the socks you usually run in. Feel inside the shoe and make sure that there are no rough areas of stitching, and that it is well padded at friction points such as the tongue and collar. Remember: if the shoe is not comfortable in the shop *it won't get any better* on the road!

Be prepared to ask questions. If the shoe has a new, wonder ingredient get the assistant to explain it to you — and don't buy the shoe if you're not satisfied with the answer to your questions.

Finally, if you find a shoe you like, and which gives you many comfortable miles, *stick with it.* Buy a new shoe of the same model before the old one is completely worn out and you should find that you don't need to 'break it in'. There's no point in turning up at your club with the newest, flashiest shoe, complete with magic ingredient, if it's going to cripple you after a few miles.

Specialist shoes

Another important buying point is that you should not sacrifice lightness for speed. That is to say, don't look at the shoes that class runners are wearing and decide that they must be right for you. Unless you are up there with the leaders, you are more than likely too heavy or too slow for ultra-light shoes and you need something more cushioning and supportive.

It is better to lose a few pounds of weight yourself than to shave ounces from your shoes and risk injury. The shoes discussed in this specialist section — lightweight flats, cross-country and track spikes — have one thing in common. You only expect to race in them. Warm up, and down, in your trainers.

Racing flats If you are the right standard and weight for a lightweight racer, there are about 20 shoes (1982) to choose from. Manufacturers' assessments of shoe use vary — thus some 'trainers' are suitable for racing and vice versa. Generally a racing flat is 200g or less, with less cushioning , and a flat-profile outsole. If you have any hint of injury but are still fit to race you are probably better off racing in your trainers, especially in a marathon.

Cross-country Road shoes with a flat profile do not grip on muddy surfaces. Waffle and ridged soles are better and can be worn on the road without discomfort. There is a studded cross-country shoe which feels like a football boot on the road. However, if you race cross-country regularly your best bet is a spiked shoe with a waffle-sole rearfoot which combines lightness and grip. On modern spikes, the spikes are both removable and interchangeable, so you can keep sets of different lengths for different surfaces. The usual range for cross-country is 9-15mm.

Track spikes Track running does not necessarily mean spikes unless you are going to specialise over shorter distances or do a lot of interval training. Above 1,500 metres you will probably feel more comfortable in racing flats. If you do buy a pair of spikes, look for the newer type with wedge heel ie., a rearfoot profile similar to your road training shoe. Without the support and cushioning you are used to in training, you expose yourself to the risk of injury, especially to the Achilles tendon, for you will still be landing heel first.

On cinder tracks, experience and condition will tell you which length spikes to choose. If the track is either very soggy or very dry and loose, you will need a longer spike. On all-weather surfaces there are very strict rules regarding the type and length of the spikes used — usually no longer than 6mm 'needle' spikes.

When you buy a pair of spikes you may see that the spike plate has seven holes but only six spikes are permitted, although you can fit them in whichever position you prefer.

In general, track shoes are tighter-fitting (more often worn without socks) with less structural support. If you have a problem like over-pronation in ordinary training shoes this will be in exaggerated in spikes.

Shoe wear and care

When you come in from a muddy run and your shoes are wet, avoid the temptation to put them on the radiator and forget about them. They won't last as long, as they may become dry and hard on your next run. Take out the insock, if it is removable, gently pack the shoe with old newspaper and leave it to dry away from direct heat.

Some people advocate putting their shoes through the washing machine. This is OK, but the detergent tends to erode the inner padding of the shoe and if the shoes are not properly rinsed the detergent can irritate sensitive feet.

No matter how attached you are to them, sooner or later the soles of your favourite shoes are going to wear out. In some cases the sole life can be extended by resoling, but this is not worth it if (a) the midsole has compacted and is no longer springy; (b) if the heel counter has become dislodged and floppy; and (c) if the uppers are full of holes.

A number of shops offer resoling services which are cheap (about £6 at 1982 prices) and usually same-day. You do not necessarily have to have the same soles as before. If it is October, say, and your wavy flat soles need replacing, think about replacing them with studs or waffles for winter training. It is worth a phone call to the shop to see what they can offer you. As a general guide, do not resole shoes more than once.

There is a number of glue-type resins on the market for do-it-yourself repair of worn-down soles, and some runners swear by these, but you will not be able to re-create the original tread pattern, so you might slip on wet pavements.

Socks

Some runners get by with no socks, or any old socks, without blisters or chafing. The rest need special socks to avoid friction between the shoe and foot. There is a number of specialist running socks on the market, but a general chain store 'sports' sock may be a better buy if it meets the following requirements: (a) non-chafing (bad seams across the toenails can cause blackness or lifting); (b) durable; (c) cushioning (some have extra cushioning at heel and toe); (d) absorbent; (e) washable.

Recently, people have tended to shy away from man-made fibres for socks. Like refined flour and sugar, they think that natural is best, but this is not necessarily so. Cotton and wool are absorbent and comfortable, but hold perspiration and need more careful washing. Synthetics are cheaper and longer-lasting and are not as hot and uncomfortable as they used to be. Du Pont's acrylic fibre, Orlon, wicks perspiration away from the foot, and can be spun into bulk fibre for use in cushion socks.

Clean dry socks mean fewer blisters. If your skin is sensitive to detergent, wash the socks in soap and make sure they are thoroughly rinsed before drying.

Clothing

Having shod your feet, it's time to look at your clothes. But if you are a beginner, don't look too hard at first. Rummage around the back of your wardrobe for some shapeless old casual clothes in which you have been promising yourself you will do the decorating some day. To start with, you can run in T-shirts, sweaters, loose shorts and slacks, until you decide you quite like running, that is, when you really want to go out and buy yourself some smart clothes for the purpose.

Underwear

Men have a choice of three types of support: (a) shorts with built-in pants; (b) plain shorts with traditional support (jockstrap); or (c) cotton briefs worn under plain shorts. The jockstrap is falling out of favour because it is cumbersome and quickly loses its shape and comfort after washing. It also comes higher up the waist than most modern shorts, which isn't very fetching. Easily-washable cotton briefs are a better bet. With these, you have to strike a balance between being too tight or not snug enough, and look for a wide crotch that does not ride up. Shorts with built-in pants suit some men and not others. Often the briefs are made of the same, non-stretch material as the shorts, which can be uncomfortable.

Women are recommended to wear snug absorbent cotton briefs unless their shorts have built-in pants which make them feel more confident.

If you are small-breasted, you may well run quite happily without a bra, provided that your nipples are protected from friction with your vest. If you are large-breasted, it is best to seek advice from the corsetry department of a large store. For the medium-breasted women in between, there are a few special sports bras on the market (look for Berlei, Triumph and Warner). Again, the best place to find a sports bra is a corsetry department, for, sadly, sports bras are not yet widely available in chain stores or sports shops. Sports bras combine the absorbency of cotton with a stretch material, usually Lycra. Look out for seamless cups, or well-finished seams, non-chafing armholes and a broad band under the cups which will not ride up. The Berlei and

Triumph models are made in the same way as normal bras, with adjustable straps and choice of three fastenings, whereas the Warner bra pulls over the head and has a back like a racing swimsuit. The advantage of this is that it has no chafing fastenings or trimmings, but the disadvantage is that if your breast size changes for any reason (eg. you might lose weight as your mileage goes up, or you might be unlucky enough to have breasts which swell up just before your period) you cannot make adjustments.

Vests If you are choosing a running vest for yourself, you want a material that is smart, comfortable, and deals with perspiration efficiently. This is where lightweight nylon tricot scores as it wicks the perspiration away from the skin, unlike cotton knit, which holds water and can become quite heavy.

Mesh vests, or tricot vests with mesh panels, have become very popular with distance runners, men and women, although there has been some controversy over the modesty of mesh panels on women's vests.

Whichever material you are choosing, make sure that the armholes are not too tight for you, and look for non-chafing seams and bindings.

Competitors in team and relay races and championships must wear vests in the registered colours of the club or team they represent. Clubs may nominate alternative light coloured vests in races of 20km or more. An athlete is *not* permitted under AAA rules to wear any advertising material.

Shorts Again it is up to you whether you opt for nylon tricot or cotton. 'Freedom shorts', nylon tricot with a built-in gusset, are becoming very popular with men and women and they are both modest and free-moving. In general, women are still wearing the towelling knicker-type briefs in track and cross-country competition but not for road running.

Always try shorts on in the shop. If the outside looks big enough, the inner pant, if there is one, may not be. Raise your leg so that it is parallel with the floor. If the shorts are not comfortable over the widest range of movements, do not buy them. Look for well-finished seams and soft waistband — the more rows of stitching the better. A different colour trim around the hem may look smart, but avoid it if it is likely to chafe the thighs.

Tracksuits come in all shapes, sizes and materials. The purpose of a tracksuit is to keep you warm before, and particularly after, running when your body temperature can drop quite rapidly. If you actually train in a tracksuit then you will need another to change into, or put on top, after you run.

Fleecy-lined cotton 'sweats' are cheap, absorbent and comfortable, although you can also get very soggy in a downpour. You may prefer a nylon tracksuit with a fleecy lining.

On top, look for a jacket that is not too short or too tight at the waist, or it may part company with the trousers, leaving your midriff exposed. The trousers should have tapered legs (not straight or flared) and long zips so that they can be removed over shoes. Pockets should be zipped so that you can safely keep a key or money in them.

Tracksters are tracksuit trousers with a drawstring waist which can be bought separately and quite cheaply so that if you have a wide range of sweat tops you do not have to buy a whole tracksuit.

Keeping dry Gore-Tex is a new fabric made into jackets and trousers which is lightweight and waterproof, and 'breathes' by allowing perspiration to evaporate. So it keeps you dry both ways. It is machine-washable (in soap flakes) and only needs to be worn with a layer of thermal underwear underneath. However, it is expensive, although it may become cheaper as more people discover it, and it is not the sort of thing you want to leave lying around in the changing room.

Lower down the price range is the proofed weather- or windsuit. This is a smart cover-up for travelling to and from races and while, not guaranteed rainproof, will certainly keep you dry in all but the most torrential downpour.

In any type of rainsuit, look out for a hood, reflective tape trim for nightime use, back ventilation, glove pockets and long zips on the trousers.

Keeping warm is particularly important if you are a newer, slower runner, when on winter days you will take a long time to warm up and then, if you drop pace, you can cool quite rapidly. Cold legs are more susceptible to injury and stiffness, and cold chests to respiratory illness. It is better in winter to be too warm rather than too cold.

For winter running it is worth investing in a long-sleeved top and long johns, either to wear under your tracksuit, or Superman-style with your vest and shorts outside. There is no mystique about the word 'thermal' — the ideal material is one that both keeps you warm and wicks perspiration away from the skin — so that you keep warm and dry after you stop running. Look for polypropylene, chlorofibre, Viloft, or mixes of these with natural fibres.

In winter you might want to wear a hat and gloves in either wool or cotton. You do not have to go to any great expense — choose a hat and gloves that can be tucked into a waistband or pocket if you take them off, and cheap enough not to worry about if you leave them in a changing room or at the start of a marathon.

Safety first

Most sensible cyclists wear some form of fluorescent or reflective clothing on the road, and the Royal Society for the Prevention of Accidents have long preached the maxim 'wear something white at night'. Yet many runners still venture out on to the road like the Invisible Man. For your own safety, and the sanity of passing motorists, it makes sense to follow the cyclists' lead.

Fluorescent colours are bright by day and noticeable — but not necessarily bright — by night. The most visible material is 3M Scotchlite which is made up of tiny, highly reflective beads which pick up the light of car headlamps. Scotchlite is incorporated into most newer rain - and Gore-Tex suits, or you can get a bib to wear over your outer clothing which has a Scotchlite strip running through it.

Look in your local cycle shops for armbands, belts and stick-on-devices. Always carry a small torch. With any luck, more running shops will soon recognise the need for this safety gear.

Other equipment

Watches The digital stopwatch or chronograph is clearly here to stay, and is now priced so reasonably that even if you prefer to wear a conventional analogue watch during the day you can afford a digital watch for running. The basic function you need for running is a stopwatch accurate to 100ths of a second. A lap counter and split timing functions are also useful. As optional extras, there are watches that work out your pace and give a metronome beat, but they are based on stride length which changes if you run uphill or get tired; others incorporate pulsemeters; and others even mini-video games. Occasionally in extremes of temperature the display on a digital watch may fade.

Pulsemeters These are useful if you do a lot of interval training or indoor bicycling, where you want to keep a steady pulse level without stopping — but they are still a comparative luxury. The conventional method of checking your pulse is just as reliable.

Vaseline If you are going to do a lot of long-distance running you will need to cut down on friction — 'jogger's nipple' is no joke as the movement of the vest against the nipples can be very painful and even draw blood. Vaseline (petroleum jelly) is the most popular and effective application, although some runners prefer nappy cream or nursing cream —

experience will tell you which is best. Before any long run or race, apply a thin layer of Vaseline to some, or all, of these areas: feet (especially around the toes); backs of the knees; inner thighs (women especially); nipples (men) — Elastoplast is an alternative protection; under the band and straps of the bra (women); armpits where the vest touches; elbows, inside and out; lips; nose; eyebrows; (to keep sweat out of the eyes). Even for men, a moisturiser or baby lotion applied all over the face can help prevent sore and dry skin if the weather is windy.

Liniments There is always a rich smell of wintergreen at the start of a big race, and a wide variety of lotions and sprays are available. Medical opinion is divided on the efficacy of heat rubs at deeper than skin level, but muscles do *feel* warmer after embrocation as a result of the dilation of the blood vessels of the skin. There is no substitute, though, for proper warming-up exercises.

Hot and cold packs Struggling with ice cubes or a hot water bottle to relieve a minor injury can be awkward. The hot/cold pack is an idea that has been used in hospitals for some time, but it is now available to the public. This is a pack or pad of material that does not freeze or vaporise if chilled in the fridge or placed in boiling water. Do not apply directly to the skin, but wrap a towel around the affected area first — and if your injury is persistent, seek specialist help.

Footcare If you have read all the earlier advice about socks and Vaseline you are less likely to have blisters. If you do, however, look out in sports shops for the Spenco range and in chemists for the Scholl footcare range to help you avoid or alleviate painful feet. Blisters on the feet can easily wreck your marathon — they can just as easily be avoided.

Diaries Once you are running regularly, it is a good idea to record your daily run — how long it took,

how you felt, how far you ran, weather, running partners. As you progress it is fun and informative to look back on your early days. You can use an ordinary diary or even an exercise book or buy one of the logs or diaries specially printed for the purpose. These are supplemented with pace charts and other useful information and are usually undated so that you can start at any time.

Your running essentials have now all been covered. You will find in shops and magazines, advertisements for all manner of other useful bits and pieces — special purses and bags for carrying on the run; home exercisers; personal hi-fi; bands for holding your glasses on…the list is endless. Enjoy shopping for running and come away with the equipment that is right for you.

Tracksuits come in a wide range of styles and sizes for adults and children alike. Comfortable and warm, they are ideal for warming up or cold weather training sessions.

CHAPTER FOUR

Stretching before and after training

by Sandra Dyson

Most people accpept that a 'warm-up' of some kind is always desirable before running without really understanding why it is necessary. Because of this, the usual procedure is to jog a couple of laps before getting started on the real training, or racing, and very often this leads to injury or, at least, a below optimum performance. This chapter is mainly concerned with stretching exercises but first of all let us have a look at where these fit into a propert warm-up procedure and what benefits you can gain from carrying this out.

Basically, there are four elements in the warm-up procedure, which are as follows:

1 Light running
2 Stretching
3 Loosening
4 Progressive speed increase

The first observation must be that very few runners indeed spend enough time on any of these elements. When the vagaries of the British weather and the fact that most training and racing seems to take place in cold, wet or windy conditions are considered, it becomes even more important that a really thorough job is made of all the warm-up aspects. Apart from the immediate dangers of injury or poor performance, there is the more insidious problem of a gradual loss of function because corrective action is not being taken during the warm-up.

The initial light running is not simply an opportunity for a chat and to make sure that the lane markings go all the way round the track! It is the first step in bringing the body's internal temperature up to its best working level. (*Towards an understanding of human performance*, E.J. Burke, Ithaca, N.Y. 1978, Mouvement Publications). Most scientific studies have indicated that there are many beneficial effects on performance from a proper warm-up (*Body temperature & capacity for work,* Asmusson E. & Boje O. Acta Physiology, Scandinavia 10:1, 1945 and *Textbook of Work Physiology,* Astrand P.O. & Rodahl K. New York, 1970). Perhaps the most important effect is the gradual increase that takes place in the coronary blood flow to the heart's myocardium, thus increasing the capacity of the body to perform work.

Also important are the changes that take place as the body temperature rises. With this increase in temperature, there is also a corresponding increase in the speed of the metabolic processes within the cells because those processes are temperature dependent. For each degree of temperature rise, there is an increase in metabolic rate of around 12 per cent. This means that at these higher temperatures, there is more rapid and complete separation of oxygen from haemoglobin and myoglobins, so improving the oxygen supply to the muscles during exercise. (*Effect of warm-up on metabolic responses to strenuous exercise* — Martin, Robinson, Wigman & Aulick. Med. Sci. Sports 7. 146 1975).

The first step in achieving all of these benefits, ie. light running, needs to last for at least 15 minutes, varying with the weather, and only then is it time to move on to the next phase — stretching. Of course, beginners should stretch to warm-up before they run for 15 minutes and then stretch again afterwards.

Stretching

What benefits can we expect to gain from always carrying out a thorough stretching routine? Good flexibility improves the ability to avoid injury by permitting a greater range of movement within a joint. If the joint is capable of a good range of movement, then its ligaments and other collagenous tissues are less likely to be strained since they can accommodate all but extreme positions. Certainly, tight-jointed athletes are more prone to muscle strains and tears than their more mobile colleagues, but fortunately the situation can be remedied since repetitive stretching of collagenous and ligamentous tissue over a long period will give that increased range of movement. However, a word of warning — hyperflexibility must be avoided. Extremes of flexibility are of no value as the joint will then be weak at certain angles, making it prone to subluxations and dislocations.

The type of exercise used to achieve this increased range of movement is important. As a muscle is stretched, a muscle-protective mechanism is invoked, called the stretch-of-myotatic-reflex, which causes the muscle actively to resist stretch. The amount and rate of this stretch is proportional to the amount and rate of the stretching force. Because of this, a vigorous, ballistic type of exercise will produce a proportional contraction of the muscle — the very opposite of what is required. Hence, the gradual and sustained stretch should be used by the runner.

So much for the long-term effects. But there are also more immediate benefits to be gained, for instance, the reduction of muscle stiffness and soreness. Muscle stiffness is a condition that most runners experience, particularly those involved in a daily running programme. When muscles are worked hard continually, fluid collects within the muscle, causing swelling, shortening and thickening, and it is a very slow process for these fluids to be absorbed into the blood stream. The process is speeded up, however, by gentle stretching, light exercise and mobilisation (which we will come to shortly).

More severe than the commonplace stiffness is the muscle soreness that can occur, either following a sudden change or an increase in the work load normally carried out. A fairly general soreness is likely to appear a few hours after exercise and this will last for about 24 hours. After this a more localised and specific soreness may be felt, which is called myositis, and usually lasts a few days before it wears off gradually. Until recently this soreness was believed to be due to minor tissue damage of the muscle fibre, or of the connective tissue. Recent research however, by deVries (*Physiology of exercise for physical education and athletes*), suggests that at least in part the muscular soreness is due to tonic muscular spasm. Therefore, slow stretching of the affected muscles will help to reduce that soreness.

We have selected some exercises specifically designed to help build up a routine which can then be used throughout your athletic career. Use the exercises as a basis on which to build, for with a little bit of intelligent application, you should be able to work out for yourself which position you need to adopt to stretch a particular muscle group.

All the exercises illustrated are of the slow stretch type and you must not be tempted to 'bounce' into position, even if you see your colleagues doing so. Some of the exercises are more suited to an indoor area, some to a soft surface, but it is your responsibility to select one or two exercises from each group, to give the balance required.

You will soon find yourself doing the exercises automatically as part of your warm-up routine. Even on days when you miss your training for whatever reason, it is a good idea to stretch and exercise your muscles. The exercises can be performed almost anywhere — in the gym, on the track, at home or even in the office.

Calf stretches

In the calf there are two major muscles — Gastrocnemius and Soleus. Gastrocnemius is the more prominent muscle, which has its origin above the knee. For this reason it can only be stretched by keeping the knee straight. The origin of Soleus, however, is below the knee and therefore has to be stretched with a bent knee. Of the five exercises illustrated, the first three are designed to stretch the Gastrocnemius muscle, and the other two, the Soleus, hence it is important that a selection from each group is included in the warm-up routine.

1 Standing — raising toes

The exercises are graded in severity. This one is a gentle stretch which can be performed anywhere, at any time, but is nevertheless very useful, and a good prelude to the later exercises. Stand with the leg to be stretched about 12 inches in front of the supporting leg and draw up the toes of the forward foot as far as possible, whilst leaving the heel resting on the ground. Hold for about 10 seconds.

2 Standing — leaning against wall

In this exercise lean against a vertical support and about four feet away from it. Points to remember are that the seat must be tucked in and the heels firmly on the floor, with the feet facing forwards in front of you. As an alternative, and particularly if one leg is rather stiffer than the other, each leg can be stretched separately, the other leg being rested on the floor about two feet in front of the other. Hold for 10 seconds.

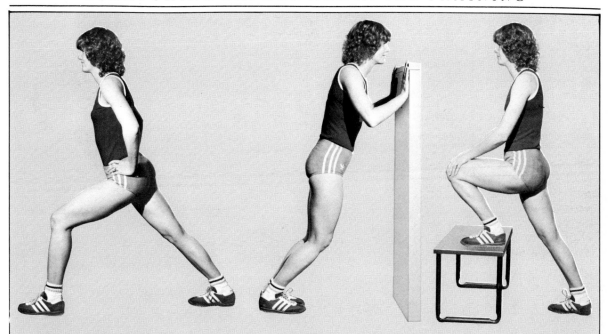

3 Lunge position
Stand in a lunge position with the back foot facing forwards, unlike a true lunge, and the heel always maintaining contact with the ground. The front foot, which must be bent, should be as far forward as the rear leg allows. The trunk must remain erect as otherwise much of the stretch is lost. Hold for 20 seconds, continuously holding the stretch.

4 Leaning against wall — bent knee
Lean against a wall or similar object, as in the previous exercise, but this time two feet away from it. The hips must be tucked in again, heels on the floor, and the knees bent until stretch is felt in the back of the leg. Tightness may be felt anywhere along the length of the calf muscle, from immediately above the knee, down to the Achilles tendon. Stretch will vary according to the degree and type of exercise.

5 Standing — resting foot on object
Stand about 12 inches in front of a stool or similar object, approximately knee height. Place one foot flat on the object with the back of the heel to the back of the support. As the purpose is to stretch the bent leg, weight can be added with both hands. Because the knee is bent, this is another exercise which stretches the Soleus muscle. Hold for 10 to 15 seconds.

Quadriceps stretching
This is a group of four muscles which are situated on the front of the thigh. As one of these, Rectus femoris, has its origin on the hip bone, these exercises should be carried out with the hip extended, (stretched).

▽ **2 Kneeling on all-fours with one leg outstretched**
Kneel squarely on all-fours with hands placed directly under shoulders, and knees under hips. Raise one leg backwards and allow knee to bend so that stretch is put on front of the thigh. Hold for 15 seconds and then repeat.

▽ **3 Kneeling — bent backwards**
Start in an upright kneeling position, then, using the arms for support, lean as far backwards as is comfortable, making sure the knees are still on the floor. If your ankles are stiff, put a cushion under the foot. Hold for 10 seconds, increasing to 25 seconds.

△
1 Standing — holding foot
Stand, as in the picture, firmly holding one foot. The trunk must be kept upright, or much of the value of the exercise will be lost, and the leg pulled gently backwards. Hold for 20 seconds.

Hamstring stretches

Of all the muscles, this group is the most neglected with regard to stretching, as shown by the number of injuries it suffers. The hamstrings are the muscles on the back of the thigh. They are biarticular, which means that they work over two joints, bending the knee and extending the hip. To stretch the muscles, the hip must be flexed and the knee straight.

1 Sitting — legs outstretched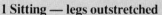

Sometimes called 'the screamers', but not deservedly so! No exercise should cause pain, just a feeling of 'getting back to normal'. Remember that forward lean must start at the hips, and not just involve the spinal joints. The legs may be held together, but there are plenty of variations — legs apart, and stretching each leg separately, or bending one leg and stretching one leg at a time.

2 Standing — one leg resting on support ▷

Stand about four feet away from a suitable support, and rest one leg on top of it. Keeping this leg straight, bend forwards from the waist and try to rest the head on the knee. Care must be taken not to reach first with the fingers, as this will only encourage the spine to bend at the top, instead of at waist level. As this exercise may well prove too difficult at first, start with the lead leg slightly bent. Hold 30 seconds.

Hamstring stretch continued

3 Sitting — hurdle position △

Sit with one leg outstretched and the other flat on the floor, with hip, knee and ankle bent to approximately 90°. If this is not possible, the hip may be placed at a lesser stretch. Ensure that the back is bent from the waist, as the object is to get the head onto the knees. Some runners cannot even balance in the starting position, let alone try to lean forwards! If so, put a hand to the floor for support and practise until you can begin the proper exercise. Hold position for one minute, then change legs.

▽ 4 The plough

Lie on your back and take bent legs, together, over your head, supporting hips with your hands. The legs should be straightened at right-angles to the floor, and carried slowly backwards to touch the floor behind the head. Lie on a soft surface to protect the neck and spine. If you cannot manage this exercise with straight legs, try it with bent knees and when comfortable, gently straighten the knees, with the feet still touching the floor. Hold 10 seconds.

Hip muscle stretching

The range of movement of the hips during running reduces as the distance involved increases. That is, the slower the running speed, the more restricted the movement. This tendency needs to be corrected and a selection from the following exercises will help to overcome this. It will be noticed that in all the following exercises, one knee is flexed. The reason for this is to reduce the pull on the hamstrings and so allow more movement at the hips.

◁ **1 Standing — knee to chest**

Stand near to where there is some support, should it become necessary. Bend one knee fully and grasp it with both hands, pulling the thigh well into the chest to give maximum stretch at the hips. Hold for 15 seconds, then change over legs.

▽ **2 Ski stretch**

Stand in a lunge position with back leg facing forwards and, bending front leg, gently lower body to floor until resting on hands. The back leg should be held straight and stretched as far back as possible. The heel should not be kept on the floor. Hold for 20 seconds, and then change legs.

Hip muscle stretch continued

3 Foot on support — knee flexed
Stand, as in the illustration, about two feet from a suitable surface. With one leg straight and supporting, place the other foot flat on the surface. This will give great stretch to the supporting leg. Hold for 15 seconds and then repeat the exercise with the other leg.

4 Side-stretching — leg on support
Stand at a distance from the support which allows the supporting leg to be at right angles to the leg on the surface. This exercise is often a difficult one for runners as it stretches the adductors, or inner thigh muscles. However, it is very effective and helps with the all-round balance required by the aspiring runner.
▽

Trunk stretching

In running, there is very little movement of the trunk, the muscles working mainly as stabilisers. This encourages them to shorten and create stiffness, which may then adversely affect their running action.

1 Side stretch — arms above head

Stand with feet comfortably apart, hands loosely clasped. Raise arms above head and bend over to one side, reaching as far as possible. Hold the position for 30 seconds, but trying to lower the trunk very slowly during this time and relax the side muscles. Change ◁ sides slowly.

2 Rotation

Stand with feet about one foot apart and parallel with hands on hips. Slowly rotate the trunk to one side as far as it will possibly go. This is NOT a 'swinging' exercise. At the extreme of the rotation, hold the position for 20 seconds before returning to the starting position, then rotate to the other side for a further 20 seconds.

◁▷

Trunk stretching continued

3 Lunge
Another lunge position, but this time the accent is on bending the back. Take a free-standing position, with both legs bent comfortably, and then bend backwards as far as possible, before holding the position for 20 seconds. For this exercise, there is no need to keep the heels on the floor.

4 Lying — back extension
Lie face downwards and rest one hand on top of the other. Holding the forehead against the hands, raise the whole of the trunk off the floor, as in the photograph, and then raise both legs as well. The object is to bend the back as much as possible. If you find it difficult to hold the position, try it first holding either legs *or* trunk, before putting the whole exercise together. Hold for 15 seconds.

Loosening

Having completed the stretching and flexibility work, it is time to carry out some loosening or suppling exercises. These are the dynamic type of exercises which take the joints through a wide range of movement rapidly. With the muscles, tendons and ligaments already stretched, this can be done safely and since one of the most effective methods of raising the internal temperature of a joint is to exercise it, this will quickly prepare the body for the last phase of the warm-up. The following mobilising exercises can be carried out quite vigorously, and are a good lead-in to the final phase:

Ankle circling Sit or stand and rotate each foot in both directions through a full range of movement. The exercise is slightly better performed sitting, as then the ankle can be grasped just above the ankle bones, to prevent rotation at the knee. Although this is a very simple exercise, and usually disregarded, it is useful in helping to eliminate the ankle 'locking' which many people experience at the beginning of a run.

Leg swinging For this exercise, it is helpful, although not essential, to have some support in case of over-balancing. First, each leg is swung backwards and forwards, systematically increasing the height of the kick, and endeavouring to maintain a straight kicking leg, although the supporting leg may bend a little. Following this, turn to face the support and swing the leg across the body in both directions. Again, try to keep the swinging leg fairly straight, although the knee will not be locked. This leg swinging exercise is particularly good for stretching the hamstrings and the inner thigh muscles.

Arm circling Stand with feet 12 inches apart and swing each arm in large, relaxed circles from the shoulder, allowing the trunk to follow the movement. Make sure that the arm is turned in both directions.

It is a good idea to do this type of exercise in a circular or pendular movement, as there is no jarring experienced at the end of the range.

Shoulder circling This involves the shoulder girdle and not the shoulder joint. Standing with feet comfortably apart, let both arms hang loosely to the side of the body, then rotate the shoulders in a circular fashion. At first it is a good idea to practise the movements separately — that is, shrug the shoulders and then let them gently down, and then roll them backwards and forwards. When these four aspects are accomplished, the shoulders can be rolled in a full, circular movement, but you should still keep the arms relaxed by the side.

Trunk circling This can be done either with hands on hips or with outstretched arms. Again, stand with feet apart and then relax from the waist, making sure the back is fairly straight and not bending in the middle. From this position, start a large circle, going as far as possible into the range. A little practice will be needed to really benefit from this exercise.

Progressive speed increase A series of runs can now be carried out, of up to 100 metres in length and gradually increasing in speed with each successive run, until running at full effort. By this means, over-loading of the muscle groups occurs, which prior to any power activity will give an increase in performance. It is thought that the increased load creates an increased excitation of the motor units of the muscles that have been called into play, and that this is then carried over into the actual performance.

All the benefits that have been gained through a conscientious warm-up will gradually wear off, so the closer the warm-up is to the performance, the more beneficial it will be. It is advisable to leave no more than 15 minutes between warming-up and the performance itself.

CHAPTER FIVE

Racing and competition
by Andy Etchells

There is one factor that unites the vast majority of runners. Athletes, joggers, marathoners, fun runners — no matter what title they give themselves — nearly all stress that their enjoyment of the sport stems not from beating other runners but from competing with themselves, from setting themselves a challenge and then matching up to or surpassing it.

To some people, that challenge may be a very personal one that no one else knows about. It could be just getting fit, or promising yourself you are going to run at least four times a week, or simply managing a certain distance in training. The challenge and the accomplishment are private, with no one there to cheer you on or applaud you at the finish; but the achievement is no less real for that. For some, that is fun running at its purest: a simple pleasure indulged in for its own sake, well removed from the workaday world where, whether we like it or not, we are forced into competition, forced to be go-getters and achievers.

Indeed, there is considerable evidence that some of the popularity of running in recent years can be ascribed to its fundamentally non-competitive nature. Many people discover running after trying a number of other sports which they find less congenial because they cannot be practised without the bother of courts or special equipment, partners or teams. Above all, many conventional sports are based on the adversary relationship whereas running in its basic form is about setting your own standards and probing your own limits. You can make your running as organised as you want it to be, with or without others for company. At the moment, in this country, there are probably thousands of people out running who have never run with others and have certainly never entered a competitive race or even a fun run. They are quite happy with this situation and long may it be so: they are the recreational or fun runners *par excellence*.

But man is, of course, a competitive animal. We like to compare ourselves with others, to have a yardstick with which to measure our performance and progress. A further advantage of running — on top of the private pleasures referred to above — is that when competition is entered into, it is not, as in, say, football, simply a question of which is the better team. Football performance can never be truly evaluated and ranked, but as runners we have the benefit of the greatest arbiter of all-time.

This does not imply that there is anything wrong with aiming to outstrip the performances of others, or with wanting to be top dog by demonstrating your greater talents or, another notable feature of running, your ability to work hard and dedicate yourself to a goal. Indeed much of anthropological, psychological and sociological research proves that we only progress as a species and as individuals by means of contest, evaluation, emulation and ambition.

And that is why people race — to test themselves, to see how good they are, for the pleasure of victory, real or imagined, large or small. And as long as we are mature enough as people to accept the customs and courtesies of victory and defeat, the experience, whichever side of the battle we end up on, is an enriching one.

For competition does not have to be cut-throat and all-embracing. Competition in a sport like running brings people together rather than setting them apart. How many other sports allow Joe Jogger to line up alongside Alberto Salazar in the same sporting competition, or his sister Jane to rub shoulders — at the start at least — with the likes of Joyce Smith? There is a genuine sense of community in running which is not possible in, for example, tennis where it is inconceivable that more than a handful of people could ever walk out on to the Centre Court at Wimbledon with Bjorn Borg.

Furthermore, people with experience of other sports often express their surprise at the good fellowship demonstrated even in the heat of serious competition. Of course, at the 'sharp' end of the sport where increasingly, under the more relaxed rules about payments and professionalism, the stakes for potential winners are high and where pride matters more to athletes who have dedicated so much of their lives to a particular end, the ethos may be slightly different. An often-quoted phrase, used to psyche runners up in the right conditions, is 'first is first and second is nowhere'. And you will often hear top runners echoing the sentiment of Jack Foster, the fastest veteran marathon runner ever, who once said: "I'd rather win a marathon in 2:15 than come second in 2:10".

Professionalism is all about aiming for the best and being able to cope with the slings and arrows of outrageous fortune with dignity and then learning from the experience. It has nothing to do with the shameful misuse of the word in what is known in football as a 'professional foul'. When some years ago, a leading athlete stated publicly that he would, if necessary, win at any costs, including pushing a rival off the track, he was not widely admired. Nor was he typical of the sport as a whole.

The competitive structure

Britain boasts not only the oldest competitive athletics structure in the world, but also the most comprehensive. Everyone should be able to find something to suit his or her needs as the system, with very few hindrances, lets you plug in at your own level. For in the wake of the running boom, competitive opportunities have multiplied by the year. As keep-fit joggers found that they wanted some gentle competition to give a point to their exertions round the block, fun runs and later 'citizens' races, such as the Gillette London Marathon arrived on the scene to fill the gap. Meanwhile, the traditional structure of club races and leagues has benefitted by increased numbers and interest and many changes have been made to the traditional format to accommodate the new wave of runners.

Equally, athletic clubs — of which there are around 2,000 nationwide — have become more accessible and less the preserve of the specialist élite. Where clubs did not exist or did not cater for all types of runners, a new tier of clubs arose to serve that need. Here we tell you what to look for and how club membership will benefit you.

We then outline the opportunities for different levels and types of competition across the running spectrum — from fun runs through road races and marathons to the specialist branches of the sport such as track and fell running. You will also find a quick guide to the basic rules of competition and advice on how to compose a racing schedule if you want to take your running progressively more seriously. Finally, there are some hints on how to handle race day and racing tactics.

Rules

Competitive athletic events in this country must be organised under the laws of the Amateur Athletic Association (AAA) and/or the Women's Amateur Athletic Association (WAAA), or one of their affiliated sub-bodies such as the English Cross Country Union. Advertisements and programmes for such events must state this fact so that entrants know that it is an officially sanctioned event. Theoretically, at least, a runner who knowingly competes in an unsanctioned event is liable to disqualification from all official events.

In practice, some unsanctioned events do take place in which runners of all standards can take part. These are the new breed of fun runs and some citizens' races which class themselves simply as runs rather than races and which do not award prizes (or if they do, there is not a hierarchy of prizes, because everybody gets the same certificate or medal simply for finishing). Perhaps the most famous such event in Britain is *The Sunday Times* National Fun Run held in Hyde Park each September. However, these events are not officially sanctioned by the AAA and their rules do not apply.

In order to comply with the rules in official AAA races, there are a minimum number of regulations of which you need to be aware. First, there is the need to be an amateur, ie. somebody who has never competed for prize money in athletics. If you have competed for money in other sports, it is now possible under new rules to apply for reinstatement of your amateur eligibility from the relevant governing bodies.

Then there are certain age restrictions setting out maximum distances for different age groups. No one, male or female, for example, is allowed to run a marathon under the age of 18 in an AAA sanctioned race. I personally do not recommend marathons for people under 18 — partly because of the possibility of damage to growing bones (a subject about which we know alarmingly little), but also because, on a practical level, the budding marathoner should first of all be very competent at all the intermediate distances with the advantage of speed that they offer. See the table of prescribed maximum distances for younger people on page 90.

Then there is the thorny question of club membership. It used to be the case that you could not compete in official events as an 'unattached' runner (ie. not a member of a club affiliated to the AAA/WAAA or other national associations) for more than 12 months. This was designed to encourage runners to join clubs and thus contribute to, and become part of, the athletics infrastructure.

Since there is no such thing as individual membership of the AAA/WAAA or similar national governing bodies, club membership is the only way in which communication can take place between the administrators and participants (including the right to vote on rule changes and other matters of importance).

In practice, though, not all clubs cater for all standards of runners and with the modern road running boom, it has proved impossible to police the '12-month-rule'. As a result, participants in road races do not have to be members of an AAA-affiliated club, but if they are not, they must pay an extra levy on their entry fee of 50 pence minimum (some races add £1) for AAA administration, which is forwarded to the area association. For the other branches of athletics, it is necessary to become a club member after your first 12 months of competition (and, in fact, as will be explained, the other branches of athletics are much more dependent on the club structure than the individual orientated road-running organisation).

If you enter more than a few races a year, it will soon make economic sense to join a club rather than permanently paying the additional levy, for club membership is often as little as £5 (less for juniors) and rarely more than £15 per annum. The question is, how do you find a club — and is it the right sort of club for you?

Finding is the easy part. Consult the list of clubs in the UK Club Directory (see page 174), and note the special ruling about veterans (men 40 and over, women 35 and over). Most clubs carry the title Athletic Club (AC) and this usually implies that they run teams across the board — cross-country in winter, track and field in summer, and road running whenever. Some, however, are season-orientated (winter only; summer only) either by design or circumstances. This may necessitate joining two clubs for year-round activity.

Teaming up with a group of people is a very

subjective thing. You have to decide what you are looking for in terms of organisation, training facilities and company, competitive opportunities and social life. For the newcomer to club running, perhaps the most important thing is the presence of others of a similar standard, or of coaches who will at least guide you if you are unsure about training, and most of the other members are already established, successful runners.

This is competition at its highest level of participation; these top internationals are competing in the 1981 European Marathon Cup at Agen, France. Huw Jones (43), winner of the 1982 London Mararhon, and John Graham (44) are both running.

Larger, more go-ahead clubs solve this problem by creating jogging or beginners' sections to ease the new breed of runner into the system. Some will stay at that level, happy to potter around on a sociable basis with others of a similar standard. Others will start to graduate to more specific and serious training groups relevant to their age, ability and interest.

Apart from the conventional town or regional athletic clubs (which usually have a base at a track and an arrangement with a local authority for changing rooms and a clubhouse) there are other clubs you might also consider. First, there is the 'street corner association', a loosely-knit group which is really just a bunch of people who meet up for training. Then someone may say 'let's enter a fun run' — and the die is cast. Such groups, along with works teams, constitute the vast majority of competing teams in the National Fun Run. If they wish to take their competition further in the same unit, the club will usually benefit by affiliating to the area association (and thus, the AAA). Silverstone Joggers are a case in point. They added AC to their name when they affiliated and within a year or so were winning medals in their county cross-country championships. Most jogging clubs eventually take this step if members show any interest in formal competition.

Then there are the associations that are not geographically specific. The Potteries Marathon Club in the Midlands is open to anyone interested in the marathon in the area — they might, or might not, already be a member of a local athletic club. The London Road Runners Club, on the other hand, is an AAA-affiliated club conferring all the usual benefits on members vis-à-vis race entry. They organise events in the London area but do not have a team as such, or indeed, a central place to meet.

On the national level, there are organisations such as the Road Runners Club and the British Marathon Runners Club. We will refer to these in greater detail under the relevant headings below.

Information and access

The national clubs mentioned above produce their own fixture lists and usually newsletters as well. These are a good source of reference when planning your own race programme. Most people rely on information within their club and in the following section there is a breakdown of the typical athletics club year consisting of championships, leagues, mob matches, trophy meetings and 'freelance' or one-off road events when a club team may go foraging for trophies and prizes ('pot-hunting' as it's known!).

If yours is an active club, you may well get all the information and races you need simply by following the fixture list, but there are public sources as well. The principal magazines are *Athletics Weekly* (long established, with a 1982 circulation of 22,192), *Running Magazine* (monthly — established 1979 with a 1982 circulation of 42,334) and *Athlete's World*. It is rare for an event not to be either advertised or listed (usually both) in one of these journals, which all carry advertisements and information featuring coming events and races.

In addition, there are now a number of annual publications listing road races and marathons. These are very useful for planning and reference, but details should always be checked nearer the time, either locally or in the specialist press.

If you are making individual contact from 'cold' with a race organiser, it is usually necessary to request an entry form (though these are sometimes printed in the magazines) and to enclose a stamped addressed envelope. Entry fees vary from 50p to £5 depending on the size and type of event. Mass marathons with all the back-up required are expensive to mount, and there is often a charitable donation wrapped up in the entry fee as well. However, it is generally agreed that runners get good value from both events and clubs; other sportsmen and women often have to pay more in club, facility and tournament fees.

Club fixtures

Most athletic clubs produce two fixture lists per year for the two major seasons — winter and summer. Let's take a look inside those for a typical club. My own club is Ilford AC in the London Borough of

The cross-country National Championships for women (left) and men (right) are very tough and attract some of the top runners, including Chris Benning, Kathryn Binns, Steve Ovett, Bernie Ford and Mike McLeod.

Redbridge, and looking at our winter 1982/83 fixture list, I can see that I am pretty well catered for as a distance runner throughout the winter.

Cross-country Firstly, we are members of the Metropolitan Cross-country League which operates north of the Thames stretching from Hillingdon in the west to ourselves in the east and as far north as Verlea AC in Welwyn Garden City.

There are five fixtures each season, starting early October and finishing late February, with three before Christmas and two after, when the cross-country championships tend to take over. Each meeting has a senior race (any member of runners per club to run, the first 12 home making the scoring team; points are aggregated over the five fixtures for final standings), junior and youth race. The ladies compete, separately unfortunately, in the Southern Women's Cross-country League and have to travel rather further afield as the name implies for their three pre-Christmas matches.

Each region or metropolitan area has its own mens' cross-country league — the Manchester League, the Birmingham League etc — whereas the women tend to organise in larger areas. Interspersed with the league is a gradually rising pyramid of championship races, from county level (December for the girls, January the men) which leads to the Inter-Counties in January for the chosen few; then area championships (northern, southern etc) in February, followed by the National Championships (late February for women, early March for men). Here nine men per club may run at senior level, with six to score. There are also junior and youth races, while the senior women (where four score) are accompanied by intermediates and juniors.

Every affiliated club can enter area and national championships, whether it has complete teams or not. The men's 'National', as it is known, attracts getting on for 1,500 runners in the senior race whereas the women's has about 250, with twice that number in the junior category. Individuals who are not members of clubs cannot usually run in any of these organised leagues or championships and unlike the open graded meetings in track running (see page 51) there are very few opportunities for the unattached individual in the cross-country season.

Cross-country and road race team scoring are very similar. Usually race positions are added up with the lowest total being the winner (though occasionally leagues invert things by awarding, say, 200 points for a win, 199 for second and so on,

Competition is fierce even at Junior level in the cross-country National Championship, as shown here in 1981 at Parliament Hill Fields, London. Spikes or cross-country studded shoes are needed for soft, muddy courses.

according to the numbers in the race and ultimately producing season point scores in the thousands).

Interspersed throughout this activity in the winter are the usual road races and there are two road relay seasons in September and October and then again in March. There is the occasional cross-country trophy race and, less and less frequently these days, an inter-club or 'mob' match — usually any number to run and perhaps six to score or count.

Some clubs have more of these traditional inter-club events, which generally started life as paper chases, the precursor of organised cross-country running before the advent of the Keep Britain Tidy campaign, if they are not members of a league or if they run a second team for those less competitive. This is the information to solicit when considering joining a club. A good question to ask of both seasons is: "What is there for me if there is a limited number of places on a given team? Will I still get the chance to run somewhere?" Younger runners should, equally, ask about young athletes' leagues and the like, though many will be catered for additionally by the schools structure.

The average senior men's cross-country race is around five miles in distance. In championships, at county level it is usually seven miles, and at area/national level, nine, compared to the ladies' standard three to four throughout. The average competitive member of a cross-country section wil find himself (or herself) running perhaps once every two weeks if he/she turned out on every club occasion. Many other runners, of course, pick up individual road races in the meantime, according to their outside commitments, but racing once a fortnight is a good norm, allowing adequate recovery and giving a regular target to aim at in your training. If you do end up racing more frequently than this, don't expect too much of yourself each time and be prepared to regard some races just as quality training. See also the comments below on planning a race programme.

Separating the winter cross-country season from the summer track season is an interim road season, but the track season is fully under way by the end of April, with county championships taking place in mid-May, leading on up the same hierarchy to national level, usually in August. Again there are leagues — national and area — with a connecting promotion and relegation system between most of them. We have five southern league matches per season, with perhaps a qualifying/knock-out meeting at the end in September. Also for the club athlete of reasonable standing, there are other knock-out cups but as with the cross-country season, there are fewer and fewer inter-club meetings, which is a pity for those wanting to experiment or find their way on the track. Instead, though, there is a burgeoning system of 'open graded meetings' where club membership, unlike nearly all the above events, is not quite so important. Certainly, making the team on such occasions is not something you have to worry about.

Track We have seen above that there is not much access to cross-country racing except through the highly developed club system, but in track running there is much more scope for the individual thanks to open graded meetings, usually run on midweek evenings by clubs with access to synthetic (or all-weather) tracks. Generally these run from April to September, but at major centres like Crystal Palace in London, they may continue through the winter on a once-a month basis.

Here, individual entries are invited for a range of track events; usually there are at least two distance races, say an 800m and a 3000m, and then more occasionally there are 5000m or 10,000m races. The meetings are 'graded' so that each race has similar standard runners in it. Sometimes there may be as many as ten 800m races in succession to cater for everyone, and even some longer distance races.

These meetings are ideal for the newcomer dipping a metaphorical toe in the water, or for someone who simply wants to experiment when there's nothing except a bit of pride at stake. If making the team is difficult, such meetings are useful to guage your progress and can be an important incentive to keeping your interest in training going.

Enquire at your local track and look in the magazines and periodicals early in the season to find out about any track meetings. The organiser will probably be able to give you a season schedule for such meetings the (programme often changes through the season as there is never time to put on the full range of distances) so that you can pick and choose in advance. Entry fees are usually less than £1 per event, generally paid in advance and most will not accept entries on the day. There is also a series of indoor open meetings in the winter at Crystal Palace, Haringey, Cosford and Gateshead. These are all run on the graded system, and advance information of events is included in the athletics periodicals.

Roads It is on the road that the individual has the greatest choice, especially in view of the 'unattached' rules referred to above. This is also the area that has benefitted most significantly from the running boom to such an extent that during most weekends between March and October there is a minimum of a dozen road races, from four miles up to the marathon. Increasingly, the large races are run on Sundays to cause the minimum of disruption to ordinary life and traffic flow, although this can have disadvantages for those with family commitments. However, there are often lots of other things to do for the rest of the family at such races and in this area there is a fair amount of background information over and above the bare bones in the magazines. Two annual, national publications cover the scene reasonably comprehensively: *The Marathon Guide* is just what it says, although it also covers half-marathons and some other road races. There are details of courses, entry procedures, indications of standards etc, and similar material is contained in the new *Road Racer's Guide*.

You can also get annual fixture lists by joining the Road Runners Club. The RRC has over 3,000 members, all of whom must first belong to an AAA-affiliated club. There is no such proviso for the British Marathon Runners Club (BMRC) but they do set standards (you must have broken three hours on a certified course if you're a male under 40, or 3:30 if you're a woman under 35). There are lower standards for veterans: The chief virtue of joining the RRC is the fixture information and reports in the newsletter that appears thrice annually, whereas the BMRC is more of an ideas and coaching body. Membership of such clubs is very cheap and costs only a few pounds annually.

Using these various sources you should easily be able to tell quite a lot about a race, especially if you are looking for information on the sort of standard of runner the event attracts, whether it imposes any time limits at the lower end etc. In addition, the RRC sets standards for many of the traditional road courses based on the severity of the terrain, and operates an awards scheme (first, second, third class etc) based on this helpful evaluation. Thus you will be able to see at a glance that the Duchy Marathon in Cornwall, where a 2:39 time for a man earns the first class accolade, is reckoned to be a tougher course than most others where 2:35 earns that award.

Fell racing The only other major branch of running that distance runners are regularly involved in is fell racing, which takes place mostly in northern England, Scotland and Wales. As a result of rule changes in 1982, this branch of the sport is administered by the Fell Runners Association on behalf of the AAA but unlike the other sub-bodies (such as the ECCU) the FRA *does* have individual membership that entitles you to fixture lists and newsletters.

The FRA classifies its events to show severity, A class events being the toughest and generally (though not always) the longest. Of course, gradient has a lot to do with this classification, and you will see in the fixture list notation such as 10m/1,000ft, meaning

Unlike the modern synthetic tracks (right) the old-fashioned cinder tracks (left) were not weatherproof. Derek Ibbotson, spattered with dirt, pursues Zimny of Poland at the White City in an exciting 5000m race.

the race is 10 miles long and involves 1,000ft of climbing all told.

Veterans competition Details of who is eligible to compete and how this blossoming area of competition is organised are to be found in Chapter 7.

Planning a race programme

For some people, racing is the be-all and end-all of their running, the reason they do it. For others a race is an occasional change from a steady background of running. Either way, a race should be accorded a special place in your diary. It is, if you like, a 'Sunday best' occasion, and for that reason your training approaching the race should reflect this.

At the very least, you should ease down the mileage in the last few days before a race so that you go into it feeling fresh and ready to do your best. Some people have a day off running the day before a race; I prefer just to go for a steady jog and use the time to visualise how it will feel in the race. If it is a particularly important occasion, you will hear people talk about 'peaking' for it. This means that their whole training programme has been geared to this one event, and training distances and quality will all have been directed towards the race. In this case, the last few

The Three Peaks Race is perhaps the most famous fell race of all. Fell racing, an increasingly popular sport, is practised mostly in the hilly and mountainous Peak and Lake Districts of England, north Wales and Scotland.

enjoyment of running their first marathon may be spoilt by a lack of background preparation. By this I mean that there is a huge difference between training, however seriously you take it, and racing when you are running faster (and often longer) than usual, and when you are carried along (and sometimes *away*) by the crowd, the atmosphere and other runners. In fact, there is an art to coping with the race experience itself and it is therefore to be recommended that you run several shorter races before tackling a marathon.

It is often said that you should be able to run 20 miles in training before running a marathon. I would add to that that you should also have raced a half-marathon at least, preferably after building up through several other distances (say, five miles, then 10) as long as these are commensurate with your training distances. As part of the tapering-down period, it may be a good idea to run a short race a fortnight (or even a week) before your big day.

Planning for race day

On the big day, you want to have the minimum of fuss and worry, so it is well worth sitting down earlier in the week to plan everything out, starting with a list of your gear and other essentials — for example, race number, maps, instructions etc. Have these all packed ready the night before, having checked that your gear is in good shape and remembering to take spare warm clothing and optional items (eg. a T-shirt and a long sleeved shirt as possible additions to your vest) on a cold day. Do not, of course, wear new gear or shoes in a race — only tried, tested and comfortable stuff which knows your shape and style.

At some of the bigger marathons, registration for numbers takes place in the days leading up to the event, rather than on the day itself. This can be a good thing as it means you will get the travelling out of the way, and being in the area will allow you to take a look at the course. This is always a good psychological advantage.

weeks (not just days) will reflect a changed training pattern: the longer the race, the shorter the distances you run in training in this period — but there will also be a greater emphasis on quality (or speed) during this period.

It is possible to over-race and become stale and tired. This is why international athletes only race sparingly, but at club level, even racing every week should present no problems — as long as the distances are not too great (obviously, there is a major difference between a brisk five-mile cross-country and a marathon).

With the massive growth in popularity of marathon running, a lot of people are arriving at the starting line with little racing experience, and some of the

If you still have to register on the day, always allow lots of spare time for travelling, queueing and changing. In particular, remember that the excitement of the occasion always leads to a mass, last-minute rush to the available toilets. Go at the last possible moment before leaving your base and then, if you are travelling, just before you arrive to try and avoid that particular problem.

There is a lot of personal organisation and logistics involved in running a marathon especially, and the specialist books on the subject in the bibliography devote some space to the vital last few days when you have to watch not only your physical expenditure of energy, but also to husband your mental resources and keep a cool head. The secret is to rehearse things ahead — work out travel plans, make arrangements for gear collection and meeting up with your friends and supporters. The aim is to be on automatic pilot on Race Day, confident that your organisation will not let you down.

The race plan

It is not possible to prescribe tactics for racing as these will change with the distance, the quality of the opposition, your state of fitness and experience, and the type of person you are. There are certain tips you can pick up, however, like do not always lead your group; let someone else take the pressure and remember that they can shield you from wind and rain to some extent.

If there is a single strategy I would recommend to less experienced runners in longer races, such as the marathon, it is this: always set off much slower than you really feel capable of and consciously restrain yourself if you find you want to bowl away in the rush at the start. The chances are, most of those ahead *are* being carried away by the occasion and that they will come back to you later. Once you have shot your bolt in a long race, there is hardly ever any chance of recovery; it goes from bad to worse. On the other hand, it is a great feeling in the later stages of the race to be passing people who are paying for earlier indiscretions. Always drink when liquid is available: little but often is the rule. As with your speed and energy levels, there is no such thing as recovering once thirst — and the possibly serious consequences of dehydration — have taken their toll.

In view of this, it may even be advisable to start warmer than you really want to be, especially in colder weather. You could dispense with a spare top once you are feeling comfortable and are sure the weather is settled, and you might even keep a pair of cotton gloves in your waistband as a permanent insurance policy. Again, there are more specialised tips for marathon runners in the specialist books.

On the track, and occasionally in cross-country, the only major difference between training and racing may be a choice of shoes. Consult Chapter 3 on equipment for details of spiked shoes but remember you should have done at least a few miles in training in the shoes you propose to wear, especially if you are normally used to heavier training shoes. For distance runners, spikes with heels are always preferable, not only because of the repeated heel strike, but also because tendons which are used to supportive, padded heels, get a rude awakening when over-stretched in a shoe with little or no support.

Competing overseas

If you want to run outside the UK in athletics competition, you must first get 'permission' from your national governing body (the AAA, WAAA, Scottish AAA etc). This is simply a certificate saying you are a *bona fide* amateur athlete who has not transgressed any of the rules of amateurism and will therefore cause no problems for the organiser of a race held under appropriate national rules elsewhere in the world. It also allows the governing body to advise you if the race or races you intend to run are *bona fide* in their eyes. In practice, once you have the certificate, you will never be asked to show it — but it is as well to be aware of the rules.

CHAPTER SIX

The challenge of the marathon

by Cliff Temple

In just a handful of years, and especially since the first London Marathon, held in 1981, the popular public image of the longest standard running event has changed dramatically. Even until the late 1970s, if you mentioned the marathon to most people they would admit it conjured up for them associations of exhausted men staggering through the closing miles, and in particular the famous film of the tragic collapse of Jim Peters within sight of the finish at the 1954 Empire and Commonwealth Games marathon in Vancouver.

Mention the marathon today, though, and the predominant image is of many thousands of people, of all shapes and sizes, happily jogging along in what for many of them has become simply a great community event. Yet the distance of 26 miles 385 yards (42.195km) is exactly the same. So what happened?

For a start, of course, there is a world of difference between an international athlete running for a gold medal in a major Games and the average man or woman aiming simply to complete the course. But even in big international competitions one rarely sees the leading runners in such severe physical difficulty as Peters these days; simply that of extreme fatigue after the race.

It is not due entirely to increased training loads either, because Peters himself was something of a revolutionary in the high quantity of his training, and also the zeal with which he tackled it. That uncompromising attitude may also have led to his undoing, because the 1954 Vancouver race was held in totally unsuitable weather conditions, with the temperatures on the unshaded course reaching the nineties. The combination of the appalling conditions in which the runners were asked to perform (only six finished), and Peters's refusal to modify his own flat-out habit of racing in the face of such conditions, led to the harrowing scenes of his ultimate collapse from heat-stroke.

Today the more responsible organisers of many marathons try to ensure that their races are held in the best possible conditions for the runners (the 1982 Commonwealth Marathon in Brisbane started at 6am to avoid the worst of the day's heat), and runners and coaches know far more about the demands of the event in so many important respects.

The other major development that has led to the booming popularity of the marathon is that it is no longer considered a race only for the elite. Indeed, it is scarcely a *race* for most participants, because the real challenge to them is not the other runners but their own ambition to complete the course successfully.

Thus the camaraderie now existing in the many 'mass' marathons that have sprung up practically everywhere is one of the prime features, as total strangers encourage each other through the difficult stages of the race, with no question of trying to beat each other, just a common will to share the experience of running the distance. For there is no doubt that both mentally and physically it is a severe challenge. No-one runs a marathon easily, and not even an Olympic champion can be certain at the beginning

These runners streaming across Tower Bridge are competing in the annual Gillette London Marathon. The relatively flat, fast course follows the River Thames and winds through some of the city's most historic areas.

of a race that he will finish. So much can happen in those 26 miles.

Yet its appeal is a mixture of many aspects to the first-time marathoner: the challenge, of course, of being able to run that far; the need for a dedicated preparation period, with a near-certainty that if you can complete the preparation then you should be able to complete the distance too; and the subsequent improvement in fitness, tone and health that is a by-product, even for those who do not quite complete the course. Above all, to the novice it has just that irritating proximity of feasibility: just out of reach at the start, but not right out of sight, such as hoping to beat Sebastian Coe or Steve Ovett at 1500 metres would be for practically all of us.

Above all, though, it is the doors that have opened in the running world itself which have contributed to the marathon boom. Now races actually cater for the vast numbers of runners who, just a few years back, would have found that the officials had packed up and gone home when they finished. At the 1978 Goldenlay Polytechnic Marathon, Britain's oldest annual event, 205 of the 220 finishers bettered 3½ hours; only one runner finished outside four hours.

By contrast at the 1982 Gillette London Marathon, 5,389 of the 15,116 official finishers bettered 3½ hours — a much smaller proportion of the field — with the last recorded finisher taking over six hours, and some others taking even longer still. But they got round.

The total number of marathons in the UK in 1978 was just 17. By 1980 it had risen to 33. But in 1982 that figure spiralled to 130! In New York, home of the prototype mass marathon, and many other parts of the world, fields of thousands of runners were already turning out.

But what of the race itself? Where did it start, and what does it represent? The first marathons were held in 1896, when the Olympic Games were revived in Athens. As a tribute to a legendary Greek messenger named Pheidippides (who was supposed to have run from the village of Marathon some 24 miles to Athens in 490BC bearing the news of the victory by the Athenians over the invading Persians, before collapsing dead from his exertion), it was agreed to stage an endurance event at the 1896 Games over the route supposedly taken by him. The event was won, appropriately, by a Greek, Spyridon Louis, and was the only Greek victory of those Games. However, the event caught the public imagination, and it became a regular part of the Olympic programme.

At the 1908 Olympics, staged in London, the marathon was run from the private grounds of Windsor Castle (so that the royal children could see the start) to the finish at White City Stadium, West London. The distance of that race, 26 miles 385 yards, was adopted in 1924 as the offical marathon distance, but until that happened marathon courses often varied considerably in length.

The one inescapable fact to be faced by everyone preparing for a marathon is that it is a Very Long Way. So what it needs primarily in training terms is basically running, running and more running. Diet and shoes can be refined to some extent to help the runner to a small degree, but you cannot eat your way to fitness, nor can the best shoes in the world run the race for you.

So for the beginner hoping to run a marathon, the first stage is to decide when, either roughly or exactly, you want to tackle the big event, and then work backwards from that date in establishing your own preparation. If you are an absolute beginner to running, then you should allow at least six months of build-up to the event. It has been done in less, but I would not recommend it, as not only will the training itself be less substantial but the risk of injury is that much greater through trying to hurry progression too quickly.

For those in their late thirties or older, a preliminary check with your doctor is strongly advisable to ensure that he knows of no medical grounds that would prevent you from undertaking the training. In most cases, the doctor will probably be delighted to hear of your increased exercise plans, as long as you intend to graduate it moderately.

If you have not taken much physical exercise for some time, then you should spend a preliminary week of walking for 30-40 minutes a day at a comfortable pace, to re-introduce your body to the internal processes of exercise.

Then gradually introduce running, by alternately walking and running for 100 metre stretches for as long as you feel comfortable. All running should be at a slow, conversational pace, because if you are puffing and panting, then you are going too fast.

Slow down until you reach the stage where you can talk and run at the same time. Don't worry if it feels as slow as the walk at first; it will improve, as your cardiovasular system gradually adapts to transporting more blood (and with it oxygen) around the body.

If you continue this for several weeks, you will notice a strengthening of the legs, an improvement in your breathing, and that you can run for longer periods without walking. The eventual aim, of course,

The Polytechnic Marathon, which starts at Windsor Castle, is Britain's oldest marathon. The course now runs through Windsor Great Park although it used to finish in the Polytechnic grounds at Chiswick in south-west London.

is to cut out the walking intervals altogether, and just run continuously for 10-15 minutes and more at a time. There is no hard and fast rule for how many training sessions this should take. Instead, be guided by your own body. Above all, the regularity of this training is of the utmost importance. Over-doing the training one day and then taking three days off to recover will not help you progress very far.

Try to envisage the increasing volume of your training over the weeks and months as that of the height of an aeroplane taking off. But no two runners are exactly the same, and some may find that they progress quite quickly, particularly those who have

recent experience of other active sports like soccer, rugby and hockey. In their cases, the main problem may be one of concentration and patience, because they are used to activities involving sporadic bursts of high energy consumption, interspersed with brief respites.

But marathon running has no quick bursts and brief rests. It is one continuous, steady, economic

Runners in the New York Marathon cross the Verrazano Bridge at the beginning of the race. This was the first big city marathon to attract a mass field, and runners come from all over the world to compete in this popular event.

run, paced as evenly as possible, and from the first day of training it is worth remembering the story of the tortoise and the hare. There is no point in rushing, because to rush in a marathon race will undermine your chances of finishing in your best possible time, or even finishing at all.

The event is 99 per cent aerobic, which is to say that oxygen is supplied to the muscles at the same rate at which it is used, as opposed to, say, an 800 metres track runner, who has to run so fast that his body simply cannot keep up and gets into oxygen debt which is only repaid by the enforced gasping for air after the race.

Sure enough, the world's top marathon runners may cover each mile in under five minutes, whereas a lot of us would be unable to run even one mile flat out in under five minutes. But these runners are so fit that to run at a pace of a mile every five minutes is their equivalent of our seven minute mile pace, or ten minute mile, or 12 minute mile; it takes no more out of them.

So let us do away with any idea that running marathons involves running fast all the way, while gasping for breath. What it does involve is running for a long period at a steady pace, and it is your ability to continue this process for 26 miles, your stamina, which is being tested. Therefore the need in training is to gradually develop the capacity to run further and further. However, as you get fitter so the distances with which you can cope become greater. So, to some extent, does the accompanying fatigue.

When you can run four to five miles every day you should start to add more variance to the training programme by continuing to increase the distance run on every other day (say to seven miles), but on the intermediate days remain at four, or even less.

The reason for this is that the body needs time for recovery and regeneration as part of nature's process of strengthening. As you train more and more, so the need for some degree of rest becomes as important as training itself, and many international runners are not afraid to take one day completely off running each week. Nor should you be, as long as you are satisfied that you are fulfilling an adequately progressive training programme on the other days.

Several months after the start of your training programme, the development of mileage per day might go something like this over a four-week period:-

Day1	Day2	Day3	Day4	Day5	Day6	Day7
5	5	5	5	5	5	5
7	4	5	5	6	4	3
8	4	6	4	7	4	Rest
9	4	7	4	8	5	Rest

Instead of miles, which are not always easy to calculate, you may prefer to work in terms of 'running minutes', i.e. total number of minutes spent running each day. But, either way, dropping down on alternate 'easy' days between the harder, progressive days not only gives you a physical but a mental break, as indeed does that rest day at the end of the week, which runners often jealously guard.

The next stage, then, is to choose one day of the week on which you could considerably lengthen your training run with a view to eventually approaching the marathon distance itself.

Most people choose Sunday morning as the time for their long run, leaving them the rest of the day to relax or recover, but any day suitable to your own routine will do. The idea is that this one run will be the session of the week in which your body adapts to running for anything up to two or three hours at a time. That may sound a vain hope if at present you can barely jog 50 metres, but in fact obtaining the first stages of fitness are often the most difficult.

Then, as you become fitter, the momentum carries you along. It is probably harder to actually build up from 30 seconds of jogging to five minutes, than it is to go from one hour to two hours. For once, your cardiovascular system is working well again, then it is simply a question of building up the necessary stamina.

Once a week is sufficient for this long run, but you should start to think about introducing a semi-long run — say, two-thirds of the distance of the long run — at a mid-point to the week. This may involve changing the pattern of the week around again, so that you might end up with:

15 miles —5 miles — 7 miles — 10 miles — 5 miles — 8 miles — rest.

As you run more and more, so you become fitter almost without noticing it. Your pace increases with no apparent extra effort, as you are simply becoming more and more efficient in your running. Without turning every training run into a time trial, it is worth keeping a record of your time for a particular course as a means of checking progress. But be fair, and do not continually try to beat your record, or you may over-reach yourself. Just run at a comfortable pace and do not look at your watch until you have finished. You will be surprised how, over the weeks and months, the times come down without any effort, other than that of getting out and running regularly. We do all have our off-days, of course, according to fatigue or temperament, and occasionally the time may be slower. But it is usually only a temporary dip, and you will soon be improving again.

According to the season of the year, you may be limited in the surfaces on which it is possible to run. In winter, for example, most people have to do their midweek running at night, and usually on the road. Apart from the potential risk with traffic (always wear light coloured training kit to help the motorists to see you), continual pounding on the roads places a tremendous strain on the legs. On every stride the unremitting concrete sends shock waves of several times the bodyweight up through the legs and the back before being totally absorbed.

Too much running on this type of surface can lead to shin soreness and eventually stress fractures in the foot or lower leg, which are common injuries among long distance runners. Thus it is advisable whenever possible to run on grassland or cinder paths where the shock is considerably less. On the other hand, a certain amount of road running has to be undertaken to adapt the legs to the shock in preparation for the race itself. So ideally the runner should use both surfaces, alternately if possible, but neither to excess.

Shoes, of course, can play an important part in reducing and absorbing the shock, and considerable attention should be paid in their selection. For a start, the most expensive may not necessarily be the most suitable for you. Look for shoes that are comfortable all round and do not pinch or squeeze the toes. Some models come in different width fittings, but all should have considerable support under and around the heel.

Most long distance runners land heel-first and then roll on to the forefoot. Good protection is needed here too and, especially if your ambition is simply to train for and complete a marathon, do not be misled by any sales pitch in which the extreme lightness of a particular shoe is stressed. You may even be told how may tons you are lifting in extra weight with a more substantial shoe in the course of 26 miles. But in fact the lighter shoes are made primarily for top class runners who tend to be both light in weight and light on their feet.

If you are neither, and if you expect to be running slower than 2½ hours for the marathon, then the extra weight in a more substantial pair of shoes will be more than compensated for by the added protection and shock absorption the heavier shoes will give. Manufacturers often achieve lightness only by leaving out some of the protective layers of padding that the foot really needs on roads.

Now that most shoes have nylon uppers, rather than the old-fashioned leather, they are much easier to break in, but even so you should ensure that before the actual marathon you do wear the chosen shoes on a few long runs to make sure there are no inner seams or other irritants that could cause blisters in the race itself. Most marathoners get blisters of some description, but in many cases they can be prevented, or at least minimised, by smearing petroleum jelly, such as Vaseline, on the tops of the toes, under the arches, and around the back of the heels. This eliminates much of the friction between the skin and any hard surfaces which causes the blisters to form.

Other areas that should be greased before a long run or marathon race include the armpits, crotch and even the nipples. There has been an increase in the incidence of the so-called 'joggers nipple', in which the constant rubbing of a sweat-soaked T-shirt or vest against the nipples can even cause bleeding during a marathon. Many runners now tape the nipples with Elastoplast for protection.

Every item of clothing that you intend to wear in the marathon itself, even underwear, should be worn at least once in a long training run beforehand to ensure that under 'battle conditions' there is no unsuspected problem with it, such as an irritating vest-seam, or shorts which you find you will have to hold up with one hand if it rains.

In general, the clothing should be loose and airy, and light coloured, particularly if the weather is hot; white is a particularly good reflector of the sun's rays, whereas dark colours tend to absorb them. Of the weather conditions you are likely to encounter, heat is the marathon runner's greatest enemy because while you can put on extra layers in the cold, enjoy the refreshing qualities of rain, or shelter from the wind, you simply cannot escape from heat. All you can do is to try to lessen its effects.

Continuous physical exercise in itself produces heat in the body, but when the air temperature is already high, then trying to lose that heat build-up becomes a major problem. Sweating is the prime method, but in excess this in turn can lead to dehydration, and the taking of drinks before and during the race on a hot day is very important to replace the large quantities of fluid that are lost through sweating.

Convection, the cooling of the skin by a slight headwind, also helps, whereas the use of a wet sponge to cool down the face, neck, shoulders and thighs is an artificial method permitted by the rules. Sponging stations are situated about every three miles in most marathon races, while in between these are the drinks stations, where cups of water, orange and similar liquids (including some specialist electrolyte replacement drinks) are available.

It is certainly worth getting used to taking a drink on the run before the race itself, because to run and drink at the same time is an art of co-ordination in the extreme. It is easier when the cup is only half full, and it is often preferable to control the contents by placing your hand over the top of the cup or pinching it until you have steadied it before starting to drink the liquid.

Obviously the leaders in a marathon will waste as little time as possible at drinks stations, grabbing a cup and perhaps only taking a few sips before dropping it down again. In smaller races, they may even have their own personal drinks waiting in small plastic bottles at the refreshment tables, having handed them in before the race. Using such a bottle means that you can squirt the contents into your mouth rather than trying to suck.

On a cool or cold day, drinking during the event becomes less important, but on a hot day it is essential, as the spiralling stages of dehydration could lead to heat-stroke. So a few mouthfuls before, and whenever possible during, the race will help prevent disaster. After the race take in plenty of liquids (but not too quickly) until a normal pattern of urination gradually returns. Ironically, the better the weather for spectators, the worse it tends to be for the runners, who would prefer a cool, damp day to a hot sunny one!

Most first-time marathoners go into the race with an uneasy feeling about 'hitting the wall'. This

In big marathons, there are feeding stations at every mile along the course, providing water and special electrolyte drinks which replace body salts lost through perspiration (above left). Splashing runners with water can have a cooling and refreshing effect on very hot days (above right).

expression refers to the point that usually occurs between 18-22 miles, when the body's supply of glycogen, the energy source stored in the muscles, has been used up, and while the body switches to fat for its fuel, the runner suddenly feels drained and may slow dramatically, even by several minutes a mile. The feeling comes on so suddenly and without warning that it is literally as though you have indeed run into a wall. The bounce goes from the legs, and in extremes you may be turned from a reasonably fluent runner at 22 miles to an aspiring survivor by 23. Some runners say they never hit the wall, particularly top class performers who may simply have trained their bodies to such a fine degree that the change-over from glycogen to fat happens so fluently that they just do not notice it.

In the late 1960s, one of Britain's greatest ever marathon runners, Ron Hill, developed a form of carbohydrate loading diet (originally used by long distance cyclists in Sweden) in an attempt to artificially increase the amount of glycogen stored in

his muscles, and thus delay the moment of hitting the wall.

The original technique involved what is called a 'bleed-out run', in which the runner covers some 20 miles at a good pace seven days before the race to deliberately deplete his supply of glycogen. For the next 2½ days he takes very few carbohydrates in his diet, concentrating instead on high protein and fat, while continuing to train lightly. From lunchtime on the third day, he switches to a high carbohydrate diet (chocolate, cake, puddings and so on) while continuing to eat proteins, minerals, vitamins and fats, and still training lightly.

The idea behind the diet is to fool the body into producing extra glycogen-storing enzymes during the period of near abstinence, so that when the diet switches to the carbohydrates section, more can be stored. Certainly Hill had some spectacular successes and ran his fastest times after developing this diet, and so the system was rapidly adopted by many other runners, even if not all of them knew exactly what they were doing.

However, this diet does have some disadvantages. For a start, during the initial stages of the week, many runners feel tired, lethargic and jaded, and may be prone to catch any virus which is going the rounds. Their resistance is lowered. Another setback is that stored glycogen needs between three and four times its own weight of water, so that by the end of the week the runner may feel bloated, and will not have trained hard for six days. Even if he has not succumbed to any germ, he will still need a lot of will-power to feel that he is going to run well in the forthcoming race. For it is not until 18 miles or so that the benefits of all that pre-race suffering come into play, and in some cases runners have reported no apparent benefit, or even dropped out before reaching that stage.

What suits one runner may not suit another. The diet still has its ardent followers, although Hill himself has moderated his original scheme, taking a little more carbohydrate earlier in the week. There is also a theory that if it is used too often, the body 'catches on' to what is happening, and the system will then not work properly. Also the drastically revised food intake, compared to normal, may lead to digestion problems, particularly as the training is simultaneously reduced considerably. Some runners now adopt only the second half of the routine — the enjoyable part! — and even then take care to increase only the *percentage* of carbohydrates in their diet rather than the actual volume.

The best advice for first-timers is to avoid tampering with your diet, and concentrate on getting everything else right. Remember, too, that it was developed by a runner who was already one of the world's best and was looking for methods that would give him that vital half per cent advantage over his rivals, having already reached saturation point in his training mileage.

Other aspects of Ron Hill's imaginative experimentation, such as the introduction of the mesh vest to improve body ventilation and to assist the necessary loss of body heat, can help all runners of different standards. But the carbo-loading diet is one that you should really only consider when you have increased your training to its maximum. You have to run, not eat, your way to true fitness.

Even if you do not use the diet, how do you prepare for the Big Day? The easing down period for a marathon — the gradual descent of that aeroplane for landing,if you like — really begins about a fortnight before the race itself. At that time you have reached, hopefully, your highest week's training mileage, and your longest individual training run.

Let us suppose that the previous week you have totalled 60 miles. The total for the penultimate week

Space age-style thermal aluminium foil wraps help keep you warm after a race when your body temperature drops and you might catch a chill. It can sometimes take 15 minutes or so to find your tracksuit after finishing a big race.

THE AAA RUNNER'S GUIDE

before the race should be about two-thirds of that, so in this case it would be 40 miles. In the week immediately before the marathon, around 20 miles would be enough.

For at this stage you want to keep ticking over, but is is too late to be able to do anything which will significantly increase your stamina on the big day without also leaving you tired for the race itself.

So, with a clear conscience, you can cut back on training as the race gets closer. You may find, ironically, that you may even feel tired and heavy on less training, whereas you might have expected (and this does happen too among some runners) to feel more energetic than of late.

If you do feel heavy and tired, though, there is no need to panic. Very often when you approach an event for which you have long been preparing you find that the body seems to have subconsciously switched off in preparation and is preserving itself for the main event. It seems to know, however much you may try to fool it into thinking otherwise, that these last training runs are not the Real Thing. However, do not worry because when the gun goes off in the race itself, all is well again.

In the last two days before the race, you should do virtually no running at all. You do not have to live the life of a hermit, but don't do anything which is going to overtax your energy supplies. You may want to have a short, gentle run on the day before the marathon, possibly just enough to make a final check on all equipment, while your last major meal should be on the night before the race; otherwise you may experience digestive problems.

What you eat on the day of the race depends very much on the starting time. If it is an early morning start, like 9.30 or 10am, then you will need to be up early anyway. Something light, like toast or cereal, will give your stomach food to work on without causing indigestion, but eat at least 2½-3 hours before the start.

Before leaving home for the race, check that you have everything you need, including (if the organisers have posted it to you) your number. At some marathons you have to queue to collect your number before the start, and this could waste not only time, but also nervous energy. Take with you as well a small first-aid kit (plasters, cotton wool, petroleum jelly, disinfectant etc) and other essentials including spare shoe-laces (they always break at the wrong time) and your own supply of toilet paper. It often seems to run out in the changing rooms, and you may want to stuff some into your waistband before the race in case of problems!

Prior to the race stay as relaxed as possible and if it is sunny remain in the shade; you will experience enough of the sun later. Work through your own pre-race routine, performing some stretching exercises, visiting the toilets, smearing on petroleum jelly, and sipping some liquids if it is going to be hot. Don't forget to pin on your number, but the amount of pre-race jogging you should do is minimal.

In major races, the competitors usually line up in groups for the start according to their best, or anticipated, times, with the fastest at the front so that the slower runners do not get trampled in the stampede. Wearing a digital wristwatch can be a great help, not only to keep an eye on the time before the start, but also to record your own time during the race itself and at the finish.

In a field of some thousands it may take five minutes or more to even cross the starting line for the runners at the back, yet the official times recorded will still take your time from the moment the gun fired. So if you start your own watch as you cross the line you will have a far more accurate idea of your total time for the 26 miles 385 yards.

The same applies to intermediate time checks, which usually come at every five miles. As you pass, you can consult your own watch. However, unless you have a very good idea of the time of which you think you are capable, you are probably best to let fate take its course in your first marathon, and run simply how you feel.

The biggest trap into which you can fall (particularly in the bigger races where there are large crowds at the start, TV cameras, radio, helicopters fluttering overhead, and the whole works), is to be carried away in the excitement and start off at a pace that is much too fast for you. Alternatively, trying to match strides with someone who is going just a little too fast for you is also a mistake. There *may* be someone in the race who is going to cross the line in exactly the same time as you, but it would be an incredible coincidence to find him (or her) at the very start.

Every single runner will have a different background of ability, training, experience and ambition, and only much later in the race are you likely to find yourself running with someone of a similar overall standard to yourself. Until then you will be passing people, being passed, and then re-passing the same people, as everyone tries to find their own individual comfortable pace.

If, for example, you have trouble holding a seven minute miling pace for 10 miles in training, then it is less than likely that on race day you will be able to hold six minutes miling for 26 miles. So if you find yourself going through five miles in 30 minutes, then ease right back because you are over-reaching yourself at this stage, and there is a long way to go. Most people can expect to run a slower second half to a marathon, unless there is a lot of downhill running in the closing miles.

If you do have a time schedule to follow, you could write it on the back of your hand for consultation during the race. But use ball-point pen, rather than felt tip, in case it rains!

Eventually comes the moment for which you have trained, as you cross the finishing line, not forgetting to stop your digital watch, as the clock over the line will not have taken account of your delayed start. Some people run dozens and dozens of marathons in their lifetime but still say that nothing ever compares

Running Tip

Marathon day kit

Two or three days before the big race, check that you have all the clothing and other items necessary for the marathon. Make sure that running gear is clean and comfortable with no loose elastic or broken shoe laces. Test everything that you are going to wear before the Big Day and do not on any account buy a new pair of shoes to race in — it could be a recipe for disaster. Wear comfortable shoes that you use for training but not so old and dilapidated that they need resoling. Do not wear your best, most expensive tracksuit to the race — you will have to leave it at the starting line and no matter how good and efficient the organisation and transportation of kit to the finish by the race organisers, things do still get lost. So wear an old tracksuit or an old sweater and track bottoms.

Marathon checklist

1 Running shoes
2 Clean socks
3 Running vest
4 Shorts
5 Tracksuit or sweatshirt and spare bottoms
6 Nylon rain suit (if necessary)
7 Hat and gloves (if cold)
8 Large plastic bag for kit
9 Plasters
10 Petroleum jelly/vaseline
11 Tissues
12 Safety pins
13 Spare shoe laces
14 Headband
15 Race maps and instructions
16 Marathon number

with finishing their first one.

The initial reaction, frequently, is one of 'Never again!' But within a few days the same runners are usually scanning the pages of athletics magazines trying to decide which one to tackle next.

Those few days of rehabilitation after the marathon can be used to good effect to speed up recovery too. On the day after the race try to jog, very slowly and however hard it may feel, half a mile. Then on the second day run a mile. By making your body work, and getting the circulation going again, you are clearing out all of the debris left in the muscles from your exertions. Blisters will heal, bruised toe nails will clear up, and the stiffness will vanish in time. Now you know you can run the distance.

Soon the spring returns to your step, too, and then it is just a question in your second marathon of not simply surviving this time but, all other things being equal, trying to run faster.

Breaking three hours

Once you have conquered the distance, then the path to improving your time will take in two other considerations: speedwork and exercise.

Not that you should abandon your established sessions of steady running, nor the one very long run during the week. If anything, they become an even more essential part of your training if you want to head towards, and under, three hours. But now that you have laid the foundations with your background of steady-paced training, you can afford to move on.

One effect of a great deal of steady-paced training, though, may be a slight shortening of the hamstrings and Achilles tendon which, during this time, are virtually never taken through their fullest range of movements, despite the many thousands of (short) strides taken on each run.

But if running faster in the marathon involves taking a slightly longer stride, then the speedwork you should undertake to further improve the cardio-vascular system (which you have so far developed purely and patiently by steady running) will involve a considerably greater stride.

So the first step, so to speak, is to gradually increase the range of movement of the hamstrings and tendons by exercises, so that you can minimise the risk of injury which is present when you do try to run significantly faster.

Simple exercises, such as standing with your feet crossed over, then bending forwards towards the ground, so that you feel the hamstrings stretch at the back of your thighs, can help. So can placing the heel of each foot alternately to waist height on a table or chair, holding each there for 10 seconds in turn, and continuing for several minutes.

To stretch the Achilles tendons, stand facing inwards on a step or kerb, with your heels two to three inches over the edge. Then gently lower your heels together, half an inch at first, then three-quarters of an inch or further, so that you are gradually increasing the stretch, but without strain. Repeat this 15 times in all. In due course, both hamstrings and tendons will regain their full range of movement.

The term 'speedwork', of course, is relative to the event. For an 800 metre runner, speedwork may mean repetition 400 metre runs in 52 seconds. Yet for even a world class marathon runner, the same distance run in only 67 seconds could be deemed speedwork. However, he would probably run far more repetitions in a session than the 800 metre runner, reflecting the contrasting natures of the two events. What speedwork (in the sense of running faster than racing pace for a given distance) does for the marathoner is to push the pulse to a higher level than it would reach in straightforward steady running. In turn, that can dramatically improve the ability of the circulatory system to shift blood around the body quickly. But it is no use trying to do that until you have established a lower level of efficiency, ie. through that steady running.

The other point is that marathon speedwork is not necessarily run 'flat out'. If, for example, you are running 400 metre intervals in an average of only 90 seconds, then you are still running six minute miling pace, or approximately 2 hrs 38 mins pace for the whole distance. So twelve or fifteen of those runs, with a two minute recovery jog in between, would certainly have some benefit for the runner aiming to better three hours.

The side effects of such speedwork on your steady sessions should be noticeable too, as you should find it possible to run them faster with no more effort. Eventually you will need to be covering some of your shorter steady runs at close to six minute miling pace, because breaking three hours for the marathon requires an average of 6 mins 50 secs per mile. So if you only ever train at 7-8 minute miling, you could not reasonably expect to be able to churn out 26 consecutive sub-7 minute miles in the race.

Gradually, the components of the ideal week come together: the long, steady run of 20 miles or so, which can be at 7-8 minute miling; then the bulk of steady mileage during the rest of the week, at least half of which should be at 6½ minute miling pace or faster if you are having a serious shot at breaking three hours in the marathon; and then the speedwork, once a week, with sessions like 12 or 15 x 400m in an average of 90 secs, with two minutes' rest in between, or 20 x 200m in 40-42 secs with a 200m jog in between, or even 6 x 800m in 3 mins 15 secs, with five minutes' recovery. All the while, too, remember those stretching exercises — daily, if possible.

If you do not have a track available for accurate measurement, you can always run for time instead by simply pushing hard for 90 seconds, then easing off for two minutes, and so on. Alternatively, a session of fartlek can substitute for pure interval training, as long as you are honest with yourself and include a reasonable number of fast stretches within the session.

A final consideration is hills. The traditional hill session of running hard up them, and then jogging back down, is probably of less value to the marathoner than incorporating some stiff climbs into the steady sessions, and then practising the art of running in a relaxed fashion up and over the top, without breaking your rhythm. The pace in the marathon, remember, has to be continuous and economic.

This special 24 week training schedule will help you build up gradually to your aim of breaking three hours on marathon day. In this way you can develop speed and strength for a better time as well as endurance to stay the course.

WEEK	WEEKLY MILEAGE	SUN	MON	TUES	WED	THUR	FRI	SAT
1	40	10	6 fartlek	4	8	5	Rest	7
2	45	11	7 fartlek	5	8	7	Rest	7
3	50	12	8	5 fast	9	6	Rest	RACE 10
4	55	12	8	6 fast	9	8	Rest	2 x 6
5	60	12	8	8 fast	9	8	5	RACE 10
6	60	14	8	6 fast	10	2 x 6	Rest	10
7	65	14	2 x 5	8 fast	10	2 x 6	Rest	11
8	55	15	8	6 fast	10	6	Rest	RACE 10
9	65	15	2 x 5	8 fast	12	8	Rest	12
10	70	16	2 x 5	10 incl. hills	12	10 fartlek or interval session	Rest	12
11	65	16	2 x 5	10 incl. hills	12	1 hour fartlek or interval session	Rest	RACE 10
12	75	17	2 x 5	10 incl. hills	12	2 x 6	Rest	8 + 6
13	65	17	8	10 incl. hills	12	1 hour fartlek or interval session	Rest	RACE 10-12
14	80	18	8	10 incl. hills	14	1 hour fartlek or interval session	2 x 5	12
15	70	18	2 x 5	10 incl. hills	12	1 hour fartlek or interval session	Rest	RACE 10-13
16	85	20	2 x 5	10 incl. hills	14	1 hour fartlek or interval session	9	8 - 6
17	80	20	2 x 6	10 incl. hills	14	1 hour fartlek or interval session	6	10
18	75	18	2 x 5	10 incl. hills	12	1 hour fartlek or interval session	4	RACE 12-15
19	90	12	2 x 6	10 incl. hills	15	1 hour fartlek or interval session	7 - 4	22
20	60	10 + 8	5	8 incl. hills	12	1 hour fartlek or interval session	4 - 5	Rest
21	70	RACE 20	8	10 incl. hills	14	1 hour fartlek or interval session	2 x 5	Rest
22	80	22-24	5	10 incl. hills	14	1 hour fartlek or interval session	2 x 5	10
23	50-60	15	5	8 incl. hills	10	6	Rest	6
24	50	10	Rest	6 incl. hills	6	Rest	2 jog	THE RACE

CHAPTER SEVEN

Veterans- running begins at forty

by Clive Shippen

'Age will not be defied' wrote Bacon, yet for the first 25 years of our lives we try to speed it up, and thereafter we do all we can to slow it down. In modern society, 40 is the age at which the individual is expected to put his feet up. How often do we hear 'I'm not as young as I used to be' put forward as an excuse for backing out of something physical; whether it be dancing or just a kick-about with a child's football. This drift into inactivity in a society that worships television, motor-cars and fast foods has led to an overall drop in physical fitness. A British government survey way back in 1969 showed that only 27 per cent of the male population took part in any physical recreation — and this referred not to the over-40s but those aged 19-22! It is not unreasonable to suppose that the situation has not improved since then.

So if you are an inactive over-40-year-old and you feel that you would like to do something about it, then you might well ask, "But why running? Surely it's a bit late for me to start now". Well, it's never too late, and the best way to illustrate why not is to give a few examples.

James Fixx, author of the best-selling *The Complete Book of Running*, was a former tennis player who allowed himself to put on three stones (42lb) of extra weight by the time he had reached his mid-30s. It took an injury in a rare game of tennis to make him realise that his body had betrayed him. He was no longer the athlete he imagined himself to be. He decided to do something about it, stopped smoking and began running three or four times a week, at first with great difficulty. He soon lost weight and began to enjoy his running more as he became fitter.

He read about training methods and eventually took to running every day. He writes that his friends started to tell him that he looked wonderful, something nobody had said for a long time. He felt calmer, less anxious and could concentrate his mind better, as he gradually felt more in control of his life. He even felt that he had acquired 'a sense of quiet power' which he could always summon up by going out running.

This feeling is experienced by many new runners and is well-illustrated in a letter written by a young US athlete, Kenton Powell, to the San Diego Track Club Newsletter in 1977:

'My father worked behind a desk for some 20 odd years. He never exercised, he was in lousy shape and smoked two packs of cigarettes a day. Meanwhile his kids were participating in a sport he could not even conceive; the sport of running. Well, I guess it finally caught up with him, he was now in his early 40s and his health was very poor. So one day he borrowed a pair of my brother's shoes, went out, and ran a quarter of a mile. When he returned he was wheezing and coughing and could barely breathe at all.

'It is now fourteen months later and my father, now 42, can run a mile in 6:10, three miles in 20:30 and six miles in 44 minutes. The first mile he ever finished took him 12 minutes. He stopped smoking and now runs 6 to 8 miles a day.

'To me this is the greatest achievement possible. He is now in excellent physical condition and sets personal bests every week. I'm proud of a man with such courage and determination and I would take a victory like that any day'.

Germany's Fritz Schreiber, who ran for well over 70 years of his life, referred to his running as the 'melody of my life, of all my life: to sweat out anger, to concentrate on the tasks of life, to feel the pleasure and delight of loneliness and freedom, to be all of a human being!'

There is little doubt that the middle-aged runner appreciates both the physical and psychological benefits of running rather more than his younger counterpart — the physical, because he knows how easy it is for the body to slip out of condition; the psychological, because he is at an age where he has experienced most of society's pressures. Age is very much an attitude of mind. George Sheehan, America's most famous running doctor, thinks that there is no such thing as growing old; his view is that you continue growing as a person or you stagnate. Thus, if you adhere to this viewpoint, you can be 'old' in your 20s. This view was similarly put by Oliver Wendell Holmes in the last century when he wrote to Julia Ward Howe on her 70th birthday: 'To be seventy years young is far more cheerful and hopeful than to be forty years old'. So the benefits are both physical and psychological. Let us consider each in turn.

So what does physical fitness really mean? A doctor might describe a patient as being physically fit if he is free from illness and disability. But he is not truly fit unless he has cardiovascular-pulmonary fitness — in other words: a large, strong heart, powerful lungs and an efficient circulatory system. This is not difficult to acquire. It can be achieved by almost everybody by the discerning use of aerobic exercise.

A fashionable word in recent years, 'aerobic' simply means physical activity in the presence of an adequate supply of oxygen. Applied to physical exercise it can be defined as any moderate but prolonged physical activity that raises the pulse and respiration rates to a degree short of being out of breath.

Endurance running, which is prolonged running at a pace your breathing can handle for long periods, is an ideal form of aerobic exercise. Its value was illustrated by Dr Kenneth Cooper in the late-1960s when he used exercise programmes to rehabilitate heart-attack victims. These men and women would have been advised at one time to take things easy for the rest of their lives, but it was found that carefully controlled physical exercise not only restored them to physical fitness but, when maintained, took them to levels they had never experienced. Many graduated to marathon running and to a life-style that they might never have enjoyed but for their heart attacks.

Dr George Knox suffered such an attack in a restaurant at the age of 55 yet says: "My heart attack was the best thing that ever happened to me". When he regained consciousness in hospital he vowed that he would never take his health for granted again. On discharge he changed his diet and began a slowly progressive jogging programme. Jogging became running — every day. Thirty pounds of weight were shed and after seven years of his new life-style he was running a marathon. He celebrated his 63rd birthday by running 62 laps of the track. "Every once in a while someone calls me a health nut," he says. "When they do, I run around the cemetery a few times. I've turned a death sentence into a life promise".

Dr. Jack Scaff, Director of Cardiac Rehabilitation at the University of Hawaii, is a veteran runner and Chairman of the Honolulu Marathon Association. His clinic has 200 heart-attack victims on exercise rehabilitation programmes at any one time. "We are saying", said Dr Scaff, "that once someone gets into marathon condition the possibility of heart disease is so remote as to be negligible. We're dealing in what we think might be absolute protection. In our programme, among those under 70, we have had zero deaths and zero heart attacks in three years."

According to US statistics more than 60 of Dr. Scaff's cardiac rehabilitation patients should have been dead! No less than 50 cardiologists are reputed to run every year in the Honolulu Marathon, which is the only major marathon to incorporate a race for victims of cardiovascular disorders. The Danish Heart Foundation also believes so strongly in the value of marathon-type training for cardiac rehabilitation that it sponsors an annual 100 kilometres road race.

Dr. Thomas Bassler is noted for his fervent belief that anyone in marathon training has an almost absolute immunity to coronary disease. He has sought out information concerning the deaths of runners throughout the world and has yet to hear of a coronary fatality among athletes in marathon training, whatever their age.

In case you still feel that it might all be a bit too strenuous, or unsafe, or that there might be something in those old wives' tales about exercise not being good for you, it is worth citing the findings of Dr Ernst Van Aaken, coach to the former Olympian Harald Norpoth, and a great believer in maximal endurance running. Dr Van Aaken carried out a survey among members of the Association of Veteran Long Distance Runners between the ages of 40 and 90 from 29 countries. In more than 1,000 reports he did not find one case of a heart attack or cancer during five years of observation.

These accounts indicate that considerable exercise tolerance is acquired by the body when it is subject to endurance running. As a result of such aerobic training, lung capacity will increase, the efficiency of oxygen transfer to the bloodstream will improve, the elasticity of the arteries is maintained, and the heart muscles will strengthen accordingly. As the circulation improves so will the body's metabolism. Waste products, toxins and excess fat will be shed and you will become fit. This fitness will produce, in turn, a general feeling of well-being.

A good illustration of the long-term benefits of running on the heart and arteries is the case of Clarence de Mar. De Mar represented the United States in the 1924 Olympic marathon when he won the bronze medal. He also ran the Boston Marathon no less than 34 times, winning on seven occasions. He enjoyed his running so much that he continued to race until he was 69 years old and to run and work right up to two weeks before his death from cancer at the age of 70. His autopsy was attended by many interested doctors and the results were very significant. Clarence de Mar's heart was considered to be a magnificent specimen, but it was his arteries which prompted the most comment. As one doctor put it: "Instead of the usual spaghetti-like vessels I normally handle, these arteries were like small-bore heating pipes — quite remarkable".

So much for the physical benefits of running, but few of us would run if they were the sole considerations, important as they are. Fortunately there are other important factors that attract the over 40s to the world of running. Lumped together they could be called 'a general feeling of well-being' but individually they are many and varied.

The psychology and philosophy of running is a subject within itself. One of the best things about running is that, unlike many other sports, age does not matter. You can still enjoy running, whatever your age. Every run is a new form of self-discovery which brings new pleasures — and pains. Although your performance as a runner may decline, there are always new challenges to face and overcome.

You may take up running initially simply because the physical benefits attract you, or you may continue to participate because you have a competitive urge which drives you on to better performances. But the most pleasurable experience of all is when you reach the stage where running becomes a vital part of living.

Fit runners of many years' experience have found that their training has a tranquillising effect on them — particularly noticeable when taking a run after a stressful situation. They finish happier, more relaxed and with their problems reduced to their proper proportions. Once running becomes part of your daily routine there are things that you are more likely to appreciate as a mature runner than your younger counterpart, particulary as you run through the countryside and observe the changing seasons.

The increased sense of fitness and body awareness and the spiritual calm that come from running are believed to be due partly to the body's improved efficiency in handling oxygen-wasting, adrenaline-like substances called catecholamines. These substances may affect the mood of the individual and it may explain why fit people are less susceptible to depression and tend to be more content and confident than the unfit.

Another factor is the ageing process. This cannot be stopped, of course, but there is evidence to show that it can be retarded. Some doctors believe that it is linked to a condition called atherosclerosis — a fatty deposit which builds up slowly on the walls of the arteries. Regular endurance exercise can combat this trend and, in some cases, even reverse it.

This does not mean that the distance runner can retain his youth if he trains hard enough, but it does mean that he will never be 'beyond his years'. His mind will be fresh and alert, his will-power improved, his body lean with good muscle tone and his heart and lungs will have plenty of spare capacity. He may well look younger than his age and he will certainly feel a lot younger.

However, this level of fitness cannot be acquired in a matter of a few weeks — you must have patience. If it took you 10 or 20 years to degenerate into your present non-active state, do not expect to be rewarded in 10 or 20 days. If you are over 40, have never run before but you would like to give it a try, what should be your programme?

If you feel that you are very overweight or unfit, then it might be a good idea to see your doctor for a physical check-up. If possible, see if he can arrange for you to have an electrocardiogram (ECG) taken at rest. If you are 50, then have the ECG taken both at rest and during exercise (stress ECG). If you receive the 'thumbs down' verdict, do not be dismayed; there are many runners training with so-called abnormal ECG traces. Seek a second opinion from a pro-exercise doctor as there is strong evidence

Vets' cross-country races can be very tough and competitive indeed. This is the men's National at Parliament Hill Fields, London, which is run over a winding, hilly 10,000 metre course, and varies, according to the weather, between thick, soft mud or frozen, snow-covered ground.

to show that almost anyone can respond favourably to exercise programmes provided that the stress is moderate, according to the individual's capacity, and is closely supervised.

Once you have made the decision to start running, it is then up to you to supervise your own programme. For general advice and some training schedules for beginners, see Chapter 2 on getting started. It is important that you recognise your own capabilities and push out the boundaries only gently at first. Remember that it will take time for your body to adapt and respond to training, so do not increase your work-load too quickly.

Joining a club

It is a great help to find someone of the same standard with whom you can run. There are times when will-power will be necessary to take you through to the next phase and a committed companion can provide the necessary encouragement. When you both, or your group, feel that you have achieved a good fitness base and can tackle 40 minutes of steady running every day, then it is time to consider the benefits of joining a club.

There are many athletics clubs in the United Kingdom and details of how to contact your nearest club are given in the UK Club Directory. Most clubs are of mixed sex and accept all ages. Veteran status begins at 35 for women and 40 for men, with age categories thereafter, but not all clubs provide competition for veterans. However, you do not have to compete when you join a club nor do you have to be a good runner either.

As a club member, you can compete in many organised track and cross-country races against other clubs. You do not have to race hard and expect to be up among the first batch of runners over the finishing line. There is no disgrace in finishing well down in the field, and it is just as important to take part in a race as it is to win. So don't worry if you're not a winner — you can still enjoy the race and the friendly rivalry of your fellow runners.

You can also enjoy the social side of joining a club. Many clubs have their own club-house and they organise social functions and events, including meetings, dinners and dances. Being a club member gives you the opportunity to meet other runners, to share experiences, swap running stories and get advice and assistance when you need it.

So much for the newcomer to running, but what of the veterans who have already been running for anything from five to 60 years? Broadly, these more experienced runners fall into three categories: long-standing club athletes who have never stopped training or competing; former club athletes who retired in their late-twenties or early-thirties and then took up running again in middle age; and people who started running later in life and have been running seriously for only a few years.

You would be wrong to think that any one of these categories has an advantage over the others. When it comes to veteran running, age is a great leveller, and former international athletes often struggle in races against runners who were not in their class when youngsters. Sometimes, of course, even the former internationals and the established veterans who have run all their lives still get beaten by talented 'newcomers' to the sport, who have been running for only a couple of years or so. So whatever your age and running experience, there are always new goals for you to aim at and overcome. Late-comers to running often progress rapidly through the ranks of respected veterans with a lifetime of training behind them. It is a question of natural ability and the driving desire to compete and win.

On average, it takes about seven to nine years from the start of serious training to reach a lifetime running peak. This applies not only to young athletes but to veterans too, providing an added spice to running for the beginner who has the advantage of not knowing his ultimate capabilities. While his more experienced rivals are striving to keep their annual decline in speed and fitness to a minimum, the newcomer has the satisfaction and incentive of observing an annual improvement in his performance. Thus, age is no barrier when it comes to enjoying the sport and taking part in competition at veteran levels.

Training

The majority of veteran runners follow distance-running training programmes. Training patterns are

You are never too old to run, as demonstrated by these competitors in veteran events (above). A wide range of competition, including marathons, road, track and cross-country races, are regularly organised for 'vets'.

much the same as the younger athlete's in terms of mileage, but different in speedwork and tempo-running where the veteran seems to do less. There are notable exceptions, of course, but in general the veteran distance runner will regard a fast 3km or a brisk 8km as adequate pace work in his training programme. It is noticeable that many experienced veterans who still enjoy competing do not have the appetite for repetition pace work and interval training that they once enjoyed. And yet, if they find it difficult to face the rigours of speedwork, they may well require more pacework rather than less.

Charles Smart, a noted runner in the 1940s, continued his speed training well past his sixtieth year. "I cannot understand," said Charles, "why, as runners slow down with age, they do less speedwork rather than more". Smart recognised that veterans after many years of training build up a reservoir of stamina through their careers and are probably better equipped to face endurance events than their younger counterparts. And yet these veterans invariably accentuate the trend by doing more steady mileage and less speed.

A noted British veteran who has not fallen into this trap is Laurie O'Hara of Belgrave Harriers. Laurie commenced running in his late twenties and although he won representative vests for Southern Counties AAA and Middlesex he never reached international status. Yet, when he became a veteran O'Hara was running life-time bests, winning world veteran track titles and finally taking the world age-best 3,000 metres track time from the great Olympian Alain Mimoun.

O'Hara (now 50) still follows the speed training patterns he was using 20 years ago, and his last-lap kick still has plenty of sting in it. Laurie joins up his short speedwork to his long distance running with 2 x 2 mile sessions on the stopwatch. "I have a good warm-up running out to a nice flat two miles stretch of grass and do a few preliminary strides. I then run the outward stretch at a fast tempo on the watch, jog for 10 minutes and then zip the homeward run, in similar time". It is O'Hara's favourite session, takes just 50 minutes, and is one that he slips into his routine when short of time.

Another veteran to show the benefits of controlled speed training on an endurance background is Harry Tempan. An average middle-distance club man in his day, Harry did not produce any really special performances in his veteran years until he was into his fifties. He began joining in his son's speed sessions and the results were dramatic. Harry used to hold the world age records for the over-55s at 800 metres and 1500 metres.

Most of the veterans who take part in track competition follow the same training principle as the younger athletes: speed is built up on a winter's diet of endurance training, fartlek and cross-country racing. This principle is very important for the veteran athlete and generally he copes well with the necessary background work, but how does he cope with speed?

Nearly 300 years ago Edward Young wrote: 'Be wise with speed; a fool at forty is a fool indeed'. Young was not speaking of running, of course, but his words are relevant on both counts. The young athlete can acquire speed very rapidly after the endurance phase. His suppleness and speed of adaptation may soon lead to his running flat out without any ill effects. However, the older athlete must proceed with more caution. He is less supple and takes longer to adapt. He must have a very high respect for the injury risk in speedwork and feed it to his body in carefully rationed doses. So be wise with speed.

Little has been written about training schedules for veterans and their wide range of age-groups, which is perhaps a good thing. It is unwise for a young athlete to follow a schedule slavishly, particularly when it has not been tailor-made for him. It would be doubly unwise for a veteran to do so. Far better to study the principles of training and, by experiment, find out what is best for you. Training is the art of combining all the ingredients previously mentioned in the right proportion for a particular individual. Arthur Lydiard, the famous New Zealand coach, constantly stresses that the athlete at peak form must be equipped with every armament from a 50 metre sprint to marathon endurance and must be able to produce anything between those distances without warning during a race. To do so, you must practise running all distances up to the event of your choice at racing pace.

The principle is the same for all ages but the veteran would be well advised to follow the advice of Bill Bowerman, the United States track coach, who advocates alternate hard/easy sessions for his young athletes. Intensive speed sessions are broken up by steady running to give the body a chance to adapt, besides giving the mind a rest too. In the case of older runners it would be prudent to keep their speed sessions even further apart, say every third day. Some veterans have taken it for granted that they can pick up schedules from their youth, step up the mileage, and then battle their way through to glory. However, most come unstuck, and the ones most likely to succeed are those who are not in a hurry to follow a modestly graded schedule. Indeed, some successful veterans have followed Lydiard training schedules but doubled their length by using them only on alternate days, with a steady run on the in-between days.

When lots of steady endurance work has been assimilated and tempo runs and some speedwork have been added in the right proportions for you, then you will eventually experience the joys of running at your true optimum pace. It will be most satisfying to realise that all the grit, determination, patience and skill that went into your training programme have produced the desired result. But don't be greedy. When an athlete is at his peak it requires more willpower *not* to train than to over-train. There have been many notable examples of international athletes reaching world-record levels in their racing preparations and squandering their newly-won resources before the big day because they did not have the courage to ease off. Runners are notorious for believing that rest means loss of form, but 'rest' is a relative term and does not mean putting your feet up! Veterans must also learn to recognise the danger signals of over-training or over-racing. If you think you feel the warning signs, then introduce a few days of easy running. You will lose nothing by this. When you are very fit and have any doubts, always err on the cautious side.

Racing opportunities

So you are now very fit, very fast, very wise and eager to test yourself against your fellow veteran runners. What opportunities for racing are open to you? Before answering that question it would be a good idea to review the evolution of the present competitive structure for veterans. Races, especially for the over-40s, have been held in Britain for well over 50 years, but prior to 1970 they were on a modest scale only. It was in 1931 that the first club was formed exclusively for veterans, Veterans AC. This London-based club has now passed its fiftieth year with a current membership exceeding 1200. In its early days the principal competitions were sprint handicaps, and although these are still a feature of the club's activities most of the modern membership is concerned with distance running. Up until 1975 there were two age-groups, over-40s and over-55s.

In 1961, on the other side of the world, Arthur Lydiard's preaching of the benefits of endurance running had begun to take effect in New Zealand

Many racing opportunities exist abroad for veterans. Here Jack Fitzgerald (3154) and Jim Caddy (3152) race against a Belgian rival in the 1977 Veterans World Championships 25km race at Bruges, Belgium.

when, in conjunction with a cardiologist, he organised a jogging programme for heart attack victims. Eight months later, eight of the group ran the full marathon distance. The following year, Bill Bowerman (USA) visited Lydiard, took back the jogging philosophy to the United States and by 1963 several thousand

Americans were joining the cult, for which Bowerman received an award from President Kennedy. Running boomed across the United States and soon there was a large demand for competition, and mass-start road races were the principal result. In 1966, the over-40s were sufficiently strong and competitive to form their own association: the US Masters Track and Field. 'Masters' is the American term for 'veteran'. The founder of this movement was a San Diego law attorney, David Pain. Fifty years old, Pain was an enthusiastic runner whose dynamism made itself felt around the world during the next 10 years. Not content with half measures, he organised a full track and field championship programme in three divisions (over-40, over-50 and over-60), and within a year he had persuaded the American AAU to absorb the Masters programme into its own National programme. The US Masters Championship programme was soon attracting veterans from Canada, Australia and the United Kingdom, and in 1972 these contacts led to the combined tour of Europe by American, Canadian, and Australian teams.

Leading veteran organisers in the United Kingdom, notably Jack Fitzgerald and John Hayward, organised a highly successful international track and field meeting at Crystal Palace (three age groups) for the tourists, and the shape of things to come was indicated when Duncan Maclean (87) and Charlie Speechley (86) complained about having to race against men young enough to be their sons in the 100 metre heats for the over-60s!

Following the Crystal Palace meeting and a cross-country race, the touring teams visited Germany where they were joined by a large British team. Besides an international track and field meeting at Cologne, the German International Association of Veteran Long Distance Runners (IGAL) were holding their annual road-running championship at the marathon distance. The number of age-groups had now increased to four and were referred to as Classes 1,2,3 and 4; the last being for the over-70s. It is worth noting that the IGAL has been holding races annually since 1968.

The following year (1973), the Association of Veteran Athletes was formed in Great Britain and through their journal, *Veteris*, they campaigned for the international rationalisation of age-groups, acceptance of ex-professionals into the sport and some form of recognition by the I.A.A.F, besides striving to bring the British regional bodies together into a British Veterans Athletic Federation. All of these aims were achived in the late 1970s together with the formation of the world body, the World Association of Veteran Athletes (WAVA). Age grouping for championships is now universally as follows:

Men	Women
Class M40 (40-45)	Class W35 (35-40)
Class M45 (45-50)	Class W40 (40-45)
Class M50 (50-55)	Class W45 (45-50)
Class M55 (55-60)	Class W50 (50-55)
Class M60 (60-75)	Class W55 (55-60)
Class M65 (65-70)	Class W60 (60-65)
Class M70 (70-75)	Class W65 (65-70)
Class M75 (75-80)	Class W70 (over-70)
Class M80 (over-80)	

No longer do veteran runners lose their motivation as they age — many can hardly wait to qualify for the next class. Instead of worrying about their age they actually look forward to getting older! Age-grouping gives the veteran a fair deal in so far as he knows that he can be beaten only by athletic ability rather than age. Now for the racing opportunities which exist at championship level.

In cross-country there are County, Area and National championships; in track and field, Area and National only, although some counties will soon be holding veteran championships. In all these championships there is no qualifying requirement. If you wish to take part you are free to do so.

This group of 'vets' are off to compete in the 1977 World Veteran Championship in Gothenberg, Sweden. Veteran runners from all over the world gather at these international events, which are held every second year.

At international level there are great opportunites for travel. World Veteran Championships are staged every two years and to date have been held in Toronto, Canada (1975); Gothenberg, Sweden (1977); Hanover, Germany (1979); and Christchurch, New Zealand (1981). The next venue will be at Puerto Rico in 1983. European Championships are also well established and have been held at Viareggio, Italy (1978); Helsinki, Finland (1980); and in Strasbourg, France (1982). The next championships will be closer to home at Brighton in 1984.

Tours are organised for all such events at a very reasonable cost. Single athletes, married couples, and even families, can combine several days of competition with sightseeing trips and other opportunities to relax and enjoy themselves. Many international friendships are struck up and each championship is a reunion for some athletes — an opportunity to meet up with old friends and relive past races and events. Whatever your standard, you are accepted as part of the scene. The championships include not only the full track and field programme but also a 10km cross-country event, a road walk and a marathon. The occasion usually includes civic receptions, banquets and other special entertainments, and the teams have their own distinctive track uniforms.

Other smaller parties regularly attend the Italian Veteran Championships and events such as the popular Bruges 25km in Belgium. Jack Fitzgerald, Chairman of the Southern Counties Veterans AAA, has been organising the Bruges trip for many years. Departing on a Saturday morning and returning the following Monday, the total expense of the trip is relatively small. A great welcome awaits all veterans at these overseas events and there are many runners who just live from one trip to the next.

While the European and World events are staged on alternate years, the German IGAL stage their road championships annually — 10km and 25km one year, followed by 10km and marathon the next. These have been held in Holland, Germany, Czechoslovakia, Romania, the Isle of Man, New Zealand, England, Japan and Sweden.

All of these events represent the icing on the cake. You do not have to be at your very best to compete, but it is more satisfying if you are really fit. As each occasion approaches, a little more spice is added to your training sessions. You wonder how that fellow in Canada is getting on and whether the German you beat in New Zealand really will turn up in Puerto Rico. Perhaps an extra session this week would be a good idea!

So, whether you wish to run just for fun, for fitness or to explore your competitive potential you will always enjoy the benefits of running, whatever your age. For the veteran runner, age is simply a stage of mind; birthdays are merely stepping-stones to the next class. There are no limits, no restrictions as running begins at 40!

CHAPTER EIGHT

Women runners
by Conrad Milton

In the last decade, more and more women have started running as barriers to their participation, particularly in distance events, have gradually been overcome despite some pretty hefty opposition from men initially. It is fast becoming the biggest growth area in running as increasing numbers of women are putting on running shoes and tracksuits and taking to the roads in search of a new fitness and self-awareness. Once the exclusive prerogative of men, running is now being invaded by women who no longer feel self-conscious or shy about taking part in active, energetic sports.

They have dispelled the myth, perpetuated for many years, that running and exercise are somehow 'unfeminine' and 'unladylike', and a new breed of women runners is springing up. They come from all walks of life and occupations — professional women, working mums, housewives, retired women — but they all enjoy running and no matter how busy they are they manage to fit it into their daily routine and work pattern. They run for a variety of reasons: to keep fit and slim; for their health; for the psychological benefits and relief from stress and tension; or simply because they enjoy it.

Women are traditionally the 'weaker' sex, but they are now proving on the track, the roads and cross-country that they are well-fitted for endurance events. In the past, most women's running focused on short, fast explosive events, such as sprinting as they were not considered strong enough to compete over long distances. This situation existed until the 1960s when many women began to challenge the accepted views and regulations and to campaign for greater participation by women in the sport, especially in long distance events. The sex barrier to women competing in marathons with men was finally broken in 1967 when Kathrine Switzer entered the Boston Marathon as K.V.Switzer and finished the race despite a race official attempting to throw her physically off the course. Although she was later suspended from the American Amateur Athletic Union, she set a precedent for women runners, and at last in 1972 women were finally allowed to run the marathon distance in the United States. Other countries soon followed suit and gradually more women started training for marathon events.

However, it was not until 1982 that the first real international marathon was officially held for women at the European Games, and the first women's Olympic marathon will not be staged until 1984 in Los Angeles. It is significant that in the last 10 years, while men have knocked half a minute off the world marathon record, women have smashed the women's record by an astonishing 30 minutes: Beth Bonner's unofficial time in the 1971 New York City Marathon was 2:55:22, but Allison's Roe's New York new world record of 1981 stood at 2:25:29. On this form, she would have won a medal against the men in the 1952 Olympics. However, it is highly unlikely that, given their physiology, women will ever overtake the men, and despite the record-breaking years of the last decade, women's running is now levelling out and new records are increasingly difficult to achieve.

Marathon running, in particular, is becoming more popular for women runners: only 300 women started the 1981 London Marathon but by 1982 the figures had increased to 1300. Moreover, many of these women were not experienced runners who had risen

The marathon women's world record holder is Allison Roe of New Zealand. She sliced 13 seconds off the world record at the 1981 New York Marathon, and her record-shattering time of 2:25:29 still stands.

top British women marathon runners, notably Joyce Smith and Libby Pfeiffer, are well into their 30s (over 40 in Joyce's case), many with children and jobs, but they still manage to run and get to the top without neglecting their other responsibilities. This is an exciting time for women runners and *you* could become part of this great running revolution as you are never too old or too young to start.

Women's physiology

A great deal of research has been done in recent years into the physiological differences between men and women runners and how this affects their running performance. Obviously, the average woman is not so strong as the average man: her heart is only 85 to 90 per cent of the size of his; she has smaller, lighter bones; a lower percentage of muscle mass(23 per cent against 40 per cent for men). As fat weighs less than muscle and her bone structure is lighter, she has less power than a man of exactly the same weight to propel her body.

As already stated, women have traditionally been confined to short, fast sprinting events which require power and speed, but these are muscle-dependent attributes and therefore more suited to men. Long distance events necessitate stamina and efficient movement and it is in this area of running that women excel, particularly in the ultra-distance events where they sometimes beat many of the men.

Women are built strongly to bear the physical strain of pregnancy and childbirth and this endurance quality and high threshold to pain makes them ideally suited to competing in long-distance endurance events. In fact, women hold the world records for long distance swimming. Dr Ernst Van Aaken believes that women may even have more stamina than men and will become increasingly competitive over long distances. Although the woman is handicapped by having less muscle, her greater ratio of body fat may be an advantage indirectly, as she can metabolise fat better than a man, making the

through the schools' or the BAAB's coaching systems for girls and had run for years. Many were relatively new to running — they had started jogging for fitness and fun and had graduated to joining a club and racing regularly, or had even started running as little as nine months before the big event with the sole aim of running and completing a marathon course.

Age is no barrier for women runners, either. Being over 30 does not make you over the hill. Some of the switch-over from glycogen to fat more smoothly on long runs when she needs to draw on energy resources.

Many women worry that if they take up running they will develop large, 'unfeminine' bulging muscles, but scientific research has shown that women can increase their muscular strength without a corresponding increase in muscle bulk. So you can run well and still remain an attractive woman. If anything, running will add to your beauty rather than diminish it, as your figure gets trimmer and you feel fitter and more healthy.

Women's running performance can be affected by their often low red blood cell count. Oxygen is transported to muscles and body tissues in the haemoglobin in the red corpuscles, and if the amount of haemoglobin present is deficient (due to monthly blood loss during menstruation) then aerobic capacity will be lowered and performance will consequently suffer. Iron supplements may be necessary to help reverse this.

Thus women can benefit from their metabolic resources by participating in endurance running where they can utilise their subcutaneous fat as a reserve fuel and so compensate for their limitations in speed and strength where men will always excel.

Running style

Something needs to be said about women's running style as many women, especially beginners, do not develop a relaxed, flowing style and lay themselves open to injuries. Because most women, especially young ones, often wear fashionable high heeled shoes, they tend to have shortened Achilles tendons which makes them particularly vulnerable to Achilles and leg injuries. Fortunately, 'flatties' are now back in fashion for day wear, so try to keep your glamorous high heels for the evenings and special occasions.

If you do wear high heels, then be sure to regularly stretch your Achilles, calf and hamstring muscles to keep them elastic and supple(see Chapter 4 for some simple exercises). Even if you do not have this

Two of Britain's top lady marathon runners are Carol Gould (left) and Joyce Smith (right). Joyce's 1982 London Marathon time of 2:29:43 ranks her as Britain's best and places her fifth on the all-time world women's list.

problem, it is still a good idea to stretch before and after you run — better safe than sorry.

Too many women run very daintily on their toes, putting too much strain on leg muscles and making themselves prime candidates for shin splints. Only sprinters run on their toes to gain power and speed over short distances. It is not the right style for long distance running, in fact, anything over a quarter of a mile or so. Try to develop a heel-to-toe style (see page 19 for further details). Landing heel-first will cushion your stride and help prevent you getting injured. Also, keep your arms relaxed and held low — don't clasp them tightly to your chest as many women do. If you need support there, then buy a better more supportive sports bra (see Chapter 3).

Running safety code

Some women are afraid to start running for fear of being mugged or, even worse, attacked and raped. However, this happens very rarely indeed to women runners, and safety is really a matter of common sense and taking a few simple precautions.

1 Always try to run in public parks or areas where there are lots of other runners and people about. You are less likely to be molested and there are more people to come to your aid.

2 If possible, run in a group or with a friend. There is safety in numbers.

3 Never run alone after dark, especially in remote, badly lit areas or unsafe districts.

4 Always be aware of your surroundings and what is going on around you so that you can anticipate and avoid any trouble before it happens. If you spot danger in time, you can take evasive action before it is too late.

5 Always run facing the oncoming traffic (on the pavement if there is one) and wear reflective strips or a light coloured tracksuit at night or even in the half-light of early morning or late evening.

6 Get someone to pace you on a bicycle if you cannot find a running partner — many parents accompany their daughters (and husbands their wives) on training runs in this way, providing pace judgement as well as security.

7 Don't rely on your speed and endurance to get away fast from dangerous situations. Although you may have more stamina over long distances, many men, however unfit, are still faster in a sprint.

8 If you are really nervous or worried, then you can buy a portable alarm device which is sold by many retailers and big chain stores to deter attackers.

Anti-mugging sprays are still not legal in Britain.

Women's minds

Women are socialised, to some extent, to be natural under-achievers, and thus many are cautious about pushing themselves to their limits. Running can help make them more self-assertive and confident, giving them a new sense of body awareness and a realisation of their own capabilities. For it takes determination and guts to push yourself through a hard running schedule and to succeed at endurance running.

Perhaps because women are brought up to be less competitive and aggressive than men, running is the ideal sport for them. In running, you do not need to test yourself out against other runners unless you want to do so — you can always run alone and set your own goals and running targets so that you are, in fact, running against yourself. By doing your own thing, you can create a new individual role for yourself and discover self–esteem and a new identity.

To be a good runner, you need not only some natural athletic ability but also some very personal qualities: character, determination, discipline, patience and honesty. Obviously some natural ability helps flavour the package. You need character to accept any set-backs and return to training and competition with renewed vigour afterwards; you need discipline to organise your life so that you never miss your training; patience to accept a long-term view rather than short-term success; and honesty with yourself and your coach (if you have one).

Many women runners worry about neglecting their family responsibilities, particularly if they have young children. It is hard work to run a home, a family, a job and go out running. So you must be prepared to be a little flexible with your training schedules and willing to compromise if need be. Train your husband and family to be supportive and understanding and you may be surprised at the help and encouragement you get. It is often married women athletes who have the greatest discipline and rise to the challenge best. Babysitters may become a way of life and are required with greater frequency than in most families. You may also need to marshal a veritable array of friends and relatives to help out on occasions if every training session is to be fulfilled.

The more seriously you take your running and the more you progress, obviously the worse this problem may become, although it can be overcome with good organisation and support from your family. However, you should not neglect your friends and social life altogether. You will probably make new friends through running and there must be a balancing factor through other outside interests which, in turn, helps keep alive your enthusiasm for running itself.

Always be positive about your running and never look for the negative aspects of any situation. Improved confidence in yourself and your running ability can bring about improvements in your performance, and this applies especially to racing where many women are not aggressive enough.

Remember that there are no short-cuts to success in running. Patient and persistent training is the only way to suceed, and it is only by building up strength and fitness that you are going to meet your goal of running a marathon or achieving a respectable placing in a race, or whatever your objective is.

Paula Fudge and Ann Ford, formerly known as the Yeoman twins, have been at the top of British women's athletics for several years. Whereas Paula was inaugural world record holder at 5000m, Ann held a 3000m Commonwealth record.

comparable men runners to compensate for their inherent disadvantages.

Coaching for women

Women's coaching is very similar to that of men, but, as Dr Ken Foreman once remarked:"Because of the differences 'between male and female performers it must be recognised that the female is not a scaled down version of the male...she is a unique and highly specialised individual." Many coaches are over-protective with their girl and women athletes and give them only a half to two-thirds of the training programme that would be prescribed for men. But given women's lower haemoglobin levels and their reduced oxygen- carrying capacity, it could be argued that they should work harder than

Starting young Of course, you have an advantage if you start running in your teens and receive qualified coaching from an early age. Many teenagers are natural runners — slim, long legged with a high power/weight ratio. Also, at this age their oxygen-carrying capacity is better than that of boys although this is reversed as they grow older. Over-training and heavy mileage at this age could have good short-term results but may restrict progress to senior competition. Pressure for instant success, especially from well-meaning but over-enthusiastic parents, is great but the coach should develop a philosophical long-term approach.

During the early teens, spells of peak growth (up to five inches in under a year) can occur when energy previously available for athletic improvement will be required elsewhere by the body and performances will level off or even deteriorate.

Towards maturity Those of you now older will probably recall that the late teens/early twenties was the time of greatest social pressure when courting, marriage, employment all commenced and an adjustment to a new life style was frequently required. By this time, peak growth has ended and the body has adjusted to its new physique. Many women starting the sport at this age do so for a complete change from home or job routine, and for the fresh air and exercise that city life in particular seldom provides.

A far more inquisitive approach is frequently seen in those carrying on from junior days and from the new senior. The 'why' becomes more important than the 'what' as the wish to understand training theory is combined with a unique exploration of the body's limits. A greater commitment develops and increasing workloads may be undertaken; this may well mean twice a day training but remember that too rapid progression can quickly lead to injury and stress problems. Even if you have the time, energy and enthusiasm for two runs a day, it is best to progress gradually in stages. I suggest the following:

2 sessions a day on 2 days a week for 2 weeks
2 sessions a day on 3 days a week for 3 weeks
2 sessions a day on 4 days a week for 4 weeks
2 sessions a day on 5 days a week for 5 weeks

This must be a generalisation and you must be ready to extend the period at any point if you are clearly becoming over-tired. Initially, this type of work might be tried during a holiday when midday rest is possible.

Because of their high discipline capability, women runners are ideally suited to double work-outs of this nature, which have the advantage of completing a major percentage of the required mileage prior to the day's main training when higher quality or greater variety can be introduced.

The lady veteran The terminology might take some getting used to, but at 35, believe it or not, you classify as a veteran and have the added opportunity of competition at each age-band without that awe-inspiring thought of facing Internationals in your first race. Serious competition might never be envisaged and by now you could be well on the open road to retain that trimmer figure and gain muscle tone. You may, of course, even be introduced to the sport by your children, gaining your first insight by watching their enjoyment from a trackside seat deciding that whilst you are waiting for their training to end you might as well don a tracksuit and join some of the other active parents. The club atmosphere of this situation can provide the company and social element to add to any other attractions; and indeed you may find it preferable to run from a club base initially until your confidence grows and you can venture forth from your own front door without feeling that the eyes of every neighbour are upon you in utter amazement.

Home and family routines are probably well established so that you can relax into your running satisfied that a healthier mind and body are resulting whatever the personal performance challenges you set. If you do have race ambitions, remember that running every mile of every run at roughly the same pace will train you to run at that pace but not necessarily any faster. Thus your training should include stretching exercises, shorter, faster runs and more intense work to ensure progress and open up further horizons.

As with any physical activity commenced later in life the veteran beginner is well advised to have a medical check before starting to train.

So exciting opportunities exist for the women runner, regardless of her age, experience and ability. If you are not content with just running around your neighbourhood and want to meet up with other women runners, why not consider joining a women's club or the women's section of an athletics club? Look in the UK Club Directory (see page 174) for further details.

Women's clinic

Our medical panel answers some of the health questions that are asked by many women when they take up running or change their training.

Can I run while I have a heavy period? The first two days are often painful with severe cramping, and I have heard that it's unsafe to run at this time. Is this true?

Unless you experience severe pain and discomfort while running, it is perfectly safe to run with a period. Medical research has shown that exercise, including running, may, in fact, help to reduce and relieve menstrual cramping. Anyway, it certainly won't make cramps worse or more prolonged. Cramping is caused by the prostaglandins which cause the uterus to contract. You can inhibit these prostaglandins and relieve cramping by taking aspirin.

I am training hard for my first marathon but I am a little concerned as I have heard that if I step up my mileage my periods may become irregular or even stop completely. Is this true and if so could it affect my fertility?

It is true that long distance endurance-type running may affect a woman's menstrual cycle and reduce, or even eliminate, her regular monthly periods. Medical evidence suggests that this phenomenon may be related to the reduction of the percentage of body fat that occurs when a woman trains hard. It is thought that a minimum of 22 per cent body fat is necessary for the maintenance of the menstrual cycle. Amenorrhoea, as this condition is called, may be the body's reaction to getting too thin and it is really pointing out that there is not enough body fat to support a healthy pregnancy and so ovulation stops.

While a woman is not menstruating and ovulating, she is not fertile, but fertility should return as body fat is restored and the menstrual cycle returns to normal. The Sports Council's Fitness Advisory Group found that there was no evidence to suggest that sportswomen have specific difficulties in conceiving and bearing healthy children. However, although amenorrhoea is not dangerous in itself, it can contribute over a long period of time to heart and blood vessel disorders. Therefore, you should consult your doctor for a gynaecological check-up if your periods stop. If you are really worried, then reduce your mileage and train less frequently, but many women, including top internationals with the heaviest training schedules, never suffer from this problem at all. On the other hand, one distance runner had not had a period for about five years when she conceived.

Can I continue running during pregnancy? I have heard that many women run right up to and including the day they give birth?

Many women do continue to run during pregnancy without any ill effects but we really do not know how much exercise is safe for a pregnant woman. As long as your pregnancy is normal and there are no complications, then you can continue running although you should run more slowly and carefully than usual, particularly in the later months. This will help to keep you fit and stop you getting heavily overweight. As soon as you feel any pain or discomfort, then stop running immediately and consult your doctor.

Many doctors think that women are mad to run at all when they are pregnant. They will tell you to put your feet up and take it easy. But if running makes you feel good and it is painless, then there is no need to stop. However, if you do have any bleeding or, in the later stages of pregnancy, don't feel your baby move for a couple of days, then stop running and seek medical advice.

When you run, take plenty of fluids and avoid extremes of heat and cold which could adversely affect body temperature. Research in the United States has shown that women who run are statistically more likely to have shorter labours and easier births than inactive women. Perhaps this is because their firm, supple bodies can handle the delivery better. Certainly they are stronger and weigh less after the birth and regain their figures more quickly than non-active women.

? **I suffer from fluid retention, especially just before my period when my stomach bulges and I feel bloated. I feel very sluggish at this time and this affects my running. What can I do about it?**

Many women have the problem of premenstrual retention, and you can now buy over-the-counter diuretic drugs to deal with this annoying problem. Regular exercise will help tone up and firm stomach muscles to make the bulging less evident. The trouble might lie partly in your diet, particularly if you tend to eat a lot of salt and don't drink enough fluids. So try and balance your salt and water intake and see if this helps to alleviate the problem.

? **I have an IUD (intra-uterine device, or coil) fitted. Is it safe to run with this or should I switch over to some other form of contraception?**

Many runners experience no problems at all while others do suffer pain and discomfort. If you do have problems, then seek advice from your family doctor or local family planning clinic, and if necessary change to another contraceptive.

? **How soon can I start running again after the birth of my baby? I have heard that breastfeeding could make running painful.**

You can start running as soon as you feel strong enough and the doctor says that it is safe to do so. Stop at once if you feel any pain or discomfort. Running is perfectly safe while you are nursing your baby and will not affect your milk supply or its quality. Some women who have very enlarged breasts at this time may have to use an extra-firm support

bra to make running more comfortable. Sorbothane insoles in your running shoes will help increase shock absorption and make running easier and decrease bouncing. A gradual return to running will soon tighten up muscles and help regain your slim figure.

? **I have been running regularly for some time and have just had a hysterectomy operation. When is it safe for me to start running again?**

You should not run until your doctor or surgeon says that it is safe to do so. When you start running again, you should run very slowly at first and build up speed and distance only gradually. You should also set yourself a daily exercise routine to strengthen stomach muscles without over-straining them. Try to run on soft ground and wear well-padded shoes for additional shock absorption. If you feel any pain, stop running and consult your doctor.

? **I think that I may be anaemic. When I run, I feel tired and listless without my usual strength and energy. Can anaemia affect running performance and what can I do about it?**

Anaemia is a common problem for many women as monthly periods deplete the body's reserves of iron. As it can lead to a reduction in the blood's oxygen-carrying capacity, it can cause poor running performances. Many inactive women who are slightly anaemic aren't even aware of it, but if you are used to training hard and making demands on your body in aerobic exercise and suddenly you feel sluggish and tired and are making no progress with your training schedule, then you may be suffering from this. See the doctor for a blood test and check-up. He may prescribe some iron supplements. It is a good idea, anyway, to include some foods which are rich in iron in your diet, such as liver, kidneys, wheatgerm (in bread or sprinkled on breakfast cereal), spinach and other leafy green vegetables.

CHAPTER NINE

Training for the club athlete
by Harry Wilson

Whether you are aiming to be the best in the world, the best in your club or the best in your road, the same principles will govern your training. The range of events covered by this chapter, ie. 5km to 20km, is quite wide, so obviously there will be certain differences in the training programmes followed. These are mainly related to the physiological requirements of the events and the physical qualities possessed by individual athletes.

These distances are predominantly aerobic events, ie. the oxygen utilised by the athlete whilst running is roughly sufficient to meet his energy requirements, and there is little build-up of lactic acid, so it is logical that the training will be mainly aerobic. However, there is a certain amount of anaerobic activity (oxygen uptake is insufficient to meet the runner's energy requirements) involved, especially in the following circumstances:

1 An inexperienced athlete who has not yet developed a high oxygen uptake and consequently moves into the anaerobic energy process sooner than more experienced runners. In this instance, he should include more anaerobic training in his programme until he has improved his oxygen uptake.

2 In shorter distance events where the speed level is much higher and the anaerobic energy process may be better utilised, particularly after a very fast start, or if fast surges are used during the race, or towards the end of the race if the overall pace has been fast.

If your main aim as a distance runner is going to be improving your oxygen uptake, then it is vital that you are physiologically suited to do this. Each person's muscular system consists of a mixture of slow twitch and fast twitch fibres. A heavy predominance of slow twitch fibres means that you will be more suited to endurance activities, whereas a predominance of fast twitch fibres implies that you will do better in explosive activities. It is no coincidence that a muscle biopsy carried out on Alberto Salazar, the world record holder for the marathon, revealed a make-up of approximately 95 per cent slow twitch fibres, and it follows that great middle distance runners such as Steve Ovett and Seb Coe would almost certainly have a 50:50 ratio of both types of fibres. So if you are naturally blessed with a high proportion of slow twitch fibres then it follows that training can bring about major improvements in your running but if you have the other type of fibres then the amount of improvement that can be effected by endurance training is limited.

It is not necessary to carry out a muscle biopsy to determine your muscle make-up — if you can do an endurance activity such as running or cycling for a reasonable length of time, say a minimum of 20 minutes without undue distress, then it is probable that you possess sufficient slow twitch fibres to bring about a good improvement with intelligent training. Other physical attributes that will help are:

1 A strong healthy heart acting as a powerful pump to circulate the oxygen-carrying blood to and from the muscles, and to carry away the waste products of exercise.

2 Large lungs inhaling large quantities of air and a good chest expansion allowing the lungs to expand as they take in air.

3 A reasonably proportioned frame; obviously the ideal is someone who has long legs attached to a short, light and powerful torso, but many people

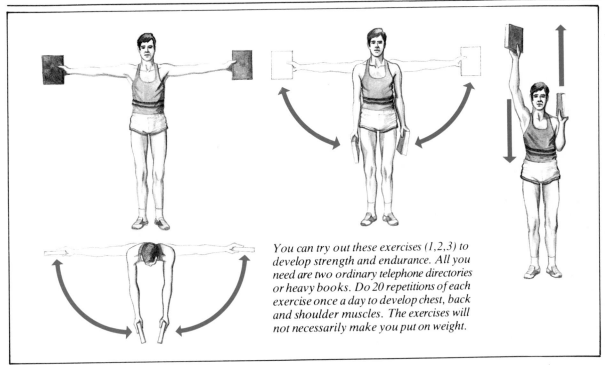

You can try out these exercises (1,2,3) to develop strength and endurance. All you need are two ordinary telephone directories or heavy books. Do 20 repetitions of each exercise once a day to develop chest, back and shoulder muscles. The exercises will not necessarily make you put on weight.

have done well in endurance events without possessing this ideal physique.

Of course, you cannot choose the heart and lungs with which you are born, but intelligent training can make healthy organs more efficient. The heart is a muscle and, like any other muscle, it will become more powerful with exercise. The inter-costal muscles, which control chest expansion, are also strengthened and made more effective by regular activity.

Running technique

It is important to develop an efficient and economical running technique early on in your running career, as it is extremely difficult to change a running action which has been 'grooved-in' as a result of thousands

of miles of running. Your style of running is related to your physical attributes. Your technique is affected by the proportion and dimensions of your limbs, by your muscular strengths and weaknesses, and by your degree of suppleness. However, any idiosyncracies of style should not alter the fact that there is a mechanically correct way to run and you should always try to be as efficient as possible. An inefficient stride is multiplied approximately 800 times for each mile run, so you can see how much difference this can make on long runs.

The basis of the runner's action is to place one leg in front of the other and for the arms to work in time with the legs, ie. left arm forward with right leg and vice-versa. You do not need to learn this technique as it is natural to all of us. Each runner modifies this basic action to produce an individual style but you should be satisfied that your own style is both efficient and economical.

Leg action Most runners naturally develop a suitable leg action and stride length without having to be taught. We have an instinctive way of adapting stride length and foot placement to suit varying circumstances and surfaces, and it is rarely necessary to tell a runner how to vary his technique according to the speed required. As you get fitter and stronger changes happen automatically in the length and power of your stride. You have only to stop running for a while and put on a little weight to see how quickly your stride shortens when you start running again. The important things to look for in your leg action are:

1 That your knees point straight ahead. Any turning inwards or outwards of the knees will result in your feet being planted similarly out of alignment. This means that instead of all the drive being in a forwards direction, a certain amount of effort is wasted in a sideways direction. Turned-out knees are often a sign of insufficient strength in the thighs, which can also seriously affect you if you attempt to sprint, or when you tackle hills on the road or cross-country. I recommend hill running for strengthening thighs, and two useful exercises are:

a. Running up a gently sloping hill, about 400m/ 500m long. Run with a normal action and resist the temptation to shorten your stride to make the exercise easier. Your knees should be pointing forwards and always keep in the back of your mind the thought that you are not running these hills to achieve fast times but to develop a sound technique.

b. Fast running up a steeper hill of about 80m/100m in length. Run with an exaggerated thigh lift, placing the emphasis on maintaining the action throughout the length of the runs.

2 Make sure that you use your feet correctly to assist leg drive. In distance events, you usually make contact first with your heels and then roll forwards to drive off the front part of your feet. To gain more speed, you probably move even further forwards so that when you sprint, the final part of the drive is from the toes. The 'flat-footed' runner lands heavily on his heels, fails to achieve any 'foot-roll', and is unable to use his feet as another lever to assist leg drive. This fault is usually due to weak calves or lack of mobility in the ankle joints and the fault cannot be overcome simply just by asking the runner to use his feet correctly. Strength and mobility must be there to enable the feet to assist the legs, and I suggest that this type of runner does rotating-type exercises to achieve greater ankle mobility, and heel-raising exercises for calf strength. Running over soft, uneven ground will also develop mobility in the ankle joints, whereas uphill runs will strengthen the calf muscles.

Remember that if you have strong and resilient legs, you are equipped to run on all surfaces and will rarely suffer from the injury problems that beset the runners who are weak and inflexible.

Arm action In distance events, a good running technique means an economical use of energy, but we often see energy being wasted by unnecessary arm movements. Your arm action balances your leg action so it is easy to visualise the necessary movements. You need a relaxed, swinging type of arm action to counter-balance the easy striding action necessary for distance events. It is only when you use violent and powerful leg movements for sprinting that you need to use similar arm movements.

For any movement of your legs there is an equal and opposite reaction by the upper part of your body, and you must ensure that your arm action gives an economical reaction. If your arms are not used properly, then your shoulders will provide the reaction, and shoulder movements are both wasteful and slow (the shoulders and upper part of the body will twist, and it should be noted that much more energy is needed to move these large masses than is needed to swing the lighter arms).

Arms should be flexed at roughly 90 degrees and should swing easily backwards and forwards slightly across the front of your body. Easy paddling movements of the forearms will have no ill effects, but always keep your elbows low and close to your body. If they come too far away from the sides, then your body and shoulders will develop a wasteful, rolling action.

For the major part of a distance race, you should carry your arms low, but I advocate a more powerful action during fast surges or the finishing burst. Then, the arms should be raised, flexed more and driven violently through a large range in an attempt to make the legs react in a similar violent way. During the final burst, speed, not economy, is the decisive factor, and it is particularly important to be able to make a quick change into this sprinting action.

Most long distance runners are usually adequately equipped to use their arms correctly for the major part of the race, but some runners are not sufficiently developed in the upper body to be able to quickly adopt the powerful finishing action outlined above. On page 89 I have suggested some exercises that you can practise in order to develop upper body strength.

Improving oxygen uptake

Earlier on in this chapter, I wrote that a great amount of a long distance runner's training will be done aerobically, and it is this type of running that brings about the greatest improvement in the athlete's ability to take up oxygen in the lungs and then dissociate it to the muscles. With aerobic training, you will raise your heart rate soon after the start of running and maintain this rate at a fairly even level throughout the session. This effect is usually achieved by long steady-state runs, but you can introduce some variety by including varied-paced sessions, provided that the fluctuations in pace are not too marked and do not bring about violent changes in the heart rate. Remember that during even-paced long runs there will be some variations in your heart rate as you

encounter uphill stretches or when you increase your pace on downhill sections. Change in terrain can also affect heart rate, as it obviously requires more effort to run over heavy plough than on flat, even grassland. This steady or near steady-state running has the effect of moving huge quantities of blood around the circulatory system, and research has shown that this form of exercise produces greater capilliarisation, ie. opening up more channels for blood to be carried to and from the working muscles.

The pace of the steady-state runs will depend on the length of the run and your level of fitness. However, I like to think that you should train over a range of distances and paces, varying from the short fast runs (3-4 miles) to the long easy run (15-20 miles). The length of the training run will be related to your racing distance and thus 5000m runners would not include so many long easy runs as those athletes who are going to race over 20km. As the speed of the runs determines the level of pulse rate, it is quite likely that a 10,000m runner would be operating at about 150 b.p.m. (beats per minute) on his long easy runs, but at approximately 160/165 b.p.m. on his short fast runs. However, there is a minimum pace that needs to be achieved in order to bring about any significant training effect, and if you do only long slow jogs for training you will not stimulate the respiratory/circulatory system enough to bring about any improvement and you will become a good 'long slow runner'! You can determine your own training threshold (ie. the intensity of exercise needed to bring about any training effect) by the following method:

1 Count your heart rate at rest in beats per minute.

2 Get someone else to count your maximum heart rate in beats per minute, eg. immediately after a flat-out effort over 300/400 metres.

3 You now know your present pulse range, add two thirds of this to your resting rate and you have a rough guide to your training threshold. As long as

Emile Puttemans (white vest) and **Lasse Viren** (dark vest), world class runners at distances from 3000m to marathon.

1 and **2** These two pictures show the finish of the 'driving phase'. The right leg extends powerfully as full use is made of the foot as a lever and the left thigh swings up prior to extending to gain stride length. High knee-lift gives extra stride length as the foreleg automatically swings forwards at the end of the knee-lift. Leg strength and mobility in the hip, knee and ankle joints play an important roles at this stage and it appears that these factors rather limit Viren's action. Leg strength enables the runner to apply great force against the ground and mobility in the joints allows him to extend the drive well behind the body and to gain good thigh lift.

3, 4 and **5** The drive has been completed and the runners are now in the ground-covering 'recovering phase'. The right leg begins to flex naturally as a result of the powerful extension. In this and the next phase ('support') we can clearly see the relaxed action of two skilled runners. There are no unnecessary movements of head or arms as such movements use up precious energy. A runner must be well conditioned to run in this relaxed way, but if he has any energy-wasting actions that affect his running, then constant attention to these details will eventually result in his running

naturally in an economic way. Both Puttemans and Viren show an efficient, compact arm action and there is no sign of tension in the neck, shoulder or hands.

6 The right leg has swung back and the left foot is coming lightly to the ground with the heel making contact first. The middle distance runner makes no attempt to reach out and pull back with the feet as this would be far too tiring.

7 As the body-weight begins to pass over the left foot, the right leg folds up into a short lever. Flexibility and strength of drive determine whether or not there is a high back-lift. There is a marked difference at this stage in the two runners and the difference can be traced back to the amount of drive shown in pictures 2 and 3. It is difficult to say which is the more correct action as in the longer distance events stride length must always be related to economy of action, ie. Viren may not cover so much ground as Puttemans with each stride but his action may use up less energy.

8 The whole of the left foot is now in contact with the ground in the middle of the 'supporting phase'. The only function of the left leg at this stage is to support the body-weight and the calf muscle gains a moment's relaxation. The legs are 'resting' and so are the arms.

9 The body-weight has now moved over and in front of the left foot at the beginning of another 'driving phase'. Note that the feet point straight to the front so that no drive is wasted in a sideways direction.

you are exercising at a rate either above the result figure or not more than 10 beats below the figure, then you will experience some training effect from the exercise.

As an example, a runner who has a resting rate of 50 b.p.m. and a maximum rate of 200 b.p.m. should be training at a pace that will produce a pulse rate of at least 140 b.p.m.

As training thresholds can vary from athlete to athlete, it can be appreciated that training in groups at the same pace will benefit some runners but not others. For some the pace will be just right; for others the pace will be too fast resulting in a gradually increasing pulse rate, and these runners will have to slow down; for others, the pace will not be fast enough to raise the pulse to the threshold level. So, in general, if you are going to do steady-state runs with other athletes, try to run with an athlete of a similar level of ability and fitness. However, running with athletes of similar ability often leads to the runs becoming over-competitive. Avoid this and reserve your competitive instinct mainly for races.

It is sometimes a good idea to check your pulse in the middle of a run and then again at the finish to see whether you are achieving a steady pulse rate at a significant level. You will soon become a good judge of the effort needed to maintain this level over a wide range of distances and will be able to measure improvement by noting how comfortable you feel at a certain pace. A five mile run in 35 minutes may feel hard to the beginner, but this time will soon feel comfortable after a few weeks of regular, intelligent training. As you improve you will find that you can maintain a given pace for a longer time and with much less effort. You will also find that you are achieving a lower level pulse plateau at this pace than previously. As soon as this is apparent, then you can step up the pace or length of your runs. Some of the runs can be timed so that you can set yourself training targets and measure improvement. However, you should guard against treating each

run as a time-trial, and the ease with which you achieve a time is as useful a measure of improvement as is setting faster times. Much of this steady-state running will be well below full effort, and you should remember that improvement is due to both the quantity and the quality of the training.

The recent vast improvements in the times of long-distance races are, in the main, due to the increased mileages run by athletes, and many apparently mediocre athletes have transformed themselves into good class runners by doubling or trebling their previous weekly mileages. Eighty to one hundred miles each week, much of it at a fairly steady pace, is fairly commonplace now, and some runners have covered even bigger mileages at certain stages in their training. This volume is certainly not necessary for all runners and each athlete should find out for himself the quantity and quality of training that brings about the best results. This can be related to several factors, such as natural ability (runners with a great deal of natural ability usually get by on less training than less fortunate runners) and mental approach (some people enjoy the shorter, faster runs, while others prefer the longer, slower runs).

It is also important to build up slowly to bigger mileages and not to switch suddenly from running 40 miles a week to 100 miles a week. The body adapts gradually, so training loads should be increased gradually. Quite often, the runner who attempts to increase his training load too quickly (either by quantity or quality) sustains an injury or experiences such constant fatigue that he gives up the experiment after a week or two. When you step up your training mileage, allow a few weeks for your body to adapt before increasing the load again. Maintaining a training load for week after week calls for great concentration and I think that it is valuable now and then to deliberately slip in easier training weeks to allow you to 're-charge your batteries', both physically and mentally.

I mentioned earlier that sessions of varied-pace

runs performed aerobically can add variety to the 'steady-state' runs. The important points to remember in this type of session are:

1 The faster stretches are not very fast and only raise the pulse rate a little higher than that achieved on a steady-state run.

2 The slower recovery stretches are quite short so that the pulse rate only falls to a level a little lower than the steady-state level.

With this type of session, the pulse rate may only fluctuate about 20-24 beats and the range involved is probably something in the order of approximately 160/165 b.p.m. after the faster stretch and then approximately 140/145 b.p.m. after the recovery.

Two typical sessions for a runner whose best time for 10,000 metres is 31 minutes would be:

1 8 x 800 metres in 2 min 20 secs/ 2 min 25 secs with a jog of 100 metres in approximately 40/45 secs between each 800 metres.

2 16 x 300 metres in 53/54 secs interspersed by 50 metre jogs in approximately 30/35 secs.

These sessions do not necessarily have to be run on a track and, in fact, I prefer athletes to run any repetitions over 400 metres on circuits on the roads, in the wood or over the country.

Improving oxygen debt tolerance

Improving oxygen uptake will raise the level at which you can run aerobically, but if the exercise is sufficiently intense and prolonged then it is inevitable that the time will come when the oxygen supply to the working muscles is insufficient to prevent the accumulation of lactic acid. Obviously the longer the distance, the slower the pace and the lower the anaerobic factor, but even on the longer distances there is something to be gained by including some anaerobic work in your training programme. In order to stimulate the body to increase its tolerance to lactic acid, you will need to reproduce the anaerobic effect in training. This means you will have to train at fast speeds to ensure that your oxygen requirements

will outstrip your oxygen intake, and training at these high speeds will in turn mean that you cannot maintain the effort for long before slowing down or resting. The training effect is usually achieved by a series of fast runs interspersed with recovery periods. Here are some of the methods used to produce this training effect.

Interval running The original concept of interval training, as devised by the German partnership of coach Gerschler and physiologist Reindell, was for the runner to repeat a set distance in a given time with a fixed recovery jog between. A typical session could be 8 x 200 metres in 30 seconds interspersed by recovery jogs of 100 metres in one minute. Pulse rates were used to determine the intensity of the fast repetitions and the efficiency of recovery after the jog. The Germans looked for pulses of approximately 180 b.p.m. after the fast session, going down to 120 b.p.m. after the recovery. The session could be made more difficult by:

1 Increasing the number of fast runs.

2 Increasing the speed of the fast runs.

3 Increasing the distance of the fast runs.

4 Reducing the time spent in recovery.

Although interval training was once primarily regarded as taking place on the track, many athletes now use circuits marked out in the woods, or grass land, or on roads. Another variation to the original concept has been in the use of varying distances during a session, eg. 2 x 400m, 4 x 600m, 2 x 800m with appropriate recovery runs between.

A further variation used by many of the long distance runners that I have coached is to split up the session into a series of sets, such as 4 sets of 2 x 1000 metres, with a very short recovery between each pair of fast runs, then a longer recovery between sets. The training effect on the heart in this type of session is shown in table 1 and should be compared with that produced by a more traditional type of interval session in table 2.

To my mind, it is essential that during interval training the fast runs and recovery jogs are accurately timed, and that pulse rates are checked occasionally to ensure that the correct effect is being achieved. The session is not producing much in the way of training effect if the pulse is not raised sufficiently high after the fast runs or if too much recovery time is allowed. However, insufficient recovery time will not allow the athlete to maintain a good quality in the fast runs.

As your body adapts, so you will find that the sessions become easier and to continue the training improvement there must be some progression by intensifying the session along the lines indicated earlier on in this chapter. In general, I like to think of distance runners improving the quality of sessions in the winter by increasing he number of runs or the distance of the fast runs, and in the summer by increasing the speed of the fast runs or by reducing the recovery times. However, to increase the speed of the fast runs may mean having to allow longer recoveries or reducing quantity. Reducing the recovery time may mean having to decrease the numbers of fast runs or splitting the session up into sets.

The distance and the pace of the fast runs should be related to the athlete's racing distance as this is the physiological effect he is trying to stimulate the body to become adapted to, so I suggest:

1 A variation in distances from 400 to 1,000 metres.

2 A pace faster than that covered in the same segment of a race. For example, during a 5,000 metre race run in 14 min 30 secs a runner would cover each 800 metres in approximately 2 min 20 secs. His training pace during 800 metre intervals should be at least 5 seconds faster than this rate.

3 Total distance covered during the fast runs in an interval session should be at least two-thirds of the racing distance and no more than one-third over racing distance, eg. for 10,000 metre runner, 4 sets of 3 x 1000 metres, or 4 x 3000 metres.

Table 1: this graph plots the pulse rates which are likely to be recorded during an interval training session of four sets of 2 x 300m with 30 seconds recovery permitted between 300s, and four minutes recovery between sets.

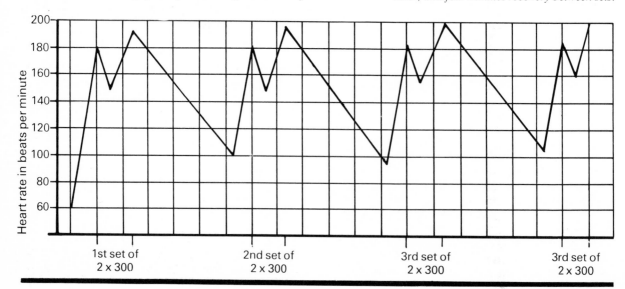

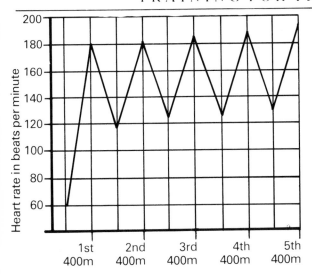

Table 2: this graph shows the pulse rates which are likely to be recorded for an athlete during an interval training session of 5 x 400m, allowing a 200m recovery jog between each.

Repetition running In this type of anaerobic training, the athlete does fast sustained runs at fairly longish distances, and because of the fast pace and the distances covered he needs a complete rest between the runs in order to recover adequately. The athlete cannot be expected to run many of these repetitions and some suggested sessions for varying distances might be:

1 5,000 metres — 5 x 800 metres at about 5 seconds per lap faster than racing pace with 4/5 minutes rest between each.
2 10,000 metres — 3 x 3,000 metres, again at faster than racing pace with 7/8 minutes rest between each.
3 20km — 3 x 5000 metres faster than racing pace with 7/8 minutes rest between each.

Quality is the important factor with these repetition runs so the numbers involved will be small, the pace fast and the recovery long.

Fartlek (speed play) This is the Swedish term used to describe informal fast and slow running, usually over hilly terrain such as woods, golf courses and parkland. The athlete runs for a period of time rather than for a set distance, and during the run he varies the pace according to the terrain and his state of fitness. Before the run, he will probably visualise the route he is going to cover and have a rough idea about which stretches are going to be run fast and which are to be used for recovery. The pace can vary from a quick knee-lifting burst up a short steep hill to a long, sustained stride over a level stretch of country. The jogs between the fast stretches should be just sufficient to allow partial recovery, so the length and the pace of these jogs will also vary.

Although, to a degree, the athlete runs as he pleases, he should ensure that there is a good variety of running at different speeds and over varying distances and that the session is not over-loaded with jogging stretches. Progression is necessary to enable a runner to increase the quality of the fast stretches and reduce the amount of time spent jogging as he gets fitter. To get the best results out of a fartlek session calls for strong self-discipline, and the inexperienced runner may spend too much time jogging. If you are new to fartlek, you should do a few sessions with an experienced runner in order to get the feel of what is required and from then on should work out alone, becoming your own judge as to the intensity of the session. You must be honest with yourself and train hard without supervision. This is a very natural and stimulating form of training, but to produce good results calls for the same concentration as a formal interval session. I suggest a minimum of 45 minutes' fartlek for the 5,000 metre runner, building up to 90 minutes' running for the 20km runner.

Race practice As the name suggests, this form of training tries to reproduce race sensations, both mentally and physically, and is of most value to the 5,000 and 10,000 metre runners. Races are very rarely run at a level pace throughout, so I think it useful to reproduce these pace variations during training sessions. It is quite common for surges to occur during the middle of a race or for the race to get progressively faster. Some typical training exercises that would reproduce race feelings are:

1 5000 metre runner capable of 15min 30 secs

6 x 1200 metres — 1st 400 in 75 secs; 2nd 400 in 70secs; 3rd 400 in 75 secs — 1 lap jog recovery between each 1200 metres

2 10,000 metre runner capable of 31 mins

4 x 1600 metres — 1st 400 in 79 secs; 2nd 400 in 77 secs; 3rd 400 in 75 secs; 4th 400 in 73 secs — 1 lap jog recovery between each 1200 metres

3 10,000 metre runner capable of 34 mins

4 x 1600 metres — 1st 400m in 86 secs; 2nd 400 in 84 secs; 3rd 400 in 82 secs; 4th 400 in 80 secs — 1 lap jog recovery between each 1200 metres

Some sample schedules

So far I hope I have given sufficient information about the various ingredients that go into a training programme, but the secret is to get the right mixture. You alone can estimate your own strengths and weaknesses in relation to the requirements of your event and then decide where the emphasis needs to be placed. You should plan your training according to the time available, local conditions and racing requirements. Some athletes will want to race pretty well once a week throughout the year, whereas others will only want to race at infrequent intervals. Some runners will race on the track, over cross-country and on the roads, while others may specialise on only one of these surfaces. As there are so many varied options, I have chosen three quite popular approaches and have given some suggested training schedules for these options. I don't expect you to slavishly copy these schedules but to examine them

carefully to see how they incorporate the various training ingredients, then use the broad principles to devise your own sessions.

1 A club level athlete who likes to race weekly, summer and winter, at approximately 5km and who can only train once each day. Best of 15 min 30 secs. The athlete capable of 16 min 30 secs can also attempt this schedule as long as he notes the time differences on the Tuesday sessions in April and July.

Week in November

Sun	10 mile steady run
Mon	6 mile steady run
Tues	8 x 1000m circuit fairly steady with 1 minute jog between each
Wed	8 mile easy run
Thurs	45 minutes fartlek
Fri	3 mile very easy run or rest
Sat	10km cross-country race

Week in April

Sun	12 mile steady run
Mon	6 mile steady run
Tues *	Hill-running—8 repetitions up fairly shallow hill—approximatley 400m long with quick jog down between each
Wed	8 mile easy run
Thurs	4 x 1200m circuit fairly steady with just 45 secs jogs between each
Fri	Rest or very easy 3 mile run
Sat	Road race, 5km — 10km

*This session can be alternated with a track session of 6 x 600 metres in which the 15:30 athlete runs the first 400 in 72/73 secs (75/76 secs for 16:30 athlete), then next 200 metres as fast as possible. He uses a jog of 400 metres as recovery between each 600 metres.

Week in July

Sun	1 hour fartlek
Mon	8 mile steady run
Tue	Track — 5 sets of 3 x 300m (52/53 secs for 15:30 runner; 55/56 secs for 16:30 runner) 30 secs jog between each 300m; 2-3 mins jog between sets
Wed	6 x 800m hilly circuit — quite fast with 2/3 mins jog between each
Thurs	6 mile steady run
Fri	Rest or 3 mile easy run
Sat	5km track race

2 An average/good runner who is going to race on the road at distances of 10km to 20km roughly every other week throughout the summer and cross-country once every two weeks in the winter. Can train twice a day.

2 week cycle

5 miles each morning Monday to Friday at a pace varying from very easy to steady according to the way he feels. Remainder of schedule:

Week A

Sun	15 mile steady run
Mon	6 mile steady run
Tues	3 x 3000m circuit fairly fast with 3/4 mins jog between
Wed	8 mile run
Thurs	6 mile run split up: 4 fast; 1 easy; 1 fast
Fri	8 mile steady run
Sat	AM 5 mile easy run; PM 1 hour fartlek

Week B

Sun	12 mile steady run
Mon	8 mile easy run
Tues	8 x 1000m hill circuit fairly steady but with just 30 secs recovery between
Wed	2 fast runs of 3000m with 7/8 mins jog between
Thurs	6 mile steady run
Fri	Rest or 3 mile easy run
Sat	Race at 15-20km

3 An international class 10,000 metre runner (28 min class) who can train twice a day and is aiming for peak cross-country performances in March, and to peak for high quality track races at 5-10km, roughly once every 3 weeks from June to September.

Week in period October/December

5 - 6 miles each morning, Monday to Friday, at own pace

Sun	AM 10 mile steady run; PM fartlek for 35/40 mins
Mon	8 mile steady run
Tues	4 sets 2 x 1000m fairly fast with 1 min jog between each 1000m, then 2½/3 mins jog between each set
Wed	10 mile steady run
Thurs	5 mile fast run
Fri	8 mile steady run
Sat	AM fartlek for 25/30 mins; PM 8 x 800m on hilly circuit not very fast but with only 30 secs recovery between each 800m. Follow this with some relaxed fast strides over 100m. Occasionally a cross-country race could replace this afternoon session.

2 week cycle in March/April

5 - 6 miles each morning, Monday to Friday, at own pace

Week A

Sun   AM 12 mile steady run; PM fartlek for 30/35 mins

Mon   8 mile steady run

Tues   4 x 1500m quite fast with 3/4 mins jog between each

Wed   10 mile steady run

Thurs   7 mile run split up: 5 fast; 1 easy; 1 fast

Fri   5 mile steady run

Sat   AM 5 mile steady run PM 6 x 1000m on hilly circuit — not very fast but with just 30 secs recovery between each

Week B

Sun   AM 8 mile fairly fast run PM 12 fast relaxed strides over 200m with 200m jog between each

Mon   6 mile steady run

Tues   4 x 2000m circuit — fairly steady but with just 1 min recovery between each

Wed   10 mile easy run

Thurs   light fartlek for 20/25 mins

Fri   easy 3 mile jog

Sat   good class cross-country race

3 weeks in summer racing season

Usual 5/6 miles run each morning, Monday to Friday

Week A

Sun   AM 12 mile steady run PM fartlek for 30/35 mins

Mon   8 mile steady run

Tues   Track: 6 sets 2 x 400m (60/61 secs) with 30 secs recovery between each 400m, then

2/2½ mins recovery between sets. Followed by easy strides over 100m

Wed   6 mile steady run

Thurs   Race practice: 4 x 1200m (lap 1 in 65 secs; lap 2 in 60 secs; lap 3 in 65 secs) 3/4 mins jog between each 1200m. Follow by easy strides over 50/60m

Fri   Fartlek for 30 mins

Sat   AM 5 mile steady run: PM 6 mile fast run

Week B

Sun   AM 12 mile steady run PM 12 fast relaxed strides over 200m with 200m jog between each

Mon   8 mile steady run

Tues   6 x 1000m hilly circuit — fairly fast with 1½/2 mins recovery between each

Wed   6 mile steady run

Thurs   Track: 8 x 400m (60/62 secs) trying to stay relaxed with 2½/3 mins jog between each. Follow by 6 x 100m split up 50 stride/50 sprint (100m walk back between each)

Fri   5 mile steady run

Sat   Club standard race at 1500m or 5000m

Week C

Sun   AM Track-race practice 6 x 800m (1st lap 65 secs; 2nd lap 58/59 secs) 2½/3 mins jog between each PM 5 mile steady run

Mon   8 mile steady run

Tues   6 x 1000m hilly circuit — not fast but with just 30 secs recovery between each followed by some relaxed strides over 100m

Wed   30 mins fartlek

Thurs   5 mile easy run followed by 4 or 5 fast relaxed strides over 200m

Among the great 5000m runners are Mike McCleod (737) and Brendan Foster (724), pictured here in an international race (left) and Dave Moorcroft (above), who holds the world record with a stunning time of 13:00:42. All these runners have the advantage of finishing speed and can therefore make the winning break for home from one or even two laps out from the finishing line.

Fri	Rest or easy run for 3 miles
Sat	AM easy 10 mins run
	PM high quality 10km race

I feel that it is a sensible idea to include a week of easy training after a solid period of intensive training, to allow the body to recuperate and adapt and also to let you relax mentally,. I would suggest a week of very easy running after eight weeks of regular training, and certainly it is better to plan for such a break rather than be forced to rest due to injury or over-fatigue.

CHAPTER TEN

The role of the coach
by Denis Watts

In the early teaching of athletics we are mainly concerned with introducing an event to a group of young athletes in the school situation. The teacher in charge of physical education plans a syllabus for the whole school and the work takes place within the boundaries of the school time-table. Because of the large number of youngsters involved and the necessity to apply strict safety precautions, the work is quite formal and concentrated on the broad, basic principles of the event or events.

In many schools the P.E. teacher forms a school athletic club where the very keen and more élite athletes can be taught in a small group or as individuals. Teaching now becomes coaching and a small number of athletes are given individual instruction over a greater length of time. However, the teacher's time is limited; there are many sports and recreational activities to be taught besides all the events in track and field athletics, and this is a limiting factor in the pursuit of excellence in a particular athletic sphere.

As one or two gifted athletes emerge, the teacher/coach may well feel unable to give enough attention to these few promising individuals. If this is the case, the boys or girls should be encouraged to contact their nearest athletic club, which can allocate a Club Coach to them. However, if the local club does not have a suitable coach available, then the Club Secretary can contact the Area Coaching Secretary who will be able to recommend a suitable coach close at hand. The young athletes now belong to a club and have a coach to guide them through the next few years of their athletic careers. They are on the first rung of a ladder which will, in time, enable them to reach their true potential. The Club Coach and Assistant Club Coach form the important base of the British Amateur Athletic Board's coaching scheme. This was established by the AAA in 1947 and later developed to embrace the whole of the United Kingdom under the BAAB.

The structure of coaching

At the summit of coaching in Great Britain there is a Director of Coaching who is responsible to the United Kingdom Coaching Committee for the development of athletics at all levels throughout the country. There are eight National Coaches situated in the following areas:

Area or region	National Coaches
South	2
Midlands	1
North	2
Wales	1
Northern Ireland	1
Scotland	1

The National Coaches all have regional responsibilities but some have been appointed as Group Directors as follows: Sprints/Hurdles; Throws/Combined Events; Coaches' Education; Endurance/Walks; Jumps/Vaults; Junior Development.

There are National Event Coaches to cover all the disciplines in track and field athletics. They are responsible to the Group Directors for progress in their particular events.

Each area has its own coaching structure and is run by a Coaching Committee. Details of how to

obtain coaching may be obtained from the Area Coaching Secretaries. Coaching manpower is at three levels: BAAB Senior Coach; BAAB Club Coach; and BAAB Assistant Club Coach. If you wish to become a BAAB Coach you may obtain the necessary information from the Regional Coaches Education Administrators. The addresses of all these and any further information may be obtained from:
The Honorary Coaching Secretary,
BAAB Coaching Office,
Westgate House, Chalk Lane,
Epsom, Surrey KT1 87AN   Tel: 78 41 775

The coach

The first requirement of the coach is to make himself available for coaching and give up his time. He may be a highly qualified and experienced coach with first-class technical knowledge, and the ability to coach and inspire the athlete through to high international honours. However, this knowledge is of no value unless he is prepared to make it available at the track. The coach must have time to attend the track regularly throughout the year. Once a week may be enough for the endurance events, but twice a week is generally necessary when technical skills have to be acquired, such as hurdling and water jump sessions for the steeplechaser.

The coach should look the part and this will mean a reasonably smart tracksuit and training shoes. He will also need a warm anorak and waterproofs, since

The coach is the athlete's teacher, mentor and friend, and this is the case even with the top international running stars. Here Steve Ovett, the 1500m world record holder, is pictured beside the track with his coach Harry Wilson.

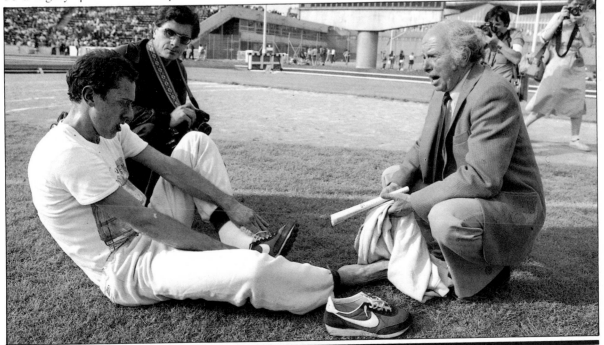

he will be spending much of his time standing around in the wind and the rain. If he is young enough, he should do at least some work with his athletes. General appearance and fitness lend authority to the coach's knowledge and understanding. The days of the eccentric giving instructions from the side of the track dressed in an overcoat and trilby hat are gone. These men did good work in their time but nowadays it is only by insistence on the very highest standards that the modern coach can achieve the required results. This begins with the coach's own example of mental alertness and some evidence of his belief in physical fitness. Some coaches, men and women, have maintained these standards close to three score years and ten!

The club coach must work to establish a good relationship with the club secretary, club officials and groundsmen at the track. This will apply in particular when there is a clash of interests over the competition plans of the individual and the requirements of the club team. Sometimes this will be over school meetings or other fixtures outside the jurisdiction of the club. Here the coach should work to achieve a happy compromise giving reasonable consideration to all concerned. Later on in life, if the athlete has progressed to junior and international honours, this may not be so easy. However, club commitments should always be given sympathetic consideration. Club life is the basis of track and field athletics in this country and, therefore, it is up to coach and athlete to give them all the support they can.

As far as individual coaching is concerned there are two recognised systems. The first is referred to as the **Escort System.** In this case the coach is learning with his athlete and, since the athlete will learn at a greater rate than the coach, the athlete may soon progress beyond the point where the coach is of much further use to him. This is due to the fact that the coach is constantly feeding the athlete with information and, at the same time, the athlete is competing in increasingly better class competition

and constantly learning from rubbing shoulders with, and listening to other competitors. This information does not always get back to the coach who now, metaphorically speaking, is having to run very fast in order to keep pace with his athlete.

The second method is the **Transfer System.** Here the athlete passes from one coach to another as he progresses. This is helpful to the athlete but disappointing for the keen young coach who wishes to reach the top of the tree himself one day. The Transfer System is probably the most effective but unrewarding for the coach and sometimes leads to bad feeling among the coaches at the lower levels. On the other hand, the Escort System can work well where you have a capable and intelligent coach, especially if he has only just retired from active participation at a good level himself. In this case, the young athlete is recommended to stay with his coach because with the passing of time he will get to know the athlete so well that he will become his guide, mentor and father confessor — someone to whom he can always return in later life for help and advice.

On any club training night when most of the facilities for track and field athletics are being used, the coach must be fully aware of all the safety precautions. The responsibility rests with everyone concerned with the development of the sport: the officials who originally planned the layout of the facilities, the groundsmen for maintaining them in good condition and the coaches who are conducting coaching in running, jumping and throwing. The running coaches must look out for any likelihood of a discus bouncing across the track. They should not allow any runners to jog across the track on their recoveries when throwing practice is taking place at either end, for example. This means that the club coaches must have an organisation of their own within the club and consult each other. They must plan the training nights so that the facilities may be used by all with complete safety. It is the coaches' absolute responsibility to insist on a code of strict track discipline at all times.

With the increasing cost of equipment, such as shoes and tracksuits, it is essential that young athletes receive good instruction on their selection, use and preservation. Shoes are the most vital part of an athlete's equipment for if they do not fit properly, he will not be able to perform efficiently. In the case of the distance runner this will almost certainly prove disastrous. The coach may advise his athletes how to get the correct size and width fitting. He must also advise on hygiene, cleanliness and care of the feet — a visit to a chiropodist once a year is a useful precaution.

Finally, the club coach should keep a watchful eye on all the runners at the club. He must keep a special look-out for any athletes whom he considers to be injured, under stress or otherwise unfit for training or competition. He should try to enlist the help of a doctor with an interest in sports medicine and work in close collaboration with a qualified physiotherapist. Competition under stress or injury can have disastrous effects on the future career of a young athlete.

The athlete

Once you have a coach it is up to you to develop a good working relationship with him. Relationships involve responsibilities and the first of these is that you should be reliable and always arrive for coaching at the appointed place on time. Punctuality on your part is essential if the coach is to work efficiently with his squad. If, by any chance, you are unable to get there for an agreed session or you are going to be late, you must let your coach know as soon as possible. This is normal courtesy on your part and a habit which you should adhere to throughout your career.

In the early days of your partnership you must do as you are told. After a year or two, you will be actively encouraged to put forward ideas of your own and discuss them with your coach, and even begin to plan your own training programme and take it to your coach for help and advice. Of course, your coach may disagree with you but you will both profit from discussing the alternatives together.

You and your coach must be loyal to each other. You may bandy words on the track and your coach may shout at you on occasions in order to encourage you to greater efforts in training! However, in public, you must show loyalty and respect for each other if your relationship is to flourish.

A running coach will almost certainly be coaching several athletes, of whom one or two may become your direct rivals in competition. Do not let this discourage you because your coach knows that the success of his squad depends largely on his fairness and impartial judgement at all times. It is advantageous for you to be training with runners who are as good as, or better than, you, and competition in training will benefit the whole group.

You will be asked to keep a training diary which your coach will want to see every week. What you write at the end of the day must be the exact truth without any exaggerations or embellishments. If you miss a session or fail to complete one, then you must record it. If you cover up, your coach will think you have completed the work he has given you and then make a faulty assessment of your level of fitness. Next time he increases your work load it could lead from one disastrous session to another and your training may be retarded for several weeks.

If there is any situation that is affecting the quality or quantity of your training you should let your coach know. It may be trouble at school, homework, a boyfriend or girlfriend who is being over-demanding and taking up too much time, or just lack of sleep through noise or worry. Sharing a room with an older brother or sister who always comes to bed late can disturb you and leave you tired and listless in training next day. All these things and others can make the difference between success and failure. With the help of your coach, try to regulate your life in such a way that you will have every chance to attain your true potential on the track.

The objective of the good coach is to advance you

and not himself. He is prepared to accept the fact that he will not get much publicity for the work he does with athletes. All this will cost him time and sometimes money, and he does it for the satisfaction it gives him to see you achieve success under his guidance. Therefore, when you succeed you should give him full credit when the opportunity arises. Public acclaim for your achievements is his just reward for his efforts on your behalf.

The coaching session

The coach and athlete normally meet once or twice a week. At one of these sessions the coach gives his individual attention to the athlete. On the other occasions he may just observe him training while he gives personal attention to another runner. The club coach has to divide his time among a number of athletes and it is not possible for him to coach every athlete individually at each training session.

The session should begin with a mass warm-up for all the athletes. This will usually be taken by the club coach with assistant coaches to help him. As you get more experienced you will be able to do your warm-up by yourself and come to your coach fully prepared to commence the work he has prepared for you. This, of course saves your coach time and enables him, in the meantime, to give some personal attention to another member of his squad. You should wear your tracksuit in cold weather for all this preliminary work and only take it off when the technical work begins. During the warm-up, all track work should be done in the outside lanes, leaving the inside of the track free for time trials, repetition runs and other forms of technical training that require the use of a stopwatch.

The club coach should come to the track with a clear plan for each member of his group. His assistants can each be given individuals or groups to help and supervise by timing, recording and just observing. In some cases they will be coaching specific skills under the direction of the coach.

It is your responsibility to check your equipment before leaving home. You must be certain that you have everything you need for the session. Remember that after training in wet conditions you must not dry your spikes or training shoes artificially. Keep them away from the drying room, any fires or hot pipes, otherwise they will be distorted and hopelessly unfit for further use. If you return them to your retailer in this condition you will not be able to obtain a credit note for another pair.

Coaching methods

The coach uses various methods to help the athlete learn new techniques and technical skills. These are listed below.

Personal demonstration This can be very useful, especially if your coach has recently retired from active athletics and is a good demonstrator. Breaking down a skill into its component parts and working on exercises that simulate the technique can be helpful to you. This will apply to a greater degree in hurdling and water jumping for steeplechase practice. Many running coaches like to maintain a standard of fitness themselves and, while you are still young, you may find your coach going for long steady runs with you and talking you through certain phases of the training session. You should accept this gladly but do not expect him to be able to keep this up as he gets older and you begin to improve rapidly.

Getting a leading athlete to demonstrate the event Here your coach can talk about the event and outline the technique and training methods being shown by the demonstrator. You will also have the opportunity to ask the athlete questions about his personal career and training schedules. This can be an exhilarating experience and you will be inspired to harder training and better performances.

Putting the young athlete in position and guiding This is all right in the beginning, particularly with steeplechasers. However, all movements are done at speed and you will find that this method has its limitations for the runner, although in preliminary field events coaching, it is widely used.

Verbal instruction Your coach will have to spend a certain amount of time in each session instructing you verbally. There are, however, certain pitfalls into which the coach must not be drawn:
1) What he says should be brief and to the point. If you have too much instruction at one time you may find it confusing. It is better if he says too little rather than too much. The short, sharp instruction will at least be put into effect because it will be heard and understood. Your coach should use phrases that convey exactly what he requires of you. For fast running he might say: "cover the ground with your thighs", or for hurdling techniques: "bring your trailing leg through late but fast". You can understand and appreciate sharp, clear instructions such as these.
2) In cold weather, instructions should be given 'on the move'. Your coach may run with you as you jog back during your recoveries and tell you what you did and how to correct any faults. In all cases, he should be quick and decisive and not come back with any second thoughts.

Asking you to report back your sensations after each period of work After you have described to your coach how your body was functioning during the run, you may be surprised to be told that your sensations were wrong. You will have to go back and try again until you get the feeling that produced the correct results. This is an important aspect of coaching because the coach builds up a mental picture of what it feels like to be the athlete. Soon you begin to understand each other and thus build up a meaningful rapport.

Getting the runner to explain the training and technique of his event to others In the club hut during the winter months this can be an interesting and profitable exercise. The more experienced athlete can help the coach by talking to beginners and giving them hints on how to proceed.

Mental practice By studying cine film and video tapes of top class athletes in action you may build up a true picture of your event. Your coach may now ask you to rehearse mentally either all or part of the skill that he considers you need to improve. This can also apply to racing tactics where you can think yourself through critical situations: what to do in a bunched start, how to move out to overtake, where and how to begin your burst down the final straight or how to look after yourself in the ruck. Mental training of this sort has been known to produce an immediate improvement in performance.

Polaroid camera This can be useful at times especially when the camera will produce a series of pictures at set intervals. However, it is of much greater use in the coaching of field events. The real benefit comes through the ability to produce pictures within minutes.

Cine camera This excellent coaching aid has now become dated. Firstly, cine film has priced itself out of the reach of most coaches. Secondly, video has largely taken over the role of the camera because of its efficiency and also the advantage of immediate playback. Films take at least a fortnight to come back and the initial impact by that time is lost.

Studying loop films and other films of athletes in action This is one of the best methods of instruction. You can sit down by yourself and see world champions in competition and training. Your coach may be with you sometimes and give comments and criticisms. All the time you will be learning and letting athletic skills soak into your system.

Video tape This is an improvement on cine film in so far as you can perform in training and then see exactly what you have done within minutes. Your physical sensations are still with you as you watch every movement reproduced on the television screen. It is the strongest back-up for your coach but unfortunately very expensive to hire. Not many clubs are able to afford one for general use.

Photographs, drawings, strip pictures and technical articles These are easy to obtain and inexpensive. They should be placed around the walls of the clubroom for their instructional and inspirational value. You should read all you can about top athletes and study their techniques in books and magazines. The club should try to make available such essential magazines as *Athletics Weekly* and, if possible, have a small club library where they may be read. You should broaden your knowledge of athletics: do not confine your reading to running alone. Get to know something about the other events and you will enjoy your sport even more.

Use of a lay figure It is possible for your coach to give you instruction in running technique by putting a lay figure in certain positions and talking around them. These would include leg drive, arm drive, arm action, body position and the use of the hips in running. Sometimes this can be useful if your group is forced off the track by inclement weather. The time need not be wasted hanging about in the dressing-room.

By personal observation Here the coach acts as the athlete's mirror and reports back to him. It is the traditional and time-honoured role of the running coach. He will either stand in the centre of the track or well back in order to observe you from a distance. He will be looking for all the good points of your technique and building on them. This is a far more profitable approach than any immediate attempt to correct the faults you have developed since early childhood. He will eliminate these gradually over a period of time.

Your aim should be to develop a fluency of style and an easy relaxed flow to all your limb movements.

In the beginning, you will find it possible to win races when you are under-striding but you will very quickly become exhausted if you attempt to over-stride. A longer stride will come naturally as you develop mobility and power. Your coach will work constantly with you to improve these two factors. By watching you in competition and training, he will be able to make an accurate assessment of all these things and many more.

Equipment for the club coach

The club running coach requires certain items of equipment, either on his person or in his bag. Some of these are listed below.

Stopwatches These vary: for speed work, a 10-second dial sweep with a split hand is preferable; for interval running and timing longer distances, a 60-second sweep measured in tenths, with a split hand for lap times, is necessary. However, most of these functions are to be found in the modern digital watch. These are now coming on to the market at reasonable prices. Before purchasing one, make certain that the figures on the dial can be seen in bright sunlight.

First aid kit Most clubs do not always have a physiotherapist available when travelling to races and there would rarely be one available on the normal training night. Hence it is a good thing for the coach to carry a small first aid kit in his bag to cover any immediate emergencies on the track or over the country. First aid qualifications can also stand the coach in good stead in times of emergency.

Starting pistol and ammunition These are not an essential for a coach who is mainly concerned with distance runners. However, flexibility of function is very useful in the club situation and a coach might be called upon to give starting practice to the sprinters or hurdlers at any time. Wooden clappers are a good substitute and avoid all the tiresome regulations which go with the use of any firearm.

Clipboard with pencil attached These can be obtained with a metal clip to hold a watch and waterproof cover for inclement weather. It is invaluable to the coach for making notes and recording lap times when taking his group on a track session.

Some useful items

Spare sets of spikes of various sizes
Regulation tool for removing spikes
Pair of pliers
Measuring tape
Penknife. ` Scissors
Safety pins of varying sizes
Spare shoelaces
Talcum powder (useful for shoes and checkmarks)
Roll of coloured adhesive tape (for checkmarks)
Whistle
Clean towel
AAA Handbook   IAAF Handbook

It is particularly important for the club coach to be fully equipped when travelling with the club team on any away fixture.

The team coach

If you progress successfully through the grades of school and club competition and become one of our leading juniors, you will come under the umbrella of junior development. This means that you will be invited, from time to time, to attend National Coaching courses and training week-ends. The progress of our top athletes in recent years has been due in no small measure to the excellent work of the Junior Commission. This was founded in 1969 and it was the unremitting work which was done and the far-sighted plans which were laid at that time, that paved the way for the excellent results which our juniors now attain in the international field.

In time you may be selected to compete for the U.K. as a junior. If you attain this standard you will find that you may be out of the country and away from home for a period of time during the season. Now you will meet a team coach for the first time.

Depending on the coaching establishment for the meeting or competition, there will be a National Coach or National Event Coach in charge of the endurance events. He will be responsible to the Team Management for your fitness and welfare; to this end he will be working in close collaboration with the team doctor and physiotherapist.

It is up to you to obtain a letter from your personal coach addressed to the team coach. This should contain a copy of your training schedule for the period of the competition and any instructions or further information he may wish to include. If any adjustments have to be made due to conditions or facilities, the team coach will go through your schedule with you and help you re-plan it to the best advantage. It is your responsibility to make the necessary arrangements with him for timed sessions on the track or for advice if you have any problems. He will know the training venues, bus times and reporting times. He will see you through your warm-up, through the reporting pens on time and see you walk into the stadium. After that you are on your own. If you happen to be involved in a protest, then you must report this to the team management immediately. The British contingent will be seated in a part of the stadium which has been allocated to the athletes. The team manager and team coach will be in this vicinity.

The team coach should be like a good full-back. He should be constantly sweeping round behind, picking up mistakes as they occur. This will include such things as a last look round the dressing-rooms before departure from the track to ensure no clothing or kit has been left behind and counting heads on the bus before it leaves for the hotel. Having said all that — you, the athlete, are also responsible. You are responsible for yourself, all your possessions and everything you do. If you have not learnt this bit of homespun philosphy before competing at this level, it will be difficult for you to muster the self-confidence necessary to perform well out there in the stadium on your own.

Running profile: Dave Moorcroft

by Andy Etchells

Once upon a time, there was a little lad from Coventry who failed to make it into the school football team and so turned to running. At the age of 14, he was introduced to Scottish coach John Anderson/who remembers him as "a pale skinny kid, not even the best of the bunch for his age". That skinny kid was David Moorcroft and 15 years on, still coached by John Anderson, he became the revelation of the 1982 athletics season with his stunning 5,000 metres world record.

By common consent, this is not just any old record. It took 15 years and four men —Viren, Puttemans, Quax and Rono — to trim just 10 seconds off Ron Clarke's 1966 record of 13:16:6. But one night in July 1982, Moorcroft single-handedly and with apparent ease lopped six seconds off the Rono record (and 20 seconds off his own previous best for the distance) in the finest piece of solo front running the world has ever see. His time was an epoch-making 13:00.42.

When looking at the British middle distance tradition, the names of Coe and Ovett might seem the logical ones to feature in a book like this. Certainly, in terms of world records and Olympic titles, Moorcroft·lags behind these two superstars. But whereas Coe and Ovett have both been described as 'geniuses', Moorcroft is a more representative product of the British middle distance and cross-country running tradition.

Ovett was running the Olympics at the age of 19; Coe broke his first world record at 22. Moorcroft, however, did not reach superstardom with his world record until the age of 29. That's not to say he was an overnight sensation — he won his first AAA junior title in 1971 — just that his development has been gradual, based on thoroughness and sheer hard work. Referring to the injuries that threatened to write him off in his late twenties, his coach John Anderson once said: "Knock him back one step and he jumps forward three."

It's been like that in his private life, too. He failed his 11-plus examination (so did Seb Coe, incidentally) and later was not considered a suitable candidate for A-levels. But he emerged from Loughborough College with an Honours degree. As well as being regarded as the complete runner — such is his ability to run from the front, or kick from the pack in a tight finish — he is also universally regarded as a nice guy to know off the track. Perhaps it's something to do with his philosophy, which he puts this way: "Most runners really respect runners who can really dig deeper and further into their depths of talent. There's not much you can do about natural ability, but there's a hell of a lot you can do about the way you apply it."

It may come as a surprise to learn that Dave Moorcroft has competed in two Olympics — he finished seventh in the Montreal 1,500m and was knocked out in the semis of the Moscow 5,000m — and that his Brisbane Commonwealth Games 5,000 metres gold medal (which went some way to atoning for his disappointing run in the Athens European Games of 1982) was his second major gold. He also won the Commonwealth 1,500m title in 1978, the same year as he won a bronze in the European Games.

So Dave Moorcroft has been around a bit — but he was never quite right at the top, by his own exacting standards at least. It was not for lack of commitment, but he was hampered by a series of

Compared to many other top athletes, Dave Moorcroft is a late developer. It is only now after years of hard training and injury for which he needed surgery that he has shown his true potential as a runner. Previously a miler, he has the ability to kick into a fast finishing speed.

injuries, including one to both calf muscles which would leave him limping and black and blue with bruising in the legs after a hard session or race. The surgeon's knife which released the muscles from their constricting outer sheath ('compartment syndrome') became the key that unlocked his real talent and allowed him to finally benefit from his perseverance and hard work.

Over the years, the various setbacks would have finished a lesser man. Now, they stand him in good stead. "I'm glad this has happened now I'm 29," he said after the world record. "I think I'll enjoy it more after all the downs in my career."

One reason is that there is far more to life than just running — important though that is to him. He has his family and a job with a cause — helping unemployed youngsters in Coventry. He is also a runner's runner who does not forget his roots in his club. "I began my career, and I will finish it, running cross-country with the lads," he says. For behind his great achievements and talents lies this simple philosophy: "If I weren't a reasonably good runner, I'd enjoy being a reasonably bad runner."

CHAPTER ELEVEN

The runner's physiology

by Dr Ray Watson

Skeletal Muscle

The kinaethesis of running An understanding of the structure and function of skeletal muscle is a basic requirement towards an understanding of how the human body responds to exercise and adapts to training. However, muscles are so completely subservient to the nerve impulse for activation, that any successful patterning of muscular activity in performing co-ordinated running actions must be preceded by an appropriate series of motor-nerve impulses. In other words, co-ordinated behaviour must arise initially as a decision by the nervous system, to be sent along predictable pathways to the skeletal muscle for action. A complete description of the nervous system is beyond the scope of this chapter, and both coach and athlete are encouraged to consult textbooks on neurophysiology for an in-depth analysis of running as a neurophysiological mechanism. Sufficient to say that the various functions of the higher nervous centres, such as the cerebral cortex and cerebellum in the brain, where movement is ultimately originated, are interconnected, co-ordinated and directed towards the periphery of the body via the spinal cord, where eventually the muscles receive a motor message resulting in purposeful co-ordinated movement.

Knowledge of nervous excitation and the characteristics of muscle will not in itself allow us to understand the essentials of running. The task in learning such a complex skill as running is to direct effort along the most efficient lines, practising the task at different speeds and rhythms until it is perfected. The body is equipped with sensory receptors that can detect information and feed it into the central nervous system. Accepting helpful stimuli and rejecting those that are detrimental makes it possible for us to learn skills and pattern the movement of running.

For too long, physiologists have stressed the motor functioning of the muscles and ignored the profound sensory mechanisms present in the muscle. Possibly, the muscle cell is our most important sensory mechanism, more important than the sensations of sight, touch, smell, hearing and taste. There are three proprioceptors in the muscles, tendons and joints that monitor body position — these are called muscle spindles, golgi tendon organs and pacinian corpuscles respectively. It is important that every runner should realise the full potential of an awareness of the 'feel of running'.

In man, the maintenance of erect posture is controlled fundamentally by the stretch reflex. Comfortable standing is largely a matter of balancing the various parts of the body on each other, in such a manner that very little muscular effort is required. As an individual sways from a balanced position there is an immediate adjustment of the muscles antagonistic to the direction of movement. Since the body requires only a slight counteracting force, the contraction needs only to be slight, and relaxation occurs again once the readjustment to balance has been made. Therefore a reflex contraction of the muscles containing proprioceptors corrects the imbalance. A more complex question in the realm of running is how the proprioceptors function in dynamically changing situations. Running is controlled by the crossed extensor reflex, and the muscle spindle has an important function in monitoring the rate of change in muscle length, whilst the golgi tendon organs monitor muscle tension. The ability to judge the appropriateness of muscular contraction, to judge where the limbs are in space in relation to each other, and to know how fast and to what extent joint angles are changing, is called kinaesthetic sense, and it is of vital importance for coaches and runners to concentrate their attention to the kinaesthesis of running during training sessions.

"Your muscles see more than your eyes," stated Arthur Steinhaus (1964).

The structure of skeletal muscle There are approximately 434 muscles in the human body, of which 75 pairs are involved in movement. A muscle is a collection of specialised cells that have the ability to change their length and develop tension. Skeletal muscles can shorten up to 10 times their length in one second, and produce tensions equivalent to over 40lb per square inch. How does the muscle produce these remarkable properties?

Advances in the development of the electron microscope have resulted in detailed studies concerning the exact nature of muscular contraction. The principal investigator has been H.E Huxley, at Cambridge University. A single muscle consists of thousands of fibres bound together in a strong framework of connective tissue. These fibres are arranged in a variety of ways, and in one example the fibres run longitudinally approximately parallel to the long axis of the muscle, although they might not reach the entire distance covered by the muscle. These fibres can vary in length, according to the function of the muscle, eg. eye muscle fibres are one millimetre long, whereas thigh muscle fibres are 40mm in length. The individual fibres are surrounded by connective tissue called the endomysium, and a group of as many as 150 individual fibres, or a fasciculus, is bound together by the perimysium. The whole muscle is encased in another connective tissue sheath called the epimysium, and this arrangement binds the muscle together in a strong framework, without interfering with the contraction or fibre arrangement.

It has been estimated that there are approximately 250 million muscle fibres in the human body, and individual fibre counts in human biceps muscle have revealed that the muscle contains over 316,000 fibres, arranged in more than 3,300 fascicles.

It is not the individual fibre per se that is crucial to understanding the contraction characteristics of muscles so much as the molecular ultrastructure of the fibre. When an isolated fibre is stained, the characteristic 'zebra' cross striations can be seen. Further magnification under the electron microscope reveals that the fibre is made up of still smaller filaments called myofibrils. When the myofibril is examined more closely, it can be seen that there are two types of filament: one of which is twice as thick as the other. The thick filament consists of a protein called myosin, and the thinner filament is the protein actin. Huxley has centred his research around the characteristics of actin and myosin that permit the fibre to shorten during contraction.

Evidence is quite conclusive that projections called cross bridges exist on the myosin molecule at regular intervals, whereas the actin consists of bead-like molecules connected together in a helical form. This makes it possible for the myosin filament to connect with the actin filament, and it would seem that a sliding movement is mediated by the myosin cross bridges pulling the actin filaments a short distance, returning to their original configuration ready for another pull, corresponding to the shortening process. This analogy seems to be the most appropriate way to interpret the complicated mechanisms at molecular level, which shows how a muscle changes its length and develops a force of contraction (see diagram).

Fast and slow fibres From a functional viewpoint muscle is not a homogeneous tissue, but is built up of fibres with different mechanical properties, of which two main groups can be identified. These have been called slow twitch fibres and fast twitch fibres. Slow twitch fibres are much more resistant to fatigue than are fast twitch fibres, and they are rich in the mitochondrid where the oxidation process takes place in the cell. The capillary blood vessel network is also more developed around the slow fibres, and the myoglobin content higher. The fast twitch fibres have a higher contraction speed, with associated glycolytic enzymes that enable the fibres to produce faster and higher maximal tension. The proportion of the two fibre types within a muscle varies greatly between individuals. The slow fibre proportion can range from about 10 per cent up to about 95 per cent in the same muscle in different individuals. Some physiologists have suggested muscle fibre profiles appropriate for an event. Top athletes in endurance events have a high percentage of slow twitch fibres, and sprinters are characterised by a dominance of fast twitch fibres. Saltin reported that two sub-28 minute 10,000m runners had 75 per cent slow twitch fibres, and that the one who could run the faster last lap had ten per cent more fast fibres. It has been concluded by some physiologists that there is a high correlation between fibre type and performance. I am not in total agreement, as this implies that the fibre profile was due to prolonged training. Histological studies have indicated that fibre composition is genetically determined, and therefore fibre typing is not a good selective instrument for predicting potential athletes.

It should be emphasised that the recruitment of specific fibres is dependent on the state of work. At low intensities of work the slow twitch fibres are activated, and at high intensities of work the fast fibres are brought into action. Slow twitch fibres are the first to lose their glycogen content during prolonged submaximal running, and then the fast fibres are recruited. This is an important observation, because when work rates are at a maximal level, both fibre types appear to be continuously involved. One can speculate that intensive training provides a balanced adaptation of both slow and fast twitch fibres, the implications of which will be discussed later in this chapter.

Chemistry of muscular contraction The fundamental principle for every runner and coach to understand must be how the molecular machinery of the myofibrils convert chemical energy into mechanical work, which can be identified with physical activity. Adenosine triphosphate (ATP) serves as the immediate and ultimate source of energy for muscular contraction. Chemical energy is stored in the bonds that hold the atoms together as a molecule. The phosphate bond is very rich in energy, and studies have shown that the actin-myosin arrangement contracts when ATP is added under the correct neurophysiological conditions.

In view of the importance of ATP it is disconcerting to find that it only occurs in the muscle in small amounts. Each kilogram of wet muscle contains about six millimoles of ATP, which is only sufficient to meet the demands of about 0.5 second of intense muscular activity. When the nerve motor neurone transmits its electrical impulse to the muscle fibre to contract, calcium ions activate the myosin cross bridges, and the ATP breaks down into Adenosine diphosphate (ADP) and phosphate, releasing energy for muscular contraction.

$$ATP = ADP + P + energy$$

Because ATP is the *only* direct source of work production, it must be resynthesised immediately, otherwise muscular contraction would cease after 0.5 second.

The rapid regeneration of ATP is provided by a second high potential energy protein called Creatine phosphate (CP). Each kilogram of wet muscle contains about 17 millimoles of CP, which is sufficient to resynthesise a further quantity of ATP, to support the demands for an additional 5.0 seconds of intense

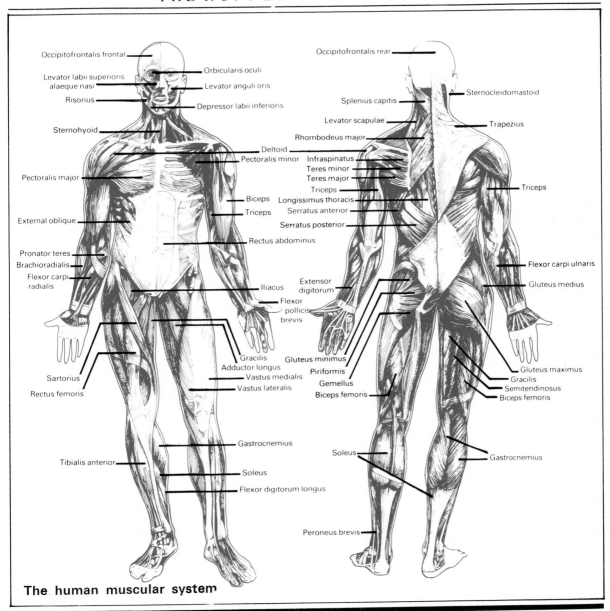

The human muscular system

muscular activity.

$$CP + ADP = ATP + C$$
$$ATP = ADP + P + energy$$

Alactacid training The energy employed in the first few seconds of running must be provided solely by the splitting of the ATP and CP molecules, and because these processes do not require the presence of oxygen, the chemical reactions are described as anaerobic. Textbooks have erroneously called this an oxygen deficit mechanism, and it is confusing to refer to the reactions as anaerobic. I would prefer to use the term alactacid debt, ie. intensive work that takes place without the lactic acid formation. In any strenuous running of short duration (less than 5.5 seconds) no lactic acid is formed and the work can be completely met by the alactacid phosphagen (ATP +CP) splitting mechanism. This alactacid debt can be completely repaid during the recovery period of about 20-25 seconds. If these conditions are met, very heavy supramaximal intermittent exercise can be carried out repeatedly, leading to a total amount of work much greater than would have been possible were the exercise protracted until exhaustion. The training of this alactacid mechanism is very relevant for all runners, but particularly appropriate for 100 metre hurdlers, ie. repetitions of five seconds running at maximal speed followed by 25 seconds recovery.

Lactacid training or anaerobic training The previous discussion has shown that the energy employed in the first few seconds of running must be provided solely by the splitting of ATP and CP. In very severe running of longer duration, the demand is met by the breakdown of muscle glycogen into lactic acid. Although a limited amount of lactic acid is found in the blood after a 100m sprint, maximal lactate values are reached in running events of a longer duration, such as the 400m sprint. The conversion of muscle glycogen to lactic acid is a very wasteful procedure, and the process can only continue for limited periods of time until muscular activity is terminated by the depletion of the glycogen

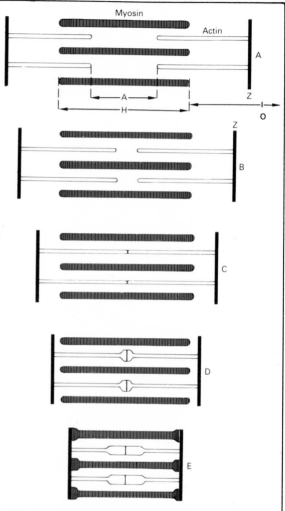

When muscles change in length, they alter the arrangement of filaments. In A, the muscle is stretched; in B, resting; in C, D, E, contracted. Under an electron microscope, a dark and light zebra-like striation is seen: A is Anisotropic band (dark); H is Haller band (clear); Z is Zwitterman band (in between); I is Isotropic band (light).

supply or by an increased acidity associated with the accumulation of lactic acid. This is anaerobic work and occurs only when there is not sufficient oxygen available to produce the energy required for an intense muscular response. Physiologically, the real significance of lactic acid production during running is an emergency mechanism for providing energy (ATP) when the oxidative mechanisms are insufficient. This would explain the great discomfort a 400m runner experiences, with an accumulation of lactic acid in the legs. It should also be pointed out that the anaerobic work capacity of a woman is lower than that of a man, and that serious thought should be given to the tactics of the 400m women's event. It may be more appropriate for the woman runner to run the first 200m slower than the second 200m, so as to avoid accumulation of lactic acid during the early stages of the event. Although anaerobic work is a very wasteful procedure, it is the only source of chemical energy available to a sub-46 second 400m male runner. The 400m runner will utilise both the alactacid and lactacid processes where the lactacid process gives a maximal capacity of about 230 cals/kilogram, which will be exhausted in about 40 seconds. Repetitions of fast sprinting for between 25-45 seconds, with four minute recovery periods, is recommended for lactacid training.

The chemical process can be summarised as follows: Glycogen stored in the muscle (15 grams per kilogram wet muscle) is converted into glucose. Glucose is reduced by a process called glycolysis into lactic acid. From this process one molecule of glucose will produce two molecules of lactic acid, which is sufficient to resynthesise two molecules of ATP.

$C_6H_{12}O_6$ Glycolysis $2CH_3COCOOH$
Glucose $\longrightarrow$ Pyruvic acid

$2CH_3COCOOH$ Reduction $2CH_3CH(OH)$
Pyruvic acid $\longrightarrow$ $COOH + 2ATP$
                        Lactic acid + energy

Aerobic work If the energy expenditure can be met by oxidation only, the work can be maintained for an unlimited time, provided that the body stores of glycogen are also unlimited. This process is aerobic work, and there are many oxidative reactions involved in the basic process summarised by the following chemical reaction:

$$C_6H_{12}O_6 + 6O_2 = 6CO_2 + 6H_2O$$

Glucose + oxygen = Carbon dioxide + water

For each molecule of glucose completely oxidised to water and carbon dioxide, 38 molecules of ATP are resynthesised. This clearly indicates that aerobic work is 19 times more efficient than anaerobic work. Most cells, including muscle, prefer glucose as their major source of fuel, and the oxidation process occurs largely in the mitochondria. These often are called the organs of respiration of a cell, and all of the enzymes involved in the oxidative process are found within the mitochondria within a single cell. The oxidation of foodstuffs is revealed by oxygen consumption, and on this principle the energy cost of running long distances can be obtained by measuring oxygen uptake. Under the aerobic conditions during which a true steady state exists, the oxygen uptake is related by a constant to the oxygen requirement and is usually characterised by a steady heart rate, steady pulmonary ventilation and negligible oxygen debt. Runners can work for long periods of time within this aerobic work capacity.

Oxygen debt If the running speed involves energy requirements beyond aerobic capacity, the maximal oxygen uptake may be achieved, but this usually occurs near to the point of fatigue and cannot be maintained for long periods of time. This maximal work capacity is accompanied by marked changes in the blood, the expired air and heart rates which are close to maximum. At this maximal level, the oxygen cost of work per minute exceeds the actual oxygen uptake, and therefore there is a build up of oxygen debt. The build up of a critical oxygen debt by the runner is a factor limiting the duration of running, and represents one form of exhaustion. An untrained person can rarely tolerate more than ten litres oxygen debt, whereas a trained runner can reach a debt of as high as 17 litres. If the running effort is to be of long duration the athlete cannot allow the continuous build up of oxygen debt until the later stages of the race — he must work aerobically at a rate low enough for the oxygen uptake to equal the oxygen demand of running

The graph according to Henry (1963) shows that calculations can be based on the oxygen cost (litres/minute) and the linear speed of running. A four minute mile run (pace 7.3 yards/second) will cost about 8.7 litres per minute or 34.8 litres of total oxygen cost for the four minute run. If an athlete has a maximal oxygen uptake of four litres per minute, as well as an oxygen debt capacity of 17 litres, the total oxygen available would be $4 \times 4 + 17 = 33$ litres, and the four minute mile would be beyond the runner's physiological capacity. Running speeds of nearly six yards per second are being achieved by top class marathon runners, and according to Henry's graph this would require an oxygen uptake of over five litres per minute throughout the marathon run!

It should be pointed out that the oxygen cost measured in units of litres/minute can be misleading. In fact interpretation of oxygen uptake results is a difficult problem to the layman, and a lot of mis-understanding has arisen. When oxygen uptake is used to examine the capacity to perform hard exhaustive running power, the value of oxygen uptake may be expressed in relation to body weight, as millimetres per kilogram per minute. Ideally, lean body weight (LBW) or fat free body weight would be a far better index to express oxygen uptake capacity.

It is important, however, to draw attention to the possible misinterpretation of results by athletes and coaches. For example, consider two subjects 'A' and 'B', with the same oxygen uptake capacity of 4.0 litres/minute, and the same body weight of 70

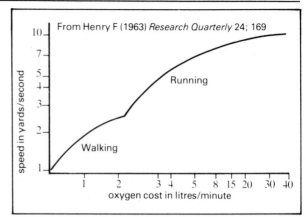

From Henry F (1963) *Research Quarterly* 24; 169

kilograms. Their identical results would give the same index of oxygen uptake if expressed in relation to body weight, ie. 57 millilitres per kilogram per minute. Then if the fat content of the body was measured and it was found that subject 'A' had 12 per cent fat and subject 'B' 20 per cent fat, the LBW of subject 'A' would be higher than 'B'; 'A' would be 61.6 kilograms and 'B' 56 kilograms. The oxygen uptakes expressed in relation to lean body weight would be 60.5 millilitres per kilogram lean body weight per minute for 'A' and 71.4 for 'B' giving the impression that 'B' has the highest value! The obese person would be under a substantial handicap during running, and the carriage of unwanted body fat would make the accomplishment of a specific running task more difficult.

Training the oxygen transport system

Worldwide research in oxygen uptake and related functions has been established, and investigations are being reported from many countries. Although existing information is fairly extensive, the data that is available is generally relevant to the male adult population, and there is a deficiency of research concerning women's response to long term training and exhaustive running.

Experimental studies have shown that the highest values for maximal oxygen uptake are achieved by long distance runners, swimmers, cyclists and rowers. An interesting question is why the best performances in endurance events are usually reached between 23-28 years of age, when the highest maximal oxygen uptake is usually reached by the age of 20? Perhaps physiological factors have been given too much credence, and it should now be recognised that performance is dependent on many factors such as experience, tactics, level of fitness and motivation.

It is obvious that athletes should include a systematic training of the oxygen transport system during their preparation for many endurance events. During very severe exercise, the cardiorespiratory mechanisms are inadequate, and the oxygen supply to the muscle tissue is insufficient. This results in an accumulation of lactic acid, developing lactacid debt, as previously explained. From this premise it would seem that hard maximal work does not train the oxygen transport system efficiently. However, it should again be emphasised that the recruitment of slow or fast twitch fibres is dependent on the rate of the work. At high intensities of work the fast twitch fibres are activated and recruited, and these fibres may be forced to depend initially on anaerobic yield, since the oxygen supply is not sufficient to cover the demand for all fibres during aerobic work.

The relationship between maximal rate of work (speed), and the rate of work that will maximally load the oxygen transport is system certainly an intriguing problem. Experiments in my laboratory have shown that there is a range of high speeds with the same oxygen uptake, but with marked differences with the production of lactic acid. Oxygen lack or anoxid in the muscle tissue enhances the oxygen uptake in the tissues, but whether the degree of anoxia is important as a training stimulus is not yet clear. The oxygen lack at higher work intensities may speak in favour of a somewhat reduced speed when training the oxygen transport system. This reduction in speed implies less fatigue, and also makes it possible to increase the volume of training. This principle has developed the concept of 'Long Slow Distance', or LSD, with numerous interpretations by individual runners.

Exclusive LSD will promote the fast fibres aerobic metabolism, but is this submaximal training effective in improving maximal aerobic power? Some athletes have devoted too much time to LSD, covering vast distances during training, but it is of questionable value to increase the aerobic potential of the fast twitch fibres.

For a long distance and middle distance runner, the optimum must be to combine three types of running in their training schedules:

1 Submaximal or LSD Running at an intensity of about 85 per cent maximal for one hour or more. Too much running at economical speeds has its disadvantages because insufficient demand is made on the muscle fibres to work anaerobically.

2 Maximal Running at an intensity of about 95 per cent maximal for up to 4-6 minutes. Recovery periods may be for up to 5-10 minutes depending on the athlete's level of fitness. Since maximal oxygen uptake can be achieved at slightly below maximal speeds, this method can be used to great effect as a training stimulus. The ability to run for prolonged periods of time, utilising the largest possible percentage of maximal oxygen uptake, is a characteristic of all top class runners.

3 Supramaximal or faster than race pace. It is possible to use running speeds exceeding 100 per cent maximal oxygen uptake, and this will involve both slow and fast twitch fibres. By running repeated repetitions of between 200-800 metres at a pace faster than is normal for the particular event, the method will train the inter-relationship between aerobic and anaerobic work. Intensity versus duration is a problem as to whether aerobic or anaerobic work should dominate. Certainly duration is limited by intensity! An athlete should be trained to tolerate the stresses implicit in his or her event. The table showing the inter-relationships between aerobic and anaerobic work for the various running events shows that aerobic work capacity is more dominant the longer the race. It has always been a long cherished belief that the training of anaerobic work is an important char- acteristic of a long distance runner. We have seen many examples of fine long distance runners who have little or no anaerobic capacity. The significance of exploiting the anaerobic metabolic processes must never be underestimated for even the most highly trained middle or long distance runner. The most urgent limitation confronting many international distance runners today is the obsession with covering such prolific weekly mileages, to the exclusion of a few dozen sprints!

Interval training Improvement in athletic attainments can be attributed to many factors, but undoubtedly the most important single factor, stimulating the current phenomenal running performances of Cram, Coe, Ovett and Moorcroft, must be due to improved methods of training and conditioning. One important contribution towards a more scientific appreciation of the principles of interval training came from the thorough work of the German cardiologist Dr Reindel, and the coach Dr Gerschler. Basically the Gerschler-Reindel method is as follows:

1 Warm up bringing the heart rate to 120 beats/ minute.

2 The athlete runs at a given distance, in a given time, to bring the heart rate up to 170-180 beats/ minute.

3 Recovery period of sufficient duration to bring the heart rate back to 120 beats/minute. The recovery period should never be longer than 90 seconds, and if it takes longer than 90 seconds it is because the effort demanded is too fast, or the distance covered is too long. Adjustments should be made accordingly.

Harry Wilson, Steve Ovett's coach, has greatly influenced my own work, and we have now collaborated with one another for over 12 years. Alternating periods of work with recovery interval training is a way of working more economically, but is more demanding on the cardio-respiratory systems. It is possible to determine objectively the optimal duration of work, and recovery, but there are many combinations and variables. It is a difficult problem to solve, and there is no single blueprint to success, but it seems inconceivable that out of the hundreds of thousands of men and women using running as a

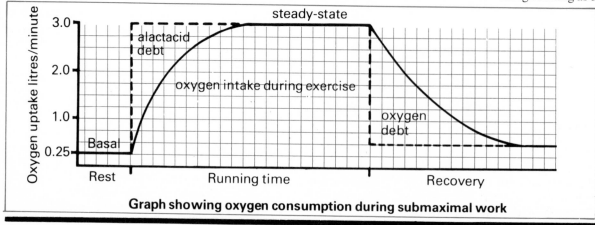

Graph showing oxygen consumption during submaximal work

Event (metres)	Characteristic	Total oxygen requirement (litres)	Actual oxygen intake (litres)	Oxygen debt (litres)	Type of work	Approx % anaerobic/ aerobic
		Table showing the inter-relationship between aerobic and anaerobic work for running events				
100	Speed, strength	10	0.5	Total	Alactacid, lactacid	100% anaerobic
200	Speed, strength Anaerobic endurance	16	1.0	15-17	Alactacid, lactacid oxygen uptake	95% anaerobic, 5% aerobic
400	Speed, strength Anaerobic endurance	20	3.0	17	Anaerobic, aerobic	84% or more 16% or less
800	Anaerobic, aerobic endurance, speed	26	9.0	17	Anaerobic, aerobic	67% 33%
1500	Anaerobic, aerobic endurance, speed	36	19	17	Anaerobic, aerobic	45% 55%
5000	Aerobic endurance	80	63	17	Anaerobic, aerobic	20% 80%
10,000	Aerobic endurance	150	130+	17	Anaerobic, aerobic	10% 90%
Marathon	Aerobic endurance	650+	650+	17	Anaerobic, aerobic	2% 98%

training stimulus that the basic concepts of quantity and quality have been largely ignored. The reader is asked to consider five training stimuli that are directly relevant to interval training:
1 The distance or duration of the run.
2 The number of repetitions of the run.
3 The speed or intensity of the run.
4 The duration of the recovery period. We would recommend a heart rate recovery index, rather than a time component. In other words, according to the heart rate.
5 The type of recovery. We would recommend slow jogging.

There seems to be little doubt that faster than race pace interval work is relevant for both middle and long distance runners, and the pyramid system, eg. 1 x 800, 2 x 600, 3 x 400, 5 x 200, 6 x 100, seems to have great merit in training the inter-relationship between aerobic and anaerobic work, subjecting the runner to stress with a continuous change of rhythm between work and recovery. The pyramid system

should also be used in reverse, starting with the anaerobic metabolic processes prevalent in shorter intervals, which should be run at faster speeds.

Exercise heart rate and its implication for training

The relationship between heart rate and oxygen consumption is in the opinion of many researchers a comparatively high one. There is a long phase of linear response between heart rate and work, which is more dominant for the highly trained athlete. In 1954, Astrand developed a nomogram to predict maximal oxygen uptake from submaximal heart rates. Coaches and athletes should realise that there are serious limitations to using the Astrand nomogram and results reprorted from my laboratory in 1972 and 1980 are not in agreement with the nomogram proposal.

However, one thing that we did find, and can be stated with complete conviction, is that 'fit' subjects had lower heart rates than 'unfit' subjects at any given work load. We also established this concept with a 20 month longitudinal study, when we found that the heart is lowered with training, together with a significant increase in maximal oxygen uptake and power output. It is difficult to understand that the response to increase heart rate is lowered with training: the lower rates may indicate that an athlete's heart is not maximally activated during exhaustive running, or, alternatively, the pumping capacity or stroke volume of the blood expelled by the heart for each beat is increased with training. If stroke volume is increased with training, there will be improved mechanical efficiency of the heart, with the result that there is no need for the same degree of activation of the heart rate during strenuous running for the trained athlete.

The ability to achieve a given exercise load at a lower heart rate with training should produce an increased maximal exercise capacity for the athlete. In other words, training will reduce cardiovascular stress at any given exercise load. This important observation can be applied to great effect by coaches and athletes by using heart rate as an index for the effects of training.

Heart rate as an index for the effects of training

Athletics literature is full of methods for calculating heart rate in beats per minute, eg. count the number of beats for 15 seconds and multiply by 4. These methods assume that the heart beat is always a whole number, that exactly coincides with the timed period. Alternatively, some coaches advocate counting the number of heart beats for the full 60 seconds. This assumes that one can count accurately when the heart may have achieved a maximal rate over 180 beats per minute, and that the rate does not change during the 60 seconds of counting! Unfortunately these methods are commonly used by coaches, athletes and physiologists throughout the world, but the results are invalid and unreliable.

In 1975 Harry Wilson and myself proposed a system that would avoid problems of validity, reliability and objectivity, as a result of our work with Olympic athletes in St. Moritz in 1972. The basis of the system is *simplicity* but *total accuracy*, and athletes and coaches are recommended to adopt the system, which is as follows:

Prerequisites:
1 Keep meticulous records of heart rates recovery data after known periods of work intensity, such as distance run and time of run. Always record the date, day and time of training session, including such details as level of fitness, injury etc. Do not forget pencil and paper, or tape recorder.
2 Purchase an accurate dual function stop watch.

Heart rate recording
1 All pulse counts should be taken no later than 10 seconds after the completion of the training run/interval run.
2 Recovery recordings should be made at 30 seconds, 60 seconds etc.
3 Use the pressure point at the wrist (radial pulse) or the neck (carotid pulse).
4 Never use the thumb for receiving the pulse count.
5 Record the recovery time *as well as* the pulse count (see 2). Dual function stop watches will enable the coach to do this easily.
6 Commence counting 10 seconds after the completion of runnning (see 1).
7 Time accurately *eleven* pulses by starting the watch on pulse one, and stopping it exactly on pulse eleven. *This gives the exact time for the completion of 10 beats or 10 complete cardiac cycles.*
8 Use the following table to convert the eleven count into heart rate in beats per minute.
9 Carry the conversion table with you at all times. The conversion is simply calculated by dividing the time for the eleven count into 600.
10 By using this method, *numerous accurate* heart rate measurements can be recorded. Everyone can count up to eleven accurately, and modern digital stop watches can even base the calculations on hundredths of a second if required!

Table of conversion into heart rate based on accurate timing in tenths of a second

Time seconds	Heart rate beats/min	Time seconds	Heart rate seconds
6.0	100	4.5	133
5.9	102	4.4	136
5.8	103	4.3	140
5.7	105	4.2	143
5.6	107	4.1	146
5.5	109	4.0	150
5.4	111	3.9	154
5.3	113	3.8	158
5.2	115	3.7	162
5.1	118	3.6	167
5.0	120	3.5	171
4.9	122	3.4	176
4.8	125	3.3	182
4.7	128	3.2	187
4.6	130	3.1	193
		3.0	200

It is proposed that the recording of heart rate is an excellent index for assessing:
1 The immediate effects of training.
2 The long term effects of training.
3 The level of fitness of an athlete from unknown previous records, giving diagnostic interpretation.
4 Specific training methods and schedules.
5 The intensity of running at different speeds.
6 The capacity of the runner to tolerate rigorous demands on the body during training and competition.
7 The level of motivation of an athlete during training. The immediate knowledge of result can be used to good effect by the coach.
8 The maximal heart rate response, and the optimal running intensity for aerobic (90% and below) and anaerobic (above 95%) conditioning.
9 A method to facilitate exercise prescription related to running intensity, with 'target' heart rates.
10 Recovery based on true physiological response and adaptive mechanisms, and not random time intervals.
11 When an adaptation to a given work load has taken place. In order to achieve further improvement the training intensity will have to be increased, either by increasing the running distance, or the required running speed.

The human heart

Previous discussion has shown that the muscles are able to store small quantities of adenosine triphosphate, creatine phosphate and glycogen to initiate exercise. There is, however, no mechanism for the storage of oxygen in the muscles, and any increase in the metabolic requirement must be satisfied by a corresponding increase in the oxygen transport to the muscles. This is accomplished by the red blood cells in the blood transporting oxygen as oxyhaemoglobin, by three methods:
1 By diverting the blood flow from less active regions of the body to the exercising muscles.
2 By increasing the heart rate.
3 By increasing the volume of blood pumped by the heart per beat (stroke volume), which will produce a concomitant increase in the total volume of the blood pumped from the heart in one minute (cardiac output).

Cardiac output = stroke volume x heart rate. At rest the cardiac output will be 5.0 litres per minute, with a stroke volume of 70 millilitres per beat, and a heart rate of 70 beats per minute. During exercise the cardiac output can increase up to and over 30 litres per minute. If maximum heart rate is 180 beats per minute and the maximum stroke volume is 150 millilitres per beat, the cardiac output would be 27 litres per minute. The heart is the muscular pump that imparts sufficient kinetic energy to the blood to move it through the thin walled capillaries, where the interchange of oxygen and food materials will take place between the blood and tissues.

The heart is a hollow muscular organ divided into

four chambers — the right and left atria at the top of the heart, and the right and left ventricles at the bottom of the heart. The atria are comparatively thinned walled chambers that are capable of exerting considerable forces. The wall of the left ventricle is much thicker than that of the right, because it has to pump blood around the whole of the body.

It is convenient to think of the heart as two halves. the venous, or deoxygenated, blood, low in oxygen and high in carbon dioxide, enters the right half of the heart via two large veins, called the superior (top) and inferior (below) venae cavae. The right atrium receives the venous blood, which is discharged from the right ventricle via the pulmonary artery (right and left) to the lungs. At the lungs the blood, though a process of diffusion between the thin walled alveoli (air spaces) and the capillaries, discharges its carbon dioxide, and takes up oxygen. The oxygenated, or arterial, blood then travels back via the pulmonary veins (left and right) to the *left heart*, where it is collected by the left atrium, before entering the left ventricle via the bicuspid valve. The arterial blood is then expelled from the left ventricle, via the aorta, to all the regions of the body.

The cardiac cycle It can be seen from the diagram that blood enters the atria is transferred into the ventricles and then pumped out. This involves two processes of contraction or systole.
1 Atrial contraction, or atrial systole, when the blood is transferred via the cuspid valves into the ventricles.
2 Ventricular contraction, or ventricular systole, when the blood is expelled from the two ventricles almost simultaneously. This procedure ensures the ejection of equal volumes of blood by the two ventricles, which is necessary if one side of the heart is not to become congested or depleted.

The completion of the systolic contractile events marks the onset of relaxation, or diastole. This results in a fall in intraventricular pressure, resulting in a relaxation of the cardiac muscle. During the diastolic

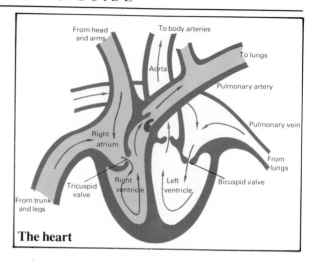

The heart

period the heart is refilled with blood.

The diastolic phase is followed by a period of rest when the entire cardiac muscle is completely inactive and relaxed. This period is called diastasis, which gives an opportunity for aerobic resynthesis of ATP in the cardiac muscle cells

The electrocardiogram (ECG)

The conversion of chemical energy into mechanical energy in the cardiac muscle cell is a similar process to that of skeletal muscle, except that the heart never works anaerobically. In contrast to skeletal muscle, cardiac muscle has no great margin of safety for its oxygen supply, and if it is deprived of its own supply of arterial (oxygenated) blood, it will soon cease contracting and beating. The amount of blood supply is all important to the heart, particularly during running when oxygen demand is increased. Evidence suggests that the functional capacities and coronary blood flow are enhanced with training, and that the cardiac muscle fibres increase in size and strength.

Cardiac muscle consists of long narrow fibres, and each fibre is made up of innumerate fibrils. The fibrils are responsible for the contraction of the cardiac muscle as a whole, coordinating millions of 'cardiac cylinders', into a rhythmic beat, which we know as the cardiac cycle.

The beat or impulse is initiated by a small electrical charge equivalent to about one thousandth of a volt, from the medulla of the brain. This electrical impulse is conducted over the heart muscle, by a network of nervous tissue, which excites a succession of cardiac

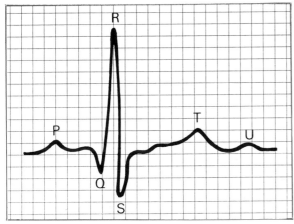

The normal electrocardiogram

P	Atriole systole	} contraction
QRS	Ventricular systole	
T	Diastole	relaxation
U	Diastasis	rest

Dr Ron Hill, the Commonwealth Games Marathon gold medallist, was an early exponent of carbohydrate-loading in the last few days before a marathon. This is done to artificially increase the glycogen stores in the muscles.

Atrial systole	0.1 second	P wave
Ventricular systole	0.2 second	QRS wave
Diastole	0.4 second	T wave
Diastasis	0.1 second	U wave

muscle fibres producing the correct sequence of atrial and ventricular contraction and relaxation.

This electrical sequence of events can be amplified and recorded as an electrocardiogram. The diagram indicates the normal electrocardiogram, in relation to the four phases of the cardiac cycle. If the heart beats 75 beats per minute at rest, it takes 0.8 seconds per beat, and the approximate time sequences of the cardiac cycle, with the electrocardiogram are:

The quantitative measurement and interpretation of the exercise electrocardiogram is a complex but intriguing problem and of particular relevance to evaluate the effects of running and training on the heart. We are currently engaged in a number of experimental techniques that will help to unravel the mysteries of the exercise electrocardiogram, and possibly the most important application has been the use of modern tape recording and computer analysis for results obtained both in the laboratory and on the athletic track.

Running profile: Joyce Smith
by Andy Etchells

Britain's fastest women's marathon runner, Joyce Smith, is coached by her husband, Brian. She is an inspiration to many women runners as she continues to set new records over the marathon distance in her forties.

It's hard to know where to begin when talking about Joyce Smith's running career. At school she was a long jumper and sprinter. In the 1950s, she was national cross-country champion. She won her first international track vest for Britain way back in 1960 over 800 metres. She returned 12 years — and one child — later to run in the first ever Olympic Games 1,500 metres. Two years later, at the 1974 European Games at the age of 36, her track career peaked with a 3,000 metre bronze medal. Then at the age of 41, she ran her first marathon — and broke the British record into the bargain.

The idea of the marathon came when she was running longer, steadier distances as part of her recovery from an injury. She had broken a bone in her foot in training for the 1978 European Championships when she was again intending to run the 3,000 metres — at that time the longest distance open to women on the international scene. It was her husband and coach Bryan's idea to run the greater distances as a means of strengthening her for the return to track running.

Perhaps he also had an inkling that women's marathoning was about to take off, but Joyce recalls, for her part, that "when I first started, I said I just wanted to run one marathon to say I'd done it." Well, that first one was the Avon Sandbach race in June 1979, the first time anyone had really taken British women's marathoning seriously. They were all there — the experimenters, the young pretenders and the merely curious — but Joyce Smith stood out head and shoulders above the lot of them. Besides which, she gave the majority of the men in the joint race a fair and square beating too!

Her time was 2:41:37 — a new British record. Her

immediate post-race comment was: "I felt I mucked it up a bit. The first five miles were a bit slow." But it wasn't bad for a beginner and she had the chance to learn from her mistakes in the Avon International marathon in Germany three months later — a trip she had earned by her Sandbach win. There, it was another win and another British record: 2:36:27.

And so the progression continued; not always in a straight line, of course, as there were hiccups like the Miami Marathon in early 1980 when the extreme heat led to her collapsing close to the finishing line. But nearly every time she ran, she lowered the British record, the two most famous and recent occasions being her two London Marathon victories which made her one of Britain's most popular sporting heroines. Not only is it her shy modesty behind that steely determination; more than anything else, she gives hope to everyone — man and woman — who is on the 'wrong' side of 40.

Despite the parade of records, Joyce is not someone who runs to time. Her mentor Bryan — he keeps her company on his bike during her long runs — explains that she dislikes the stress of running against the clock. What counts is racing against other people.

She takes each training session, and each race, as it comes, knowing that the marathon, above all other events, has plenty of traps for the unwary, and that she cannot continue competing at such a high level for ever. It was, however, a great disappointment to her and her many fans that she was injured before the European Championship of 1982, the first time the women's marathon appeared on an international championship programme. Although it would be the perfect end to a fabulous career, she herself doubts if she will compete in the first Olympic marathon for women at Los Angeles in 1984.

In some respects, her age and experience within the sport stand her in good stead against her younger rivals. For while many people are attracted to the event and rush into it with very little background preparation, Joyce has years and years of miles in

Joyce was the first woman to cross the finishing line in both London Marathons. Here she is beside Tower Bridge en route for a record-breaking British time of 2:29:43.

her legs. "You won't run fast marathons without running fast 10-miles, and you won't run fast 10s before you can run fast 5,000 metres," says Bryan.

Remember, too, that a decade ago Joyce was British record holder for 1,500 metres — and she still includes one track speed session per week (say, 4 x 800m or multiple 400m repetitions) amid all her mileage. That may reach 100 miles per week at a peak before a big race; on average, it's closer to 80, all fitted in round the routine life of a mum who also works a couple of days per week.

Her 2:29:43 London 1982 time ranked Joyce sixth on the world all-time list and is several minutes superior to the next best British time. So, in performance terms, she has already carved her place in running history. Less tangible, but no less important, is her pioneering role in inspiring other women to have a go. If she isn't in the Los Angeles starting line — and I wouldn't bet against it — she deserves the place of honour in the stands for her part in the women's running revolution.

CHAPTER TWELVE

Nutrition and diet

by Dr Ray Watson

Nutrition of the Athlete

The basic ingredients of a balanced diet consist of six categories:
1 Carbohydrates
2 Fats and oils
3 Proteins
4 Vitamins
5 Mineral salts
6 Water

Carbohydrates

Carbohydrates are compounds made up of atoms of carbon, hydrogen and oxygen. A carbohydrate always contains two atoms of hydrogen for each atom of oxygen. Glucose is a commonly known carbohydrate, with the chemical formula $C_6H_{12}O_6$. Carbohydrates can exist as simple sugars, such as glucose, fructose and galactose, and are known as monosaccharides. Fructose is present in large amounts in all kinds of fruits and honey. Sucrose, maltose and lactose are examples of double sugars, or disaccharides. Sucrose is common granulated table sugar, and lactose is present in milk. The more complicated sugar molecules are called polysaccharides, and these may consist of 300 individual sugar molecules joining together. Starch and glycogen are the most common polysaccharides. Starch is found in grain foods such as bread, cereals and pasta, as well as in potatoes, rice, beans and peas. Glycogen is not present in the foods we eat, but is transformed from glucose, and then stored by the liver and muscles as glycogen.

The digestive system breaks down the complete polysaccharides into simple monosaccharides such as glucose, maltose, lactose and galactose. These simple sugars are then transported by the blood stream to the cells of the body to provide the basis for cellular metabolism and function to take place.

Fats and oils

Fats are compounds made up of atoms of carbon, hydrogen, and oxygen, with a relatively low oxygen content. A fat consists of two different clusters of atoms, namely a glycerol and a fatty acid. Glycerol is composed of three atoms of carbon combined with hydroxyl (OH) groups. A common fatty acid contains between 16 and 18 atoms of carbon in each molecule.

There are two types of fatty acid, ie. saturated and unsaturated. The saturated fatty acid, such as cholesterol, is derived mainly from meat fats, dairy products and shellfish. Unsaturated fats are usually present as liquids and are derived mainly from veg-

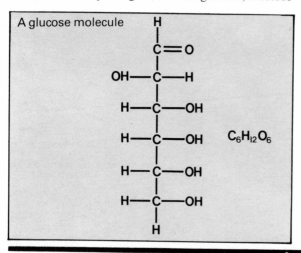

A glucose molecule

$C_6H_{12}O_6$

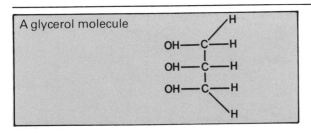

A glycerol molecule

small amount of fat should be recommended to people on a reducing diet.

5 Production of linoleic acid for correct skin and kidney functioning.

Table showing percentage of carbohydrates in common foods.

Sugar	100%
Chocolate creams	85%
Cereals, flour	75%
Biscuits, jams	70%
White bread	50%
Rice, spaghetti, beans	32%
Potatoes, apples, grapes	17%

Table showing percentage of fats in common foods

Cooking oil	100%
Butter, margarine	81%
Salad dressings	80%
Chocolate	53%
Peanut butter	50%
Pork sausages	45%
Cream cheese	32%
Ice cream	12%

Table showing percentage of proteins in common foods

Meats, poultry	20-30%
Fish	20-30%
Cheese, liver	25%
Nuts	16%
Eggs	13%
Cereals	7-14%
White bread	8%
Beans, peas	8%
Potatoes	2%

etable oils. Modern man consumes more animal fat than is required, and the role of dietary fat in the development of heart disease and cancer of the colon are controversial topics for scientific debate.

In terms of capability for energy storage, fat is more efficient than carbohydrate, in that over twice the energy is stored in a kilogram of fat compared with a kilogram of carbohydrate. This is because the fat molecule contains more hydrogen atoms than the carbohydrate molecule. A typical fatty acid has a chemical formula $C_{55}H_{104}O_6$, whereas a simple sugar has a formula $C_6H_{12}O_6$. A human being would be considerably heavier if our energy reserves depended on carbohydrate storage.

Fats in the diet fulfil several functions, some of which can be summarised as follows:

1 Protection of the vital organs such as the heart, liver and kidneys.

2 Insulation to protect the body against cold.

3 The carriage of fat soluble vitamins A, D, E and K to the cells. Diets low in fat content may lead to a deficiency of the fat soluble vitamins.

4 Depressing the feeling of hunger, due to their slow transit through the small intestine. This is why a

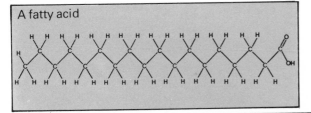

A fatty acid

Proteins

Proteins are compounds made of atoms of carbon, hydrogen, oxygen, nitrogen, sulphur and sometimes phosphorus. The major difference between the protein molecule and the carbohydrate or fat molecule, is that the protein molecule contains the nitrogen atom. The nitrogen atom together with two hydrogen atoms (NH_2) make up a basic radical called an amino acid. There are 20 different amino acids present in proteins, of which eight cannot be synthesised by the body and must be obtained through the intake of food proteins. These are called 'essential' amino acids, and eggs are recommended to contain the best balance of these essential proteins. Meat, fish, soya beans, milk and rice also contain essential amino acids. The most active and abundant tissues of the human body, the organs and muscles, are very high in protein content. Skeletal muscle contains about 70 per cent water, but by far the most important solid constituents of muscle are proteins myosin, actin and myoglobin (20 per cent). The protein contained in trained muscle is significantly greater than the protein content in untrained muscle. This increase in protein content contributes to an increase in muscle size, which is apparent following a rigorous weight training schedule. However, large amounts of dietary protein do not cause the muscle to become larger.

The amount of protein contained in different cells varies considerably and the protein content in the muscle cell is greater than that of the red blood cell, which contains the protein haemoglobin. Most enzymes and hormones that control cellular functioning consist of proteins. The principal uses for amino acids in the body are:

1 For building new cells and tissues. This is very relevant in growing children, during pregnancy, intensive athletic training, illness and injury.

2 To maintain the functional capacity of tissues, such as blood proteins, enzymes and hormones.

3 Providing energy, but only if the energy intake from carbohydrates and fats is inadequate. Contrary to popular belief the contribution of protein to the energy requirements of muscular activity is negligible, and energy is more economically supplied by carbohydrates and fats.

There appears to be a wide range of protein intake to which adults can adapt and be maintained in good health. The consensus now is that a liberal margin over the minimum requirements is good insurance against times of stress, but that excessive supplies provide no added advantage. Sherman in 1920 examined the protein requirement of maintenance in man, and estimated that probably 0.5 grams of protein per kilogram of body weight would suffice to meet the minimum requirements. A summation of all later data supports Sherman's estimate, although it would be unwise to limit the protein intake to the minimum maintenance level over long periods. A person of small body weight requires less, and one of larger than average lean weight needs more, than the standard allowance. The recommended intake for the United Kingdom is 10 per cent of energy intake. For example, if an athlete is training hard, and his energy requirement is 4,400 kilocalories per day, his protein intake should be 10 per cent x 4,400 ÷ 4, or 110 grams per day, given that 4 kilocalories is the calorific value per gram of protein. In the United States allowances for normal adults are based on 0.8 grams of protein per kilogram body weight, so that an average 70 kilogram adult male would require 70 x 0.8 or 56 grams of protein per day, and the average adult female 55 x 0.8 or 44 grams per day. One ounce of meat or poultry or cheese will give 7 grams of protein, one pint of milk 17 grams of protein and one egg 6 grams of protein. A vegetarian diet can be

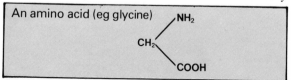

An amino acid (eg glycine)

NH_2

CH_2

COOH

made entirely adequate in proteins, with the liberal use of legumes and cereals, supplemented with plenty of milk and eggs.

Vitamins

Vitamins may be defined as organic compounds, other than any of the amino acids, fatty acids or carbohydrates that are necessary in small amounts in the diet, for normal growth and the maintenance of health. There are 13 vitamins that perform many different functions, but generally serve as essential links in the chain of metabolic reactions within cells. If there is a dietary vitamin deficiency, this results in a defect in cellular function, which manifests itself in a variety of symptoms (see table).

There are two groups of vitamins, classified as fat soluble vitamins and water soluble vitamins. Vitamins A,D,E and K are fat soluble. The water soluble vitamins are transported in the fluid medium of tissues and cells, and because of their solubility in water, these vitamins cannot be stored in the body to any appeciable extent and are normally excreted in the urine. Therefore all water soluble vitamins must be consumed within the daily diet, and any excess will be excreted in the urine. Excess intake of the fat soluble vitamins is maintained within the body tissues, and in some instances may produce a toxic vitamin overdose.

Table showing 13 vitamins, their source, function and symptoms of deficiency

Vitamin	Source	Function	Deficiency
Fat soluble vitamins			
A	Fish liver oil, egg yolks, dairy products	Vision and growth	Poor growth and vision
D	Sunshine, fatty fish, butter, margarine, vegetables	Bone calcification	Bone diseases
E	Seed oil, wheatgerm	Prevents cell damage	Connection with fertility
K	Green vegetables	Blood clotting	Difficulty with blood clotting
B complex vitamins			
Thiamine B1	Brewers yeast, wheatgerm, peanuts	Cell metabolism	Nerve and muscle degeneration
Riboflavin	Brewers yeast, wheatgerm	Cell metabolism	Skin, eye, mouth lesions
Niacin	Brewers yeast, nuts, fish, meat	Cell metabolism	Skin and nervous diseases
Pyridoxine B6	Brewers yeast, nuts, fish, meat	Amino acid breakdown	Abundant in food-nil deficiency
Pantothenic acid	Milk, brewers yeast, liver, eggs	Metabolism of foodstuffs	Fatigue, restlessness, muscle cramps
Folacin	Leafy vegetables, almonds, eggs	Red blood cell formation	Anaemia
B12	Liver and muscle meats, dairy products	Normal growth, Blood formation	Anaemia, mental and nervous disorders
Biotin	Liver, egg yolk	Removal and addition of CO_2	Dermatitis
Vitamin C	Citrus fruits, tomatoes vegetables, blackcurrants	Collagen formation	Nausea, high cholesterol levels, scurvy, poor healing of wounds

Vitamin therapy with runners It is well established that the B complex group of vitamins interact with various enzymes that are important in the energy yielding reactions during the metabolism of fats and carbohydrates. This has led many coaches to believe that supplements of these vitamins will enhance energy production, and improve performance.

Eastern European research certainly advocates the taking of vitamin B complex group and vitamin C by both endurance and explosive athletes. Brewers yeast is used for the vitamin B complex group, and ascorbic acid for the vitamin C supplement. Unfortunately, general medical advice in the United Kingdom does not support the eastern European point of view, but there is a lack of valid objective research to formulate objective advice.

Little is understood about the role of vitamin E, but recently it has been suggested that it helps to dilate the blood vessels at the site of injury, and reduce the development of any scar tissue. If this information is correct, it has obvious implications during recovery from injury. There is also evidence to link vitamin E with the supply of red blood cells, and the prevention of all membrane damage. Wheat germ and seed oils are rich in vitamin E.

Pollen extract in the form of tablets called Pollitabs has been used by Finnish athletes for a number of years. The Swedish company Cernelle have manufactured the pollen extract as a multi-vitamin tablet containing trace elements and essential amino acids. 'Flower power' is a mysterious concept, but many athletes claim beneficial effects.

Mineral salts

In addition to the non-metal elements of carbon, hydrogen, oxygen, nitrogen, sulphur and phosphorus, there is a group of 22 metallic elements present in the body. Although the total quantity of minerals present in the body is relatively small, each of the metallic elements is vital for proper cell functioning.

Minerals are part of enzymes, hormones and vitamins, and are found in muscles, tissues and body fluids. Seven minerals, calcium, phosphorus, potassium, sulphur, sodium, chlorine and magnesium, are all required in larger quantities than the trace elements such as iron, copper, zinc, cobalt and iodine. A diet deficient in iodine results in an inadequate production of thyroxin from the thyroid gland, causing a decrease in metabolic rate. Calcium taken in combination with phosphorus can give rigidity to bones and teeth. Phosphorus is an essential component of the high energy compounds adenosine triphosphate (ATP) and creatine phosphate (CP)

Haemoglobin and iron There are approximately five million red blood cells per cubic millimetre of blood, and each single red cell contains about 280 million molecules of haemoglobin. The haemoglobin molecule contains only four atoms of iron, and it is this ferrous iron that gives haemoglobin its capacity for combining with molecular oxygen to form oxyhaemoglobin in the red blood cell. The life span of the red blood cell is about 120 days, and therefore the destruction of senile red cells is a continuous process. When iron is not sufficient, the red blood cells lack the normal content of iron-containing pigment, and anaemia results. The total iron in the body of a 70 kilogram man is about four grams, from which the body loses about one milligram per day. Obviously, physiological requirements for growth, menstruation, pregnancy and constant training make additional demands for iron. The average daily intake of iron in a normal diet is about 14 milligrams; this should provide a generous margin, even for pathological losses. However, a runner may be in precarious balance, particularly as only about 10 per cent of total iron intake is actually absorbed into the body's stores. Intensive training may increase red cell destruction, which in turn will increase the demand for the important iron-containing pigment, resulting in disturbed iron metabolism. Coaches and athletes should be aware of the following three phases of iron depletion, and apply the recommendations judiciously.

In one phase, sideropenia, the person usually reacts by increasing iron absorption from the gut, thus avoiding anaemia. Normal diet is sufficient to make the required adjustments, and recommended foods are wholemeal bread, lettuce, spinach, soyabeans, eggs, fish, veal, chicken, plain chocolate, raisins, liver and liver pâtés. With all athletes I would recommend a transferrin saturation blood test, which indicates the iron binding capacity of the blood. Normal transferrin saturation is usually about 350 micrograms per 100 millilitres of blood.

If the transferrin saturation or iron binding capacity increases, as an adaptive reaction, the individual usually suffers from iron hunger. The high transferrin will also be associated with a low serum iron in transport. Normal serum iron is about 350 micrograms per 100ml blood, and a reading below 100 should warrant further investigation. It is important to point out that at this stage of iron depletion, a normal haemoglobin level may be obtained. In other words, haemoglobin measurements are a waste of time unless they are combined with additional information from transferrin saturation and serum iron levels. Should iron hunger occur in an athlete, prophylactic iron supplementation should be the treatment, eg. folic acid, feospan, ferrous gluconate, or ferrograd C. Vitamin C will help increase the iron absorption from the gut.

Food iron may be insufficient to maintain normal haemoglobin levels and this is associated with anaemic problems. If anaemia is suspected the following routine tests will diagnose the condition accurately:
1 Haemoglobin — below normal.
2 Red blood cell count — low.
3 Transferrin saturation level — high.
4 Possible infection?
5 Diet or vitamin deficiency?
6 Excessive blood loss, eg. menstruation?
7 Too much training? Deterioration in racing performance?
8 Headaches, lack of sleep?

If anaemia is suspected, immediate medical advice is required. Women are more vulnerable than men.

I am convinced that iron depletion without anaemia does occur quite often in athletes, and that this is due to the increased destruction rate of the red cells with intensive training, together with a further loss of iron during sweating. Judicious diet should be sufficient to meet the demands of diminishing iron stores, with occasional supplementation with iron tablets and vitamin C. However, do not use iron tablets indiscriminately as too many have a harmful effect on the liver.

Water

Water is second only to oxygen in importance to the body. A healthy adult may live for weeks without food, but only a few days without water. It is common sense that fluid intake must be replenished regularly to make up for the continuous loss from the body. Water is excreted from the body by the kidneys in urine, by the lungs as water vapour in expired air, by the skin as sweating. The minerals sodium and chlorine are present in the fluids outside the cells, while potassium is found predominantly within the cells. These three electrolytes control and maintain the correct rate of fluid exchange within the various fluid compartments of the body. In this way, the constant flow of dissolved nutrients into the cells, and the removal of waste products from the cells is regulated. Therefore the proper maintenance of both fluid and electrolytic balance is of critical importance during running. During excessive sweat loss, the body loses both electrolytes and fluid, and these must be replaced regularly in sufficient quantities to avoid dehydration or depletion.

Salt depletion Dehydration is a more serious problem than salt depletion, and I am against the liberal use of common table salt with food as an attempt to supplement any salt depletion. We get sufficient electrolytes in the food we eat, without resorting to using excessive amounts that can be harmful. Recent evidence suggests that sodium may cause kidney damage and there is a high correlation between salt intake and high blood pressure. Sodium-free diets are being recommended by many doctors nowadays. A trained runner will adapt to salt loss through sweating by simply reducing the quantity of salt loss in the sweat, as a physiological adaptation. My advice is maintain your fluid intake, but do not take salt tablets unless you are exposed to hot climatic conditions.

Manufactured drinks Various manufactured drinks are available, and these are designed to replace fluid, electrolytes and provide an immediate source of energy in the form of glucose. These may be helpful to a marathon runner, as research has shown that marathon runners deplete trace elements such as magnesium.

The glucose based drink used under medical supervision is useful if an athlete is a diabetic. The hormonal control of the blood sugar level is maintained by insulin. If there is an excessive amount of blood sugar, the level is lowered by insulin. If excessive amounts of glucose are ingested by an athlete, this will simply stimulate the hormone insulin

to remove sugar from the blood when the level becomes too high, with the result that an unwanted low blood sugar level may be achieved, ie. insulin induced hypoglycaemia.

Vegetable fibre

Although fibre roughage is not digested by the body, it is useful for absorbing bile acids, and for increasing the water content in the colon at the end of the alimentary canal. Most modern dieticians recommend high fibre diets to improve bowel movements, and possibly reduce the incidence of rectal cancer. With the regular use of bran breakfast cereals and other foods high in vegetable fibre, runners avoid problems of constipation that may occur with excessive fluid loss during training.

Training and eating

Club athletes have not the privilege of full-time training that some of our international runners can arrange. This creates the problem of fitting training sessions into a normal working day, and also giving sufficient opportunity for adequate meal times. Pre-breakfast, pre-lunch and late evenings are popular times for training with the club athlete. Under no circumstances must food and fluid intake be neglected to afford training time. Never train on a full stomach immediately after a meal, and avoid training if food

Table showing dietary analysis for athletes, the average UK and USA citizen, Keys' ideal diet, and the diet of the underprivileged Third World population

	Athletes	UK average	USA average	Keys recommended	Third World
Carbohydrates %	40	50	46	69	80
Proteins %	20	11	14	16	10
Unsaturated fats %	21	23	23	11	9
Saturated fats %	19	16	17	4	1
Total kcalories/day	4,500	3,200	3,000	2,300	1,900

Table giving a few examples of normal portions for nutritive values of selected common foods (1oz=28.35grams)

Foods	Weight (grams)	Energy (kcal)	Proteins (grams)	Fat (grams)	Carbohydrates (grams)
Milk	245	155	8.0	8.5	11
Apple	150	80	0.3	0.8	20
Avocado	125	190	2.0	18.0	7
Bacon	25 (rasher	140	6.5	12.5	1
Banana	120	100	1.5	0.2	25
Beans, tin	130	190	8.0	6.0	25
Beans, green	65	15	1.0	0.2	3
Beef steak	85 (3oz)	220	24.5	13.0	0
Hamburger	85 (3oz)	240	20.0	16.5	0
Beer, bottle	360 (12oz)	150	1.0	0	14
Biscuits	30	90	2.0	3.0	15
Bread, brown	45 (slice)	95	2.5	0.6	20
Bread, white	25 (slice)	70	2.2	0.8	13
Butter	5 (1pat)	35	0	4.0	0
Cabbage, raw	70	17	0.9	0.1	4
Chocolate, milk	30 (1oz)	140	2.0	9.0	16
Bran flakes	35	100	3.5	0.6	30
Cheese, cheddar	30 (1oz)	115	7.0	9.5	0.4
Chicken	95 (½ breast)	160	25.5	5.0	1.0
Cream	60	210	1.0	22.0	2.0
Egg	50 (1 large)	80	6.0	5.5	0.6
Fish, cod	110 (4oz)	180	30.0	6.0	0
Fish, mackerel	110 (4oz)	250	23.0	17.0	0
Grapefruit juice:					
unsweetened	180 (glass)	75	0.9	0.2	18
sweetened	180	100	0.9	0.2	25
Ice-cream	65	135	2.5	7.0	15
Lamb, lean	85 (3oz)	160	24.0	6.0	0
Lettuce	90	10	0.8	0.1	3
Margarine	5 (1 pat)	35	0	4	0
Orange	140	80	1.8	0.1	18
Peanuts	30 (1oz)	65	7.5	14.0	5.0
Apple pie	160	400	3.5	17.5	60
Custard	150	330	9.5	17.0	35
Pork, lean	85	310	21.0	24.0	0
Chips	20 (10 chips)	115	1.0	8.0	10.0
Rice, white	135	150	3.0	0.1	35
Ham and cheese					
sandwich	140	350	20	19	30
Sausage, pork	40 (3 links)	185	7	17	0
Spaghetti	210 (1 tin)	250	10.4	12.8	23
Tea, no sugar					
or milk	1 cup	3	0	0	1
Tomatoes	135 (1 raw)	25	1.5	0.2	6
Wheatbran	30(1oz)	60	4.5	1.0	17
Yoghurt, fruit	230 (8oz)	225	9.0	2.6	42

has not been taken during the day. Research has shown that athletes are vulnerable to accidents when the blood sugar is low. A Mars bar late afternoon will help runners who have to train after work. Eat fresh fruit, vegetables and meat as far as possible, as nutritional values are reduced with freezing, canning and preserving, and do not rely on fast convenient foods as a means of fitting in training schedules. The biorhythm of the body is a finely tuned mechanism, and you should plan your daily meal times, training sessions and sleeping habits on a regular basis. Careful planning and respect for your body will produce better results than haphazard irregular habits. Athletes should plan their diets with their coaches, in the same way that they plan their training schedules; much more awareness should be given to quantity, quality and variety of food.

The pre-event meal The basic principle should be that the pre-event meal is one that is easily digested and contains a high energy level. Despite popular beliefs, foods such as steak, eggs, milk and fish should be avoided, as well as fats and high fibre vegetables. Plain simple carbohydrates such as mashed potatoes, spaghetti, bread/toast and jam or honey, and biscuits taken with tea or coffee, or fruit juice, at least three hours prior to competition will be adequate.

Glycogen loading for marathon runners Diets based on the principle of improving the fuel for muscular work have been developed and enthusiastically adopted by marathon runners. This is the result of work by the Swedish physiologists Bergström, Hermansen, Hultman, Sultin and Astrand, who, in 1967, claimed that dietary manipulation would increase the muscle glycogen content. The system recommended was as follows:

1 One week before competition, run to exhaustion, with a long, fast sustained level, to deplete the glycogen stores in the legs (day 1).

2 For the next three days, eat a diet consisting exclusively of foods high in protein and fat, with negligible carbohydrate. The glycogen stores will remain at a low level (days 2,3 and 4).

3 For the final three days, add large quantities of carbohydrate to the diet. It should be emphasised that at this stage while carbohydrate is added, the intake of fat and protein is retained. Some athletes have not followed this routine, and have interpreted this stage as an intake of only large quantities of carbohydrates (days 5,6, and 7).

The Swedish tests claimed that muscle glycogen can exceed four grams per 100 grams of muscle with this technique, and that the total muscle glycogen stores could be ·as high as 700 grams. This would represent a reserve of about 2800 kilocalories, or double the normal reserve capacity in trained runners. The normal glycogen muscle store is about 400 grams.

Although I have guided a number of international marathon runners with this technique, there are a lot of problems that may cause side effects, and coaches and athletes should experiment with the procedure before it is used for an important major competition. Some points to consider are:

1 The depletion phase may be too severe, and the resulting fatigue may be too close to the actual competition for good mental and physical preparation.

2 The three days of protein/fat diet can be a difficult period for the athlete to handle mentally. Some have reported listlessness and tension, and even light exercise is difficult at this stage.

3 The carbohydrate loading phase needs to be supervised carefully because some athletes complain of feeling heavy and stiff. This is because of the rapid weight increase associated with the build-up of glycogen stores in the leg muscles. Fluid intake must be increased to accommodate the raised glycogen stores in the muscles, and if this is neglected the runner may get slightly dehydrated. In order to store one gram of glycogen, 2.7 grams of water are

required. The rapid weight increase will also raise the basic metabolism, as well as disturb regular bowel movements. The process may not be the appropriate preparation for peaking for tapering to take place effectively.

4 The method should not be used by older marathon runners, as there have been indications that cardiac glycogen may also increase, causing chest pains with abnormalities in the electrocardiogram.

There may be some merit in excluding the second phase of protein/fat diet, and using a four day system. The depletion long run would take place on the first day, followed by three days of high carbohydrate diet with adequate fluid intake, protein and fats.

The following quote is an extract from a report in 1978, by the British Marathon Runners Club, which stated:

'The pre race glycogen diet was discussed at great length. It was concluded that there was no sound evidence to confirm or deny the validity of the claimed superior energy sources available to the athlete at distances exceeding 20 miles. There are so many variables capable of complicating the effects of diet that it is impossible to assess its effectiveness conclusively.'

As a physiologist I can see that problems concerning the modification of endurance by over-nutrition is a fascinating area of research. What is required is a carefully planned experimental design, some very willing and conscientious subjects and financial support. With the current popularity for marathon running, this would be a most worthwhile project. I leave the final word to one of the world's most renowned physiologists, A.V. Hill (1968), who said:

"The moral is, if you have a bright idea, try it and see; the result may be more amusing than you expected."

Pre-race pasta dishes

It is a good idea to eat foods which are high in carbohydrate before running a marathon. This increases the normal glycogen content of your muscles (see Glycogen loading for marathon runners opposite).

Pasta is ideal in this respect, and pre-race pasta parties are now common. We have chosen three tasty dishes which you can make with commercially produced pasta or, better still, with the genuine home-made article. This is simple to do if you have a pasta machine. The quantities given are for four people, so double or treble them if you are expecting guests.

Tagliatelle in avocado sauce

450g/1lb mixed green and yellow tagliatelle
30ml/2 tablespoons olive oil
100g/4oz streaky bacon
100g/4oz button mushrooms, thinly sliced
1 shallot, finely chopped
100ml/4floz single cream
salt and freshly ground black pepper

pinch of ground nutmeg
1 avocado, peeled, stoned and thinly sliced
squeeze of lemon juice
50g/2oz grated Parmesan cheese

Cook the tagliatelle in plenty of boiling salted water until is is *al dente*. Drain and keep warm. Heat the oil in the same large pan and sauté the bacon, mushroom and shallot quickly until tender. Replace the pasta in the pan and gently stir in the cream and seasoning. Heat it through gently, tossing the tagliatelle in the sauce.

Pile in a warm serving dish and decorate with the avocado slices. Sprinkle with a little lemon juice and Parmesan.

Spaghetti carbonara

450g/1lb spaghetti
30ml/2 tablespoons olive oil
8 rashers streaky bacon, chopped
3 eggs, beaten
salt and pepper
45ml/3 tablespoons cream (optional)
50g/2oz grated Parmesan cheese
30ml/2 tablespoons chopped parsley

Cook the spaghetti in boiling salted water until tender. Drain and keep warm. Heat the oil in a large pan and sauté the bacon until it begins to brown. Add the spaghetti.

Stir in the beaten egg and seasoning over gentle heat until the egg starts to set. Add the cream and grated cheese. Pile on a serving plate, sprinkle with more cheese and parsley.

Tuna and pasta salad

175g/6oz pasta shells
200g/7oz tuna, canned in brine
100ml/4floz mayonnaise
salt and pepper
5ml/1 teaspoon curry powder
juice of ½ lemon
2 spring onions, chopped
few sprigs of parsley, chopped

Cook the pasta shells in boiling salted water until tender. Drain and cool. Cut the tuna into small chunks. Blend the mayonnaise with the seasoning and lemon juice and mix with the tuna, pasta shells and spring onions.

Running profile: Jack Foster

by Andy Etchells

At the age of 32, Jack Foster looked at himself in the mirror and didn't like what he saw. A stone overweight, he felt "seedy and out of shape" and he decided to do something about it. This is how he describes the start of a new life in his book, *Tale of the Ancient Marathoner:*

"One day I had the bright idea that I'd have a run for a while. It was summer time and the good weather inspired me. We were out for a picnic and a swim. I set off before lunch, thinking I'd have the run and then a swim. What I thought to be many miles later, I arrived back at the car.

" 'What's wrong, have you forgotton something?' my wife asked.

"I didn't understand.

" 'You've only been gone seven minutes,' she said.

"Impossible. I was sure I'd run at least six or seven miles. I was soaked in perspiration and felt tired. I'd thought I wasn't in too bad shape physically. Not really overweight though heavier than when I was riding the bike regularly. Now I was worried. If I was like this at 32, how would I be when I was 40, or worse still, 50? So I began running, or jogging as I realise it was now."

But soon, it really *was* running. From the feeling lots of beginners get ("it's nice when it's over") he graduated to liking the run itself, and wanting to go further and faster. In 1966, within a year of that first jog, he ran his first marathon in the astonishing time of 2hrs 27mins 50 secs.

There was nothing very special about Foster that suggested he would be capable of such a feat. Born in Liverpool, he had worked in a factory for 10 years from the age of 14 — "a dreary existence" that led to his emigrating to New Zealand. Both his parents had suffered from tuberculosis in England but the big thing in his favour was his early cycling — a sport and pastime he still enjoys. Still, that hadn't stopped the flab getting to him.

Having started running at 32, he didn't reach his peak for almost 10 years for his greatest moment came in the 1974 Commonwealth Games Marathon where, running in and for his adopted country, he took the silver medal in 2:11:19 behind Britain's Ian Thompson. That time was third best in the world that year and at the time ranked him in the top 10 marathoners of all time. Needless to say, it was a world record for a man aged 41.

Now turned 50, it's his ambition to be the first over-50 veteran to break 2:20. He missed that target by a tantalising 28 seconds when he made his first attempt in 1982.

He has run in two Olympic marathons — his first at age 40 when he was eighth (Munich 1972, 2:16:51) — and won some of the top international races and yet he says: "Others saw me as a marathoner. I always saw myself as a cross-country runner". Perhaps that's because of his background and his love for the local trails and hills near his Rotorua home.

When he flirted with the commercial possibilities of running in the USA — promotions, races and full-time training — he didn't last long. "Running has got to be fun," he says. "So I just said stuff it — I'll go back, run on Hunts (the local hills) and work at the Ministry of Works".

Despite the pressure of "carrying on his skinny shoulders everyman's hopes of beating the years" as the *New Zealand Runner* magazine once put it — and of being a national hero — Foster has always had a balanced approach to his running. He describes

himself as ''devoted, but not 100 per cent'', and he'll often stop on a run to take in the view. He once told a reporter he never trained — just went for runs!

These days he still cycles, has taken up sailing and hang gliding and still puts in the miles though not with the same consuming passion as before. Even so, virtually every time he runs, he creates a new veterans record. He takes it all in his comfortable

When he won the silver medal in the Commonwealth Games marathon at Christchurch, New Zealand, in 1974, Jack Foster was already 41. Four years later at 46, he came sixth in the New York Marathon in a stifling 80° heat with a · world class time of 2:17:29!

stride, commenting: "I never took the age factor into account. Other people have always made more of it."

CHAPTER THIRTEEN

Running and your body
by Dr Adrian Whiteson

It has been recognised for many years that exercise, preferably of the non-competitive type, is beneficial both from a physical and a psychological point of view to people of both sexes, of all ages and of all walks of life. With a tendency towards shorter working hours, more time is available for leisure activities and what better way to spend it than following a pursuit that can only do you good provided that you approach it sensibly?

Ancient man was a physical being relying on physical fitness and strength and mental cunning to survive in the swamps and the jungles of prehistoric times. Unfortunately as we have progressed, we have become more reliant on mechanical equipment for our survival. Modern transport has replaced the need to walk or run other than from the front door to the garage and back. Lifts or escalators remove the need for climbing stairs and are present in most, if not all, blocks of flats and department stores these days. There is no need to hunt for food other than on the shelves of a supermarket, and even the garden is no longer a source of activity as the majority of menial tasks can now be performed by mechanical devices. However, our diet, with its large intake of carbohydrates and fat, is still based on the need for physical activity, but with less activity man has become obese and lazy causing some health problems

Obesity causes breathlessness which slows the overweight person down and leads to even greater obesity. The heart, along with other muscles, is not used properly and complains. Poor circulation, heart enlargement and high blood pressure can then occur and even mentally and emotionally, the obese person can become sluggish and old before his/her time.

The heavier one becomes, the more strain is placed on the musculo-skeletal system, and this results in a wide range of problems from minor aches and pains to arthritis. The famous comment "when I feel like exercising I close my eyes, lie down and wait for the feeling to pass" is a formula for disaster as more and more of the medical profession and the informed general public are now beginning to realise.

Any form of physical activity must be better than none at all and the view is now held that non-competitive aerobic exercise is probably more beneficial than competitive exercise and certainly far less stressful. What better way is there of getting fit than employing man's inherent physical attributes — running does just that. For many years, doctors have been encouraging their patients to become more active, but now the doctors themselves are starting to follow their own advice as more and more of the medical profession take to the roads and country paths or the seashores.

A great deal of research is being carried out to discover the benefits of regular exercise and there is very little adverse comment in the medical press. Of course, some unfortunate accidents do occur infrequently among runners and receive great publicity but these happen mainly to the untrained individual or those runners who have some inherent medical condition and thus should not be undertaking the type of exercise that they are attempting.

Most of us experience the effects of stress and pressures in the competitive world of today. We know that such positive emotions as anger, aggression, frustration and competition cause the body to release a hormone called Noradrenaline, whereas anxiety or uncertainty release a similar hormone, Adrenaline. These hormones are released in order to stimulate the body to either fight or run away from threatening situations. The result of this release of hormones is to make you more alert, act as a general mental stimulant and aid concentration, and as such they can be addictive. The effect on the cardio-vascular system is to cause an increased heart output and a rise in blood pressure, as well as increasing the amount of circulating blood fats in a manner that will be described later. Exercise is probably the safest way of producing these hormones as you not only get mental stimulation but also prevent any undesirable side-effects by burning up the fat that these hormones release into the blood stream. Blood is diverted to the muscles of the body, and blood pressure is, in fact, thought to be lowered.

We know now that exercise can play a very important part in cardio-respiratory rehabilitation following heart surgery and heart disease, and many people who have recovered from heart attacks and other heart problems are now running long distances and even marathons regularly without experiencing any ill effects. Moreover, their health has benefited from running, both from a physical and psychological viewpoint. The capacity for physical performance depends on three different factors:

(1) The capacity for energy output.
(2) The strength, technique and co-ordination of muscular activity.
(3) Emotional or psychological factors, including motivation.

The adaptation to exercise involves not only energy output and heart-lung efficiency but also the musculo-skeletal system of the body. The capacity of the lungs and the cardio-vascular system to transfer oxygen from the air to the working muscles of the body (that is, the peak rate of oxygen delivery) is the principal factor limiting activity which involves large groups of muscles, and thereby limiting prolonged exercise. Aerobic capacity, or maximal oxygen up-

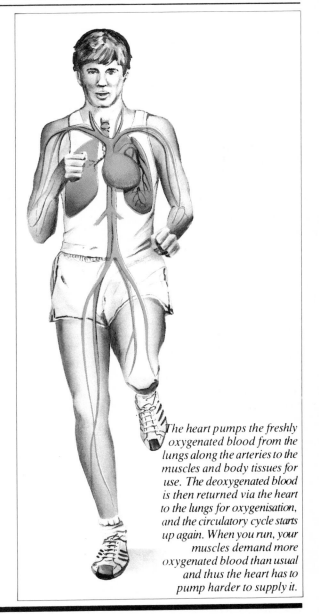

The heart pumps the freshly oxygenated blood from the lungs along the arteries to the muscles and body tissues for use. The deoxygenated blood is then returned via the heart to the lungs for oxygenisation, and the circulatory cycle starts up again. When you run, your muscles demand more oxygenated blood than usual and thus the heart has to pump harder to supply it.

take, is the level of oxygen uptake at which an increase in work load or the rate of energy expenditure no longer produces an increase in oxygen uptake. Short duration work is supported by anaerobic mechanisms, and oxygen transport during this work is not critical. High aerobic capacity in muscles will not produce superior physical performance unless it is matched by a high capacity to transport oxygen, i.e. a higher heart output.

The initial store-house of energy within the muscle fibre is an organic phosphate known as Adenosine Triphosphate (ATP). This is stored in the muscle and can support activity for a few seconds only. Stores of Creatine Phosphate provide a readily available reserve of high energy phosphate, but the total amount is also small and the combined stores can be depleted by a 100 metre sprint. Continued muscular activity requires a constant source of ATP and the major sources are Glycogen, Glucose and Free Fatty Acids. Amino acids, resulting from the break-down of protein, may also be used as a fuel but this is a very minor contribution. Carbohydrates are aerobically oxygenised to water and carbon dioxide and yield 10 times the amount of ATP and energy as does the anaerobic pathway that produces Pyruvate and Lactate.

The duration and intensity of exercise determine which fuels are used. At rest, equal amounts of energy are derived aerobically both from fats and carbohydrate. During low level, steady state exercise free fatty acids are important. As effort increases, the proportion of energy derived from carbohydrates increases, and during maximal work only carbohydrates are burnt up. A well-trained person will use far more fat and much less carbohydrate than an untrained person. The glycogen content of skeletal muscles is a limiting factor during continuous work at high submaximal intensities. Maximal work time is related to the amount of glycogen in the muscles at the onset of exercise, and at the point of exhaustion glycogen is at a minimum. The glycogen content of muscles, and therefore the endurance time, can be increased significantly by an initial phase of glycogen depletion by means of an extended period of heavy exercise followed by eating a diet rich in carbohydrates for a few days — this is known as carbohydrate loading.

This form of dietary manipulation was developed in Scandinavia and can approximately double the glycogen content of muscle fibres. This technique involves one or more bouts of vigorous and sustained effort, which thoroughly depletes the muscles of glycogen for a period of two or three days while on a protein and fat diet, so creating hunger of the muscle cells for glycogen. The last three days prior to any competitive race, a diet rich in carbohydrate, such as pasta, bread, cakes and biscuits, is substituted but the volume for each meal should not alter. There is, incidentally, great controversy concerning the value of carbohydrate loading when in relation to exercise performance over marathon distances.

Anaerobic metabolism with glucose and glycogen is the main source of energy in early exercise when the phosphate-rich stores have been depleted but the blood flow to the muscle has not yet reached the necessary level to maintain aerobic metabolism. It also bridges the gap between the demand for energy and the energy actually available at maximal exercise levels. Anaerobic metabolism can only be used to a limited extent. A build-up of lactic acid remains low during exercise intensities of up to three-quarters of maximal capacity, but at high work rates the lactic acid concentration in muscles increases sharply, and there is a strong relationship between the accumulation of lactic acid and a reduction in the break-down of glycogen and therefore the contractability of the muscle. The affected muscle becomes weak and painful, the cramp that is experienced does not disappear and further activity cannot take place until a steady supply of oxygen is restored.

Human skeletal muscle contains two major types of fibre, slow twitch red fibres and fast twitch white fibres. The higher the concentration of slow twitch red fibres the better the endurance performance of an athlete; whereas an explosive high speed, high intensity type of exercise requires mainly white fibres. These vary greatly from individual to individual and are thought to be genetically determined. The ability to supply high energy phosphates to both red and white fibres can be increased by physical training.

The maximal oxygen uptake is a very important measurement in exercise physiology and in exercise testing. It measures the maximum amount of external physical work a subject can perform in a given period providing that the work involves large muscle groups and lasts for more than two minutes. Differences in body size, age, sex and the continuing level of physical activity account for much of the physiological variation in maximum oxygen uptake. The effect of age is also significant. It is at a peak between the ages of 15 and 20, and then a gradual decline occurs as one gets older. The average maximal oxygen uptake of a 60 years old man is two-thirds that of a man aged 20. Even endurance athletes who continue training and competition beyond their forties and fifties do not alter the decrease, but the values tend to remain higher compared to those of the less active population of the same age.

The maximal oxygen uptake in young children shows little difference as far as sex is concerned until puberty when the values for girls show a marked drop associated with a reduction in the level of physical activity and body changes that occur at that time. Other than that, changes with increasing age in women are similar to those in men, although the lower average values for an adult woman are due to a smaller muscle mass and also to the fact that most women have lower haemoglobin due to blood loss at period time. This also results in a decreased oxygen-carrying capacity of the blood.

The persistent level of physical activity involved in regular training is important in controlling maximal oxygen uptake. A 20-25 per cent drop can occur in young normal people following three weeks' bed rest. Increase in regular physical activity involving moderately heavy work and large muscle groups will produce an increase in maximal oxygen uptake, determined by the intensity of the exercise, its frequency and duration, and, of course, the initial level of maximal oxygen uptake. Age has some effect on the response to training, changes tending to be smaller in older age groups but there is a significant improvement in men over 60. Strenuous physical training can produce a 35 per cent increase in maximal oxygen uptake.

The change from rest to maximal exercise in an average young healthy man causes the metabolic rate to increase 10 times. The increased oxygen demand during exercise is met by increased transport and extraction of oxygen from the blood. Cardiac output is also raised as a result of increased heart rate and stroke volume. Blood is shunted away from non-working muscles, the skin and the gut, and is delivered to exercising muscles. There is a progressive decrease in blood flow to the liver and the kidneys, with increase in work loads.

Cardiovascular control during exercise involves the nervous system as well as local mechanisms. The onset of exercise and the anticipation of effort cause a reduction in parasympathetic, or resting, activity, and increase sympathetic drive with the resultant release of adrenaline and noradrenaline. This hormonal change results in an increased heart rate and cardiac output and there is also a redistribution of blood flow from inactive to active tissues.

The greater demand for oxygen peripherally during exercise is met by an increased blood flow through skeletal muscle and an increased extraction of oxygen. The heart muscle extracts a greater amount of available oxygen at rest and this means that the rise in heart muscle demand has to be covered mainly by an increase in coronary artery blood flow. The resistance in coronary artery flow decreases markedly with exercise, and the more exercise that is taken, the better the coronary artery blood flow and the more efficient the heart muscle.

It is important to know the difference between the two types of exercise: in isotonic exercise, the load on which the muscles are acting can be moved fairly easily; in isometric exercise, the load cannot be moved or only with great effort, and the tension in the muscle increases because it cannot shorten. The latter sort of exercise is generally thought to be more dangerous to those at risk from heart disease because it abruptly pushes up the blood pressure and also increases the amount of work the heart must do.

Walking and running cause only a moderate increase in arterial pressure, but the blood pressure in a normotensive subject may increase markedly during heavy isometric exercise. This is also more likely to produce irregularities of heart rate than is heavy dynamic or isotonic exercise.

Intermittent periods of strenuous activity are not beneficial. Cardiac output and oxygen uptake reach a steady state after two minutes and the blood pressure response is also gradual. The working efficiency of the heart muscle is better during a steady state effort.

More people are now taking up exercise, especially running, than at any time in the past. Exercise is no longer only for school-children, and in the long run this trend may save Britain an enormous amount of money spent on health, owing to the beneficial effects of exercise on the body in general and the cardio-respiratory systems in particular. Cardiovascular accidents ranging from mild angina to full-blown heart attacks associated with high blood pressure are now reaching epidemic proportions in the Western world, and there is now increasing evidence that regular exercise can prevent coronary artery disease, not only directly, but also by reducing the amount of fat in the blood as a result of decreased cigarette smoking and by restricting the tendency to high blood pressure.

Excessive cigarette smoking, high blood pressure, previous heart disease, obesity, a raised blood sugar level and a raised blood fat level have all been considered risk factors of a significant degree in coronary artery disease, and there is a three-fold increase in risk among inactive younger people. Combined low energy output, cigarette smoking and high blood pressure increase the coronary risk by as much as 20 per cent, but if you eliminate these factors the population would have an 88 per cent reduction in the rate of fatal heart attacks over 22 years. Other studies have found that the coronary artery risk is directly related to activity level at work, especially in younger people. As already stated, exercise reduced the circulating adrenaline and noradrenaline and is important in reducing the risk factor. Further studies have shown that the greater the physical fitness of the individual, the lower the percentage of body fat, blood fats, blood sugar and blood pressure, and as a result of this fitness there is a much lower coronary artery risk.

Regular aerobic exercise associated with long distance running results in a number of changes in the body that are beneficial to health. The heart muscle is found to enlarge beneficially and there is also an increased blood flow from the coronary arteries to the heart muscle with beneficial effects. The biochemical changes include a reduction in the clotting tendency of the blood, a decrease in circulating blood fats, including cholesterol and triglycerides which have long been thought when present in excess to be associated with heart disease and are released as a result of the hormonal effect of adrenaline, and also an increase in high-density lipoproteins. When these are present in high concentrations, they are thought to be beneficial in preventing the tendency towards, and the onset of, heart disease.

These are all beneficial changes which are brought about by physical conditioning. An exercise programme will decrease indirectly the tendency to cigarette smoking as the nicotine effect is no longer required to 'steady the nerves'. The requirements of the body for energy during running or prolonged exercise of any type causes mobilisation of fat around the body and therefore obesity gradually disappears. The emotional tensions secondary to the stresses of modern life are also beneficially affected. In any exercise training programme, the end result depends on a number of factors, which include the level of physical fitness, the age and general health of the individual at the onset of the programme and previous physical training. Any aerobic performance is dependent on the improvement of the oxygen transport system, i.e. the lungs, heart and blood vessels, and is largely due to improvements in the overall capacity of the cardiovascular system.

The frequency of exercise should be a minimum of three times per week, preferably building up to five times if possible. The time of exercise or run is very much up to the individual depending on his own preferences, his occupation, work load and social diary, but it is never sensible to exercise within three hours of a heavy meal. For exercise to be of value its duration should eventually be a minimum of 20-30 minutes, and in any recommended exercise programme there should be three phases, the warm-up phase of three to five minutes, followed by a work-out phase when training with an intensity of 70-80 per cent maximal heart rate, and then a cooling-down phase for about three to five minutes consisting of slow working. Obviously for those people who are below average fitness the intensity of training should be less and the duration of warming-up and cooling-down exercises should be longer.

Prior to taking up any form of exercise, let alone running, you should seek advice from your family doctor as to whether you are suffering any underlying medical problem that needs treatment. Providing you have been cleared, then hopefully you should have no problems, although should any untoward side-effects occur and persist then medical advice should be sought. The build-up to regular running, either over short distances or even to marathon level, should be done gradually bearing in mind the needs of the body to adapt to this prolonged exercise.

Prolonged exercise does make you cardio-respiratory fit, but should you have suffered rheumatic fever as a child, have a history of high blood pressure, angina or any other heart problem, then seek medical advice before you start a running programme. As any runner will tell you, it is not unusual to get the odd aches and pains in and around the chest area or elsewhere in the body. These are normally insignificant but should they intensify during exercise or persist at rest or cause any untoward distress, faintness or other related symptoms, see your doctor before continuing exercise.

Heart disease and high blood pressure

Even if you have suffered from heart disease or high blood pressure, provided that your physician knows about your running and is prepared to counsel you, exercise is not contra-indicated although you should not run at a competitive level too soon. Running, even up to marathon distance, may be of benefit to you. These days, graduated exercise is encouraged for those recovering from heart attacks, but a careful and gradual rehabilitation programme should be followed in conjunction with the cardiologist. It is now recognised that gentle exercise at an early stage is helpful in encouraging the collateral coronary artery circulation as well as being psychologically beneficial. Providing exercise is not over-done, then brisk walking and gentle running can be undertaken within the limits of any discomfort, pain, breathlessness or other symptoms.

Varicose veins

The occurence of varicose veins can be prevented either directly or indirectly by exercise: indirectly as a result of a reduction in weight of the individual as his running increases and he takes more care with his dietary intake; and directly as a result of increased circulatory and general muscular tone. Minor varicose veins should certainly not prevent you running.

Anaemia

This can be a problem in endurance athletes and there has been speculation that iron losses in sweat are at least partly responsible, as, of course, is the blood loss in women which occurs at the time of their periods. This should be corrected wherever possible as maximal heart efficiency is not attained with a low haemoglobin. The exact nature of the anaemia should be determined and the correct remedy sought. Not all anaemias respond to the regular taking of iron tablets which may in fact be contra-indicated. The failure of an athlete, especially a woman, to improve performance levels despite correct diet and training should suggest that anaemia may be an underlying cause and the correct treatment may make all the difference between outstanding and mediocre athletic performance. It may be advantageous for a runner to increase his intake of iron through choice of food, such as liver. Cereals are also rich in iron if they are not unduly processed but they also contain Phytic acid, which prevents absorption of minerals by the body.

Obesity

This is probably one of the biggest health problems that occurs in the Western world today and is due to a poor diet and lack of exercise. Exercise, and running in particular, obviously will be beneficial to weight loss as long as a sensible eating pattern is adopted simultaneously, and advice from a dietician may be all-important. The runner is usually very aware of the need to eat a well-balanced diet with adequate supplies of roughage and vitamins, and also the value of eating regularly. It is very unwise to run within two to three hours of having eaten, as exercise of the prolonged type will divert the blood supply from the gastro-intestinal tract to the muscles and heart and disturb and prevent digestion with resultant abdominal upsets. Should you be more than 30 per cent overweight for your height and build (this can

be discovered by referring to the height and weight tables opposite), then you should embark on a sensible eating pattern prior to taking up running. A well-balanced and sensible diet containing adequate amounts of protein, vegetables, fruit, salads and carbohydrate in association with regular exercise will soon restore that trim figure which disappeared many years ago due to dietary indiscretions and laziness.

Fluid intake

An adequate supply of fluid should be taken in training and especially when running competitively. This can be in the form of tea, coffee, fruit juices or water. When racing, especially in hot climates, you should take advantage of the regular drink stations as it is all too easy to dehydrate with disastrous effects towards the end of the race. Fizzy drinks are not sensible as they produce a vast amount of gas and can cause abdominal cramping. Very sweet sugary drinks should also be avoided as they tend to increase thirst. Alcohol, although a fairly good source of calories, is not recommended for long distance running although it is well known that some of the top marathon runners in the world enjoy and even train on alcohol. An excessive amount of alcohol can cause relative dehydration and it is certainly not sensible to try and run or train 'the morning after the night before'. A minimum amount of three pints of fluid per day should be taken and, of course, this must be increased in hot, humid climates and also if any gastro-intestinal upsets have occurred.

Dietary supplements

The majority of athletes are great believers in the value of dietary supplements, especially vitamin pills. The reasoning seems to be that if small quantities of vitamins are good for the average performer, large quantities will produce an international champion. Unfortunately, competitors have at times been persuaded to include in their diet such bizarre items as seaweed cakes, rice polishings and celery leaf powder as well as wheatgerm oil, liver pills, yeast, large quantities of fortified cereals and various more specific vitamin preparations. The power of faith is such that athletic performance has sometimes been improved thereby but the gain has usually had a psychological basis and has not been duplicated when neither the athlete nor his coach knew whether the capsules administered contained the dietary supplement or some inactive substitute.

Vitamins

One manifestation of **vitamin A** deficiency of concern to the athlete is a blocking of the sweat glands and the skin by horny plugs. In additon to carrots, vitamin A is found in such foods as tomato juice and melon, and, in fact, many athletes eat 10 times the body requirements of vitamin A in a normal diet and certainly do not need supplements.

The **B group of vitamins,** such as Thiamine, Riboflavine and Aneurine, are closely involved in the energy-producing reactions the body needs during prolonged exercise. However, if the added energy requirements of the competitor are met by a good mixed diet rather than by empty calories, such as glucose, alcohol and sweet or soft drinks, then the necessary additional vitamins will be provided by normal food without the need for supplementation.

Vitamin C, or ascorbic acid, is concerned with the healing of injuries and large doses may reduce the period of disability from the common cold. It has been argued that athletes suffer more minor injuries than the average person and thus they need more vitamin C for healing and recovery. However, the quantity of vitamin C needed to ensure rapid healing is very small. No difference has been found in the number of injuries or in the duration of disability

Men's ideal weights				Women's ideal weights			
Height	Small frame	Medium frame	Large frame	Height	Small frame	Medium frame	Large frame
5'2"	112-120	118-129	126-141	4'10"	92-98	96-107	104-119
5'3"	115-123	121-133	129-144	4'11"	94-101	98-110	106-122
5'4"	118-126	124-136	132-148	5'0"	96-104	101-113	109-125
5'5"	121-129	127-139	135-152	5'1"	99-107	104-116	112-128
5'6"	124-133	130-143	138-156	5'2"	102-110	107-119	115-131
5'7"	128-137	134-147	142-161	5'3"	105-113	110-122	118-134
5'8"	132-141	138-152	147-166	5'4"	108-116	113-126	121-138
5'9"	136-145	142-156	151-170	5'5"	111-119	116-130	125-142
5'10"	140-150	146-160	155-174	5'6"	114-123	120-135	129-146
5'11"	144-154	150-165	159-179	5'7"	118-127	124-139	133-150
6'0"	148-158	154-170	164-184	5'8"	122-131	128-143	137-154
6'1"	152-162	158-175	168-189	5'9"	126-135	132-147	141-158
6'2"	156-167	162-180	172-194	5'10"	130-140	136-151	145-163
6'3"	160-171	167-185	178-199	5'11"	134-144	140-155	149-168
6'4"	164-175	172-190	182-204	6'0"	138-148	144-159	153-173

when long distance runners take large doses of vitamin C. The possible influence on the course of respiratory infections is a more valid argument since a common cold can make all the difference between victory and defeat, and on this basis some athletes take as much as one gram of vitamin C per day.

Vitamin E contributes to the normal health of the muscle in some animals. However, its precise role in the human body is a mystery, and although there are substantial amounts of this vitamin in normal food, additional dosage is popular among athletes. There is no evidence that such treatment helps performance either in the laboratory or on the track.

Respiratory complaints

Severe respiratory complaints such as chronic bronchitis, asthma and emphysema where the elasticity of the lungs is impaired, may well limit the runner's ability to exercise, and medical advice should be sought prior to embarking on a regular exercise pattern. Certainly the beneficial effects of weight loss, improved cardiac efficiency and relief of stress through increased exercise can greatly benefit lung function as will the indirect effect of reducing cigarette smoking which occurs when one attempts to get really fit. Minor degrees of asthma and bronchitis and also upper respiratory catarrh greatly improve by regular exercise. Hayfever and other allergic upper respiratory problems do not necessarily preclude one from running but should antihistamines or any other form of decongestant be required, medical advice should be taken as these do have a slowing-down effect on the body in general, and the drugs contained may also have an untoward effect on cardio-respiratory function.

It is certainly not wise to train or run competitively during the acute phase of colds, flu or any other upper respiratory-related infections or in fact in any febrile illness. Very rarely do you run off a fever and in fact due to the reduction in general efficiency of the body as a machine, problems could arise. It is a rare but recognised complication of running with a feverish illness that an inflammation of the heart muscle, myocarditis, can occur, and this often results in rather unpleasant problems for the sufferer! Minor muscular ligament and joint problems can also arise during the feverish stage of an illness and it is far better to take a few days off until you are fully recovered rather than put your whole training schedule and athletic career in jeopardy.

Gastro-intestinal problems

Peptic ulcers, gall bladder disease and other related problems and stress-related diseases such as colitis may be greatly improved by embarking on a regular exercise regime such as running. The regularity of diet that runners adopt and the frequency of their meals balances and improves the gastro-intestinal metabolism. The beneficial effects of reducing stress from prolonged running and the reduction in the need for artificial stimulants, such as cigarettes and alcohol, again greatly improve the general well-being of the runner.

Stomach stitch is a rather distressing problem, the actual causation of which is unknown, but it is normally easily overcome by reducing the pace of a run and taking deep breaths until the discomfort eventually wears off.

Hernias should be repaired prior to embarking on regular running as the constant jarring of the feet on the pavement can in fact aggravate this condition and may at times cause abdominal pain. More and more cases of inguinal (groin) hernias are being reported as having been mistakenly treated as groin strain, some with disastrous results.

Gastro-intestinal disturbances do occur in runners and they are normally relatively mild, consisting of abdominal cramp or bloating and frequent watery bowel movements. They often occur either during a rapid increase in the level of a running schedule, or if physical performance is suddenly increased, particularly during a race. Most runners accept that these problems will occur but occasionally they are severe enough to create alarm. The most likely explanation for them is the reduction of blood flow to the gut which occurs during maximal exercise and in fact can be as much as 80 per cent. This, associated with a tendency for the body temperature to rise during prolonged and severe exercise, is probably the cause of these distressing symptoms. A reassuring aspect of this problem is that provided high levels of training are maintained, the symptoms will gradually disappear. Another possible cause of this runners' diarrhoea is the tendency in many runners to take massive doses of vitamin C in order, so they think, to reduce any symptoms associated with musculo-skeletal problems. However, it is known that large doses of vitamin C frequently produce diarrhoea and once again a reduction in intake will relieve this somewhat debilitating problem.

Genito-urinary problems

These are not unusual in long distance runners. Concentrated urine, especially in hot humid weather over increased distances, is quite common, and after long distance races, including marathons, it is not unusual for the desire to pass urine to be delayed for several hours. This is due to a reduction in the volume of urine produced as the body mechanisms for regulating temperature during exercise are activated by fluid loss through the skin and a reduction therefore in fluid available for kidney filtration. The urine tends to become more acid and may cause some discomfort and burning, although if adequate fluids are taken during and after the run, both the flow and acidity will revert to normal within a few hours. Albumin is found in a great number of athletes whose urine is tested after extreme exertion, and again with adequate rehydration this normally clears within a few hours or days. Should this not be the case, then further investigations of the genito-urinary tract should be undertaken.

Haematuria, the passage of blood in the urine, is often very alarming to the runner but fortunately is only very rarely due to any underlying genito-urinary problem. Nevertheless, should this occur, medical advice should be sought if only for reassurance. The actual mechanism of haematuria is unknown although several theories have been advanced, but it nearly always occurs only with severe exercise and again within a few days will clear up completely. In 1978, out of 41 athletes who were examined after running the Norwegian Marathon, 13 showed a positive test for blood in the urine but within one week it had completely cleared in all cases. The actual causation of haematuria is not fully understood. It may be due to increased vascularity in the region of the bladder or actual trauma of the bladder against the pubic bone. It has also been associated with the breakdown of blood that occurs in the soles of the feet as a result of prolonged and repeated trauma during long distance running. Another theory proposes that it may be due to increased renal vein pressure resulting from the renal vein kinking at its junction with the main abdominal vein during exercise. Occasionally, clot colic can occur which is exceedingly painful and this is due to the build-up of clots associated with an increased acidity in the urine and an increased urinary concentration. Loin and groin pain can probably occur due to dehydration but may also indicate the passage of small amounts of gravel or a stone if in the past fluid intake has not been adequate. There are, of course, simple musculo-skeletal causes for loin and groin pains and these are considered by a doctor when any of these alarming symptoms occur.

Head problems

Dizziness and light-headedness are not symptoms that should be taken lightly during training sessions or during a race. They may signify the onset of some feverish illness or could be the first manifestation of dehydration or cardio-respiratory insufficiency and if they persist, despite a reduction in training, medical advice must be sought.

Tension headaches and migraine are often relieved by regular exercise as a result of reducing overall stress which initially precipitates them, but again, should headaches or migraine persist or intensify, or occur as a result of exercise, then medical advice must be sought.

Skin and nail problems

Minor skin and nail problems do occur and can be exceedingly distressing for the runner. Fungal infections of the feet (athlete's foot) or of the groin are very common. They can be prevented easily by adequate care of the feet and groin both prior to and after running. Feet should be properly washed and toes dried carefully so that no fungus is allowed to grow, and the same rules apply to the groin area. Should an infection occur, then an antifungal ointment or powder can be applied to the affected area and sprinkled in socks and in the running shoes themselves. Should this not improve, then there are now antifungal tablets available which can be taken daily with excellent results.

Blisters on the toes and feet are normally due to inadequate choice of footwear or poor preparation, and if care is taken in the selection of footwear and a gradual build-up to exercise is followed, then they should not occur. Very occasionally bleeding occurs into the blisters which can be rather alarming but is self-limiting and of no significance. Small blisters can be covered with plaster or dressing, but if large they should be pricked with a sterile needle and a firm plaster applied over it. Should blisters become infected and this will be shown by an area of redness, swelling and increasing pain in the area with probably

a red line running away from it, then an antibiotic plus an antibiotics ointment is probably required and medical advice should be taken.

Cracked nails, black nails and the loss of toe nails are almost inevitable in long distance running. They are caused by irritation of the nail bed through constant trauma and bleeding at the growing area, usually as a result of persistent friction of the toes against the front of the running shoes. This condition is never dangerous, is unsightly and somewhat alarming to both the runner and his family but is of no serious significance. Eventually the black nail will drop off but a new one will soon grow to replace it. Again, adequate footwear and careful preparation can prevent these problems occurring.

> ### Tip: Training after colds and flu
>
> Always treat colds and particularly flu with respect, and never run if you have a fever. It is best to stop running for a few days while you are feeling really under par, and then resume training very gradually, starting with perhaps only 10 or 15 minutes' gentle jogging and building up your distance slowly to pre-flu levels. You might feel quite weak and drained after a bout of flu or even a common cold, so do plenty of strengthening and stretching exercises to recover any lost fitness and suppleness.
>
> Build up your mileage gradually. It might be a good idea to rest or just do some exercises on alternate days between running at first. If you run too hard and too far too quickly, then you might overdo it and the cold or flu virus will strike you down a second time. If you start to feel run-down, then cut down on your training and rest.
>
> Colds and flu often happen when a runner is at a training peak and running extremely well. Because runners are nearer their physical limits than non-active people, they may be very susceptible to viruses and bugs.

Chafing is an annoying problem and many marathon runners in particular are affected by the sore nipple syndrome. This can be avoided easily by a liberal application of vasoline over the area or, covering the nipple with elastoplast. Other friction areas, such as the groin and under the arms, may also become chafed and sore, and vasoline applied prior to running will prevent what could be a painful problem.

Muscle cramp

This is almost always due to a build-up of lactic acid in the muscles resulting from inadequate oxidation in a particular group of muscles. This may be due either to inadequate training (the most common cause) or the depletion of glycogen stores in the muscles as a result of the massive muscular effort that occurs during a race.

Should these cramp-like symptoms occur in elderly people during the build-up to moderate exercise, then it is an outside possibility that there is some impairment of circulation to the limbs, and medical advice must be sought.

Diabetes

For many years, diabetes has been considered a strong contra-indication to anyone intending to take up running. Fortunately, nowadays, diabetics can exercise, provided that they are under medical supervision. It has even been shown that improved glucose tolerance can be associated with regular exercise. The obese diabetic and also those who are controlled by tablets may both show a marked improvement in their disease due partly to care taken in dietary intake and a reduction in weight as a result of regular exercise. Diabetics who take insulin must take great care as prolonged exercise will reduce the amount of blood sugar circulating and induce a condition known as hypoglycaemia, which is well known among insulin-taking diabetics and results in light-headedness, faintness, headaches, excessive

Tip: Foot maintenance
A runner's feet are very important and it is always a good idea to look after them and even to pamper them. Prevention is the best cure, and many foot problems can be avoided if proper care is taken. Many running injuries, including pulled leg muscles, knee and back pain, start in the feet so keep them in top condition by following these helpful tips:
1 Prevent cracked skin by applying cream.
2 Avoid blisters by wearing comfortable, wide-fitting shoes and applying Vaseline. Many runners find that nylon socks are too abrasive and cause blisters, so opt for cotton or wool socks.
3 Use an emery board or pumice stone to rub away dead skin, callouses and corns. If this does not work, visit a chiropodist or podiatrist.
4 Cut your toenails very short — this is important for downhill running when long nails may break on the toe-box and go black or grow inwards.
5 A generous dusting with talcum powder between the toes and around heels will help prevent blisters.

sweating and a disturbance in behaviour pattern at times. Should insulin-dependent diabetics want to embark on regular exercise, then either a reduction of insulin or an increase in carbohydrates or both are required and must be taken under medical supervision and not by the individual himself. It is now not unusual for professional footballers and tennis players who are diabetic to continue in their chosen careers, and I see no reason why, providing adequate medical advice is sought, this should not also apply to athletes and in particular long distance runners.

In conclusion, running can only be beneficial to the general health of the individual, provided that it is built up gradually. No longer is the lonely figure pounding the pavements a source of laughter and derision as more and more people take to the roads in order to improve their general health.

Running profile: Anne Brown
by Andy Etchells

Anne Brown is not a runner of whom you will have heard. She is an ordinary person who, until recently, took little or no physical exercise and who is never likely to become famous through running. But that is true of 99.5 per cent of all runners. Anne's story is typical of so many newcomers to the sport of running — and it might encourage anyone who is thinking about taking up running.

She is a 29-year-old midwife who works nights at a hospital in Epsom, not far from her Chessington home. She gets home in time to make breakfast for husband Bill — himself a runner and one of the reasons she started — four mornings a week, which means her training can be somewhat sporadic. She tries to make up for this at weekends and on days off.

Bill, 37, was prompted by the first London Marathon to start running and while he was training for this event, Anne would occasionally pace him on a bike — "but with great difficulty" — carrying a water bottle for him on distances up to 19 miles.

"Bill never put any pressure on me, but I wanted to try it. I had a couple of jogs and was very puffed out. I really didn't think I liked running," she recalls. After all, apart from a spot of hurdling and the obligatory school hockey, the only exercise she'd taken since the age of 17 was the occasional swim in the pool and a bit of dancing. ("I dance energetically," she insists!)

"Then Bill spotted an article in *Running Magazine* appealing for beginners who were going to be trained up for the National Fun Run and given fitness tests along the way to monitor their progress. He suggested I try it and I went out on my first run in the programme on my birthday, April 18. Well, actually," she admits, "it wasn't really a run, more like what we used to do in Guides — 10 paces trotting, 10 of walking."

On her second run, she managed just over a mile with Bill, though she prefers to talk in terms of 'points' for Anne is one of millions of runners all over the world who have used Dr Kenneth Cooper's *New Aerobics* to guide them through their early runs. Cooper awards aerobic points according to the duration of your exercise and this was the system the Fun Runners — as the magazine's group was called — used. "It drove Bill mad." she says. "He's into miles in a big way and I was always announcing points totals!"

One of the best bits of advice she got from the more established runners who gave up their time to help the newcomers like herself — and one of the nicest things about running, she reckons, is the social atmosphere and the way others do go out of their way to help — was to keep a training diary to log the miles (...or points). This reveals that within six months of that first run in April, she had, despite the occasional backsliding in training, successfully competed in the National Fun Run (just under 21 minutes for the 4km, earning a silver certificate) and then went on to run in the Avon 10 (the national women's championship) in which she placed 199th in one hour 29 minutes, the Nike 25km in London and even the Paris-Versailles 20km.

"Generally I run no more than four or five miles in training," she says, "but I put in a couple of 10s in practice for the Avon. And as for the 25km — I was so shocked at finishing... I thought I might do just one lap because I'd missed so much training, but I just kept going." It was after that that the idea of

Anne Brown likes to train in her local park and puts in a high weekly mileage. Although she has to work nights in a busy hospital as a midwife, Anne still manages to fit her training into a busy schedule.

running a marathon started to take hold. "I'd thought about it but didn't think I could spare the· time. Maybe London '83" she muses.

Anne didn't take up running — as some do — with a specific cure or result in mind. Her starting fitness was above average and it wasn't that she felt bad; as much as anything, it was to keep up with Bill. But now that she is a runner, she can see certain benefits. She sleeps more soundly (though still survives on remarkably little), can swim 35 lengths of the pool without getting breathless and, despite eating more, has lost weight.

Above all, though, it's satisfaction that running gives her — not just the time when Bill promised her a pair of flashy training shoes for reaching a specific target, but the inner feeling of satisfaction — what she calls "feeling chuffed within˙ myself" — after completing a long run.

What of her friends? What do they think? Firstly, she now has more friends through running; secondly, quite a few of the neighbours in her street were already runners so that was no problem; and one or two of those at work who said all along she must be crazy have recently started to sidle up and say: "If you take it slowly, do you think I could join you...?"

And there's a definite addition to her confidence. At first she went out bundled up in a heavy tracksuit, even at the height of summer. Then she saw that other women in the group were happily wearing shorts and she joined them. "I didn't like the sort of comments you sometimes get, but now if anybody says anything, I just wave back and run on."

CHAPTER FOURTEEN

Running injuries

by Dr Patrick Milroy

By the very nature of running, most injuries found in distance runners occur in the lower limbs and back and these are the areas we are going to discuss in detail. In this chapter, we are not going to deal with diseases of the whole body that may make it unwise for certain individuals to run. Some diseases, such as asthma, may well be helped by running. However, if you do have a medical problem or

In a freely moving synovial joint, the ends of the bones are encased in a capsule and ligaments. The synovial fluid which lubricates the joint is secreted by the synovial membrane inside the joint cavity. This helps prevent friction.

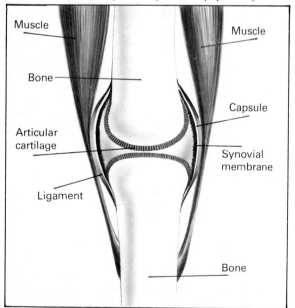

Muscle

Muscle

Bone

Capsule

Articular cartilage

Synovial membrane

Ligament

Bone

condition, seek advice from a general practitioner before taking up the sport. For further information, see Chapter 13 about running and your body.

In all branches of medicine, prevention is often easier than cure, and this is certainly the case with runners' injuries. Time and thought spent on planning clothing, shoes and training may well prevent the frustration that injury can cause.

Running is a complex mechanical action of the body involving many movements, which do, however, have a common principle involving the alternate contraction and relaxation of muscles — the meat of the body. These are attached by thinner silvery tendons to two bones, which themselves are in contact at a joint — an enclosed space filled with synovial fluid, oiling the movement of one bone against the other.

On this basis, you can see that a torn muscle in the thigh will involve the same pattern of treatment and rehabilitation as one in the calf, so before detailing specific injuries it is important to understand how the individual elements work and in what way they may become damaged.

The running body

Muscle damage in runners commonly occurs as a result of sudden internal stretching forces tearing muscle fibres, connective tissues and blood vessels. This may extend either partially or completely through the muscle, and the resultant bleeding within the muscle will cause a rise in tension and pain if it is contracted. The muscle bundles are enclosed in a sheath which, if torn, will allow the blood to escape. In a partial rupture this is not the case and the ensuing internal bruise or haematoma causes a considerable reduction in the ability of the muscle to contract or be passively stretched. Ideally, in order to minimise the damage, any treatment should be immediate. Cold from an ice pack and then pressure bandaging will prevent internal bleeding whilst elevation of the limb and rest will decrease the local blood flow. After two days, when the bleeding has ceased, healing will be speeded by an increase in the blood flow using physiotherapy and some graduated active exercise.

After injury the haematoma is invaded by repair cells which lay down inelastic scar tissue. If this is untreated it may shorten the muscle permanently . Total recovery is thus dependent upon progressive mobilisation and stretching of the muscle with corresponding flexibility of the neighbouring joints. A shortened muscle has less power, thus putting extra stresses on other parts of the body which, in turn, can ultimately lead to further injury.

Tendons link muscles to bone and consist of bands of collagen fibres surrounded by a paratenon, outside which is a further tendon sheath. Like muscles, the tendons may split under sudden stretching and this may be either complete or partial.

The tendon, paratenon and tendon sheath may also become inflamed and hence swollen, causing a tendinitis, peritendinitis or tendovaginitis respectively. It is the tension of the swelling which causes pain and this is discussed in the section dealing with Achilles tendon injuries.

Bones are not commonly injured through running except as the result of a stress fracture, which may occur with a sudden increase in training load, but pain is not invariably felt at once. The pain is usually localised and a tender spot may be palpated, but the diagnosis is not always clear as X-ray changes may not appear for several weeks.

The bones most affected are the tibiae and the metatarsal bones of the foot. These fractures must be rested, at the physician's discretion, sometimes in plaster, so that symptoms may subside and training can be cautiously and progressively resumed after a few weeks.

Most **limb joints** have the same basic structure. Each knee also contains internally two half moon-shaped cartilages and ligaments but these are discussed later. It is not common for joints to lock in runners, unless a loose body of bone from an underlying disease such as arthritis is floating within it.

However, an increase in synovial fluid with swelling of the joint may well occur after the demands placed on it by road or long-distance racing. This sign of chronic inflammation is particularly likely in the older runner and an expert medical opinion must be sought.

In a sprain, excessive movement of the joint damages the capsule or a ligament. The ankle is particularly vulnerable in cross-country runners, with pain, swelling and protective muscle spasm. This type of injury will need a longer period of rest and even immobilisation before active training can be resumed. Some strapping may be needed initially in training, but must be progressively discarded before competition.

A bursa is a protective lubricating sac of fluid found where tendons or muscles move over a prominent bone. If these become inflamed by excessive rubbing they may swell and form a bursitis.

They need early treatment with physiotherapy and anti-inflammatory medication to prevent them becoming chronically inflamed. If this happens, only surgical removal may effect a cure.

Causes of injury

Not all injuries are preventable, but certain factors may make injury more likely, these being:

1 Congenital deformities may be noticed only as a

result of running. Recurring knee pain may be due to a genu varum, or bow leg — which may easily be corrected by wedging the outer side of the shoe heels. In many cases of chronic knee pain the only abnormality may be a genu valgum, or knock-knee, which can be associated with excessive pronation of the foot. Limb length discrepancy may cause pain from the back downwards. Correction requires accurate measurements of the limb by a competent physician with a built-up shoe to compensate for the asymmetrical stride. Although a minority may need podiatric advice and an orthotic device, simple first aid with a sorbothane heel wedge can effect an almost miraculous recovery by equalising the leg lengths.

2 Training is discussed elsewhere, but unless it is stepped up gradually over-use injuries will occur.

3 Running surfaces Too much running is performed on hard and uneven roads. The effect on the body of always running on one side of a cambered road will cause forces similar to those found in the congenital

When a runner pronates (below right) the foot and shoe tilt inwards and this can lead to injury, especially in the shins and knees. Good shoes, special inserts and orthotic devices can help to prevent or alleviate this problem.

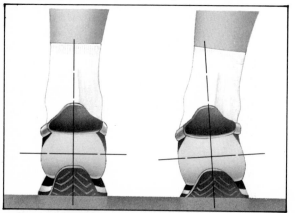

deformities. Running uphill places excess strain on the Achilles tendon; running downhill on the thigh muscles. The intelligent runner will alternate between running on roads and soft paths or grass, and mix in some hill work judiciously.

4 Shoes must be well-fitting and comfortable. Thick-soled shoes with broad, flared heels will absorb much of a runner's impact, whereas the thin-soled, flat racing shoes offer little protection between foot and ground and are a potent cause of injury. Runners who pronate excessively usually benefit from a straight lasted shoe or one which prevents the shoe tilting inwards, such as the Nike Equator. The ideal shoe has a high rounded toe box to protect the toes and nails, a flexible mid-sole helping to prevent Achilles problems, and arch support for metatarsal pain and a well padded tongue to lessen irritation on the extensor tendons beneath. Heel tabs are discussed under Achilles tendon injuries.

Achilles tendon injuries

This tendon, connecting the calf muscles to the heel, causes more distress to runners than any other injury. Some of the most common injuries and their treatments are discussed below.

A complete rupture is felt suddenly as a blow on the heel and the runner is lame. He is unable to stand on the toes of that foot and it is usually possible to feel a gap in the tendon. It is now usual to repair this surgically, although some specialists still prefer to put the ankle in a plaster cast for several weeks and allow it to heal naturally.

A partial rupture is felt as a pain in the tendon which recurs every time the runner pushes off from

The illustration (right) shows the bones and also the muscles of the legs. A detail of the Achilles tendon, a common area for injury, is shown (inset), together with the tendon sheath. Muscles are made of contractile tissue and give the legs their strength and mobility when running.

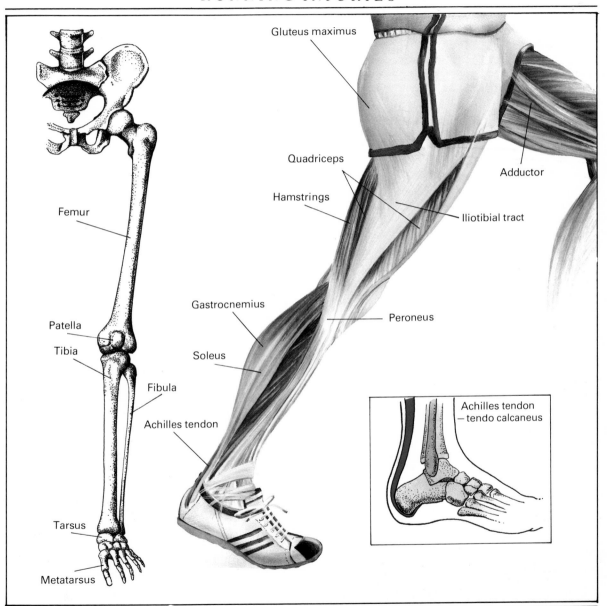

Gluteus maximus

Quadriceps

Hamstrings

Adductor

Iliotibial tract

Femur

Gastrocnemius

Peroneus

Patella

Soleus

Tibia

Fibula

Achilles tendon

Tarsus

Metatarsus

Achilles tendon
— tendo calcaneus

his toes. It often occurs with a sudden change in pace during a race. The scar tissue formed during healing is often painful and may require surgical removal, although some partial ruptures will respond to rest and judicious ultrasound or short wave from a physiotherapist.

Simple **tendinitis** may occur after unaccustomed strenuous exercise and is associated with local pain and tenderness but no swelling or crepitus (a feeling of 'crackling' in the tendon as the ankle is alternately moved backwards and forwards). Heel wedging and a few days' rest are required to prevent the injury becoming chronic.

In **peritendinitis** there is swelling and crepitus especially in the bottom two inches of the tendon.

Achilles bursitis, or Pump Bump, is caused by irritation of shoes against the calcaneus. It is felt as a tender nodule lateral to the lower attachment of the Achilles and if it fails to settle with the measures listed below it may need a steroid injection.

Treatments not discussed above include physiotherapy, initially a cold compress to reduce inflammation and stop any bleeding, followed by ultra-sound or short-wave. Friction rubbing should not be used, as it only causes extra inflammation. A doctor may prescribe anti-inflammatory drugs but more chronic causes may need steroid (cortisone) injections into the tendon sheath, never the tendon itself. Desite the bad press these injections have received, they do have a place in treatment by an experienced sports physician.

If the Achilles injury is the result of excessive pronation, an orthotic device may be needed, though the heel wedge may be just as effective. Continued stretching exercises are vital even if the injury is quiescent if it is not to recur. Trying to 'run through' Achilles tendinitis may convert a mild injury into a

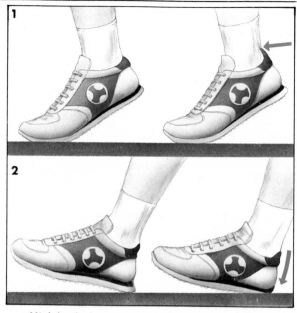

High heel tabs (1) can damage, rather than protect the Achilles if they protrude above the ankle. Rounded heels (2) may cause the Achilles to stretch excessively so avoid these shoes or those with badly worn heels.

severe one with subsequent nodule formation and a greater risk that surgery will be required for cure.

Causes and prevention Achilles problems may be prevented in many cases by simple heel padding, adequate warm-up and stretching exercises. The so-called 'heel-protectors', the high heel tabs found in many running shoes, may do exactly the opposite of protection. If when wearing the shoes and pointing the toes the heel tabs dig into the tendon, they will give a microscopic bruise with every step. In this case the only course is to refashion the back of the shoe by cutting off the heel tab. It would appear that shoe manufacturers are unwilling to accept this problem for fear of litigation.

Leg injuries

Ankle sprains are common, often with sufficient pain and swelling to make one suspect a fracture. If there is an internal sprain 'inside the joint capsule' the joint may need aspirating, followed by rest then extensive mobilisation to prevent a stiff joint forming. As well as conventional physiotherapy a 'wobble-board' may be of great benefit, and this can be easily made by taking a wooden board two feet square and nailing two concave pieces of wood underneath.

Shin splints may have separate causes which must be

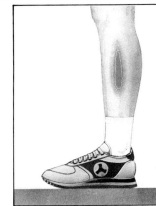

Shin splints may occur in the anterior compartment of the lower leg, between the tibia and fibula bones. They tend to affect those runners who are under-conditioned and over-train, and are often related to a weak foot or even Morton's toe.

A wobble-board can be constructed easily with a wooden board, two feet square, and two pieces of wood cut to a concave shape as shown in the diagram. This will help increase ankle mobility following an injury.

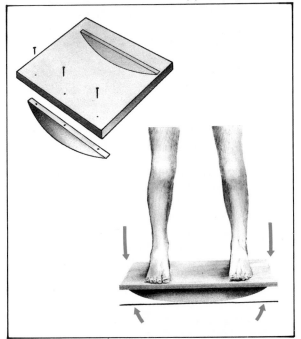

differentiated. In the anterior tibial syndrome the muscles between the two lower leg bones become swollen if the beginner steps up his training too fast, and cut off their own blood supply. Rest and elevation may alleviate it, but if it becomes chronic a surgical decompression may be vital to save the muscle dying for lack of blood.

In the posterior tibial syndrome, pain occurs on the inner border of the shin bone which may be acutely tender to touch. It is due to muscle pulling away from bone with weak scar tissue forming which again pulls away from the bone with even minimal exercise. Rest, ice and taping the leg followed by alternating hot and cold soaks must be used before returning to training on soft level ground. The shoes may need a wedge or orthotic device to prevent hyperpronation which is often responsible.

Stress fractures of the tibia and fibula have already been discussed and must be suspected if shin splints fail to settle. These injuries may largely be prevented by avoiding sudden increases in running activity.

Foot pain

This can often be a simply corrected problem. Shoes have already been discussed, but where feet are of unequal sizes it is better to buy a pair in which the larger foot is comfortable and to pad the other internally than buy a tight-fitting pair.

In the so-called **Mortons Foot**, the second toe is longer than the first and is easily bruised and stubbed. Again there is a tendency to pronate the foot, but it can be relieved by wearing sensible shoes with or without an orthotic device.

Metatarsalgia is very often due to wearing tight or incorrectly laced training shoes and responds to wider shoes and a metatarsal arch support.

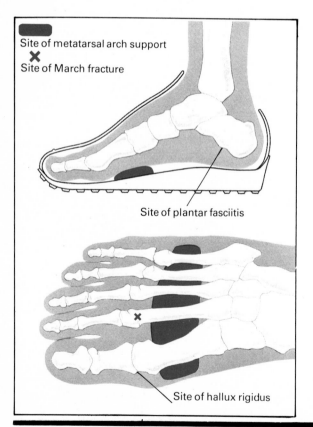

Site of metatarsal arch support

Site of March fracture

Site of plantar fasciitis

Site of hallux rigidus

Hallux rigidus, osteoarthritis of the first metatarso-phalangeal joint, is also a runner's complaint as it prevents forefoot mobility and causes splinting of the foot. If it is not corrected by the metatarsal bar, surgery may prove necessary.

Plantar fasciitis is associated with biomechanical problems caused by stiffness of the mid-foot. If heel pads or heel cups, rest and ice fail to cure it, this is successfully treated with a steroid injection.

A **March fracture** is a stress fracture of the second metatarsal bone. Treatment obviously consists of rest, accompanied by a walking plaster cast or a thick pad under the sole which is strapped from the toes to below the knee.

More leg injuries

Chrondromalacia patellae, or 'runners knee', is by far the commonest cause of knee pain in runners. Without going into all the anatomical complexities, the patella normally runs in a groove at the bottom of the femur as the knee is flexed and extended. However, because the hips are separated compared to the ankles and knees, there is a lateral force on the patella as the knee is extended, which rubs it against the outside of the joint.

The pain is typically described by the novice runner increasing his mileage as an aching around the knee-cap, aggravated by climbing stairs, though easing with training only to recur later in the day. The knee-caps may appear to 'squint' at one another.

Treatment initially must consist of ice, rest and aspirin. Further prevention is obtained by strengthening the quadriceps muscles — especially the medial ones. This is done by sitting on a bed, the knee held straight with gradually increasing weights, from 1lb to 8lb, suspended from the ankles. The weights are lifted up to 30 times a day until the pain disappears and only then may running be recommended. Training should avoid hills and still be allied with the above quadriceps exercises and suitable orthotic devices. Surgery is only needed in the most extreme cases.

Other causes of knee pain are not peculiar to runners but may still occur in the athlete. For example, it may be a sign of injury elsewhere but cartilage injuries in particular are rare due to running.

Hamstring tears may appear suddenly during any speedwork but more commonly develop insidiously due to inadequate stretching before and after training. The usual ice, rest and strapping are vital until pain subsides. When rehabilitation is started, ultrasound, coupled with gentle active exercises, will restore full fitness most quickly.

Calf muscle tears are treated no differently and prevention by stretching is much easier than treating the strained muscle.

Adductor strains occur in runners who have to take a big stretch as in steeplechases and cross-country races. The pain is felt on the inner upper side of the thigh as the stretch is made. Energetic physiotherapy with ultrasound and adductor stretching exercises will usually effect a cure, but occasionally some manipulation under general anaesthetic is required.

The principal problem is in differentiating this from other pain in the groin. Osteitis pubis is a pain between the two pubic bones caused by the shearing action of the bones on each other. Rest and steroids may be required. Runners are not exempt from inguinal herniae or hip disease which can also cause pain in this region.

General injuries and health problems

Sciatica is potentially serious in runners, nerve compression causing back, buttock and/or leg pain. It appears to be exacerbated by an uneven running gait and running on downhill surfaces which transmit excess shock through the spine. Although a few days

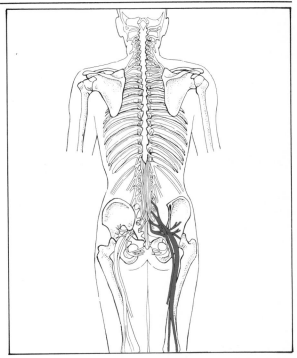

Sciatic pain occurs when the sciatic nerves at the base of the spine, which serve the legs, are pinched or irritated. It may be caused by excessive speedwork or uneven running. Regular stretching exercises can help prevent this condition.

of rest and anti-inflammatory tablets may settle the condition if only the joint between the vertebrae is injured, an intervertebral disc prolapse (slipped disc) must be excluded to avoid any potentially disastrous nerve damage.

Stitch appears to occur most commonly in the unfit runner who trains too soon after a meal or takes inappropriate drinks whilst running. Many causes are suggested, including spasm of the diaphragmatic muscles. It is treated by abdominal strengthening exercises, trunk curls or step-ups and allowing two or three hours between eating and running. If it occurs during a race, it may be possible to avoid stopping by bending forwards, holding your breath or twisting your trunk.

Stiffness is universal, associated with unaccustomed running, but of unknown cause. A good warm-up is essential in prevention, although some people have a definite propensity to stiffness, uncommon in others. A hot bath and the occasional use of aspirin will ease it, but no runner should train under the influence of anti-inflammatory medication. Long, slow distance training appears to be more effective in prevention but many distance runners are inherently stiff (eg. they cannot touch their toes) and would benefit considerably from both flexibility exercises and weekly reduction in mileage.

Haematuria is well known in distance runners who do a lot of road work. Whilst all runners with blood in the urine should be investigated it is usually benign and should not hinder training.

Heat injury is not uncommon despite the British climate. If sweat losses do not match the increase in body core temperature from muscle-generated heat, air temperature or rise in relative humidity, cramps, exhaustion or stroke may supervene.

Heat cramps require rest and replacement of fluid and electrolytes. The signs of heat exhaustion are light-headedness, confusion, nausea, vomiting and cramps. The skin is cold and clammy, the pulse rapid but weak. Runners with these symptoms should be made to drop out of the race and cooled in the shade and then rehydrated, if necessary by the use of intravenous fluids.

Heat stroke may be fatal, with fits and loss of consciousness occurring in addition to the above symptoms. Acclimatisation, adequate pre-race fluid intake, brief, light, loose clothing, a slower pace and sufficient drinks during the race should be preventive

measures. Many runners like to take pre-race salt tablets on hot days.

Cold injury shows itself as inco-ordination, confusion and lethargy. It was very common after a sudden storm during the 'National' at Sutton Coldfield in 1972. Sensible clothing, covering exposed parts with petroleum jelly, and rapid post-race warming should help to prevent it.

Skin

Blisters occur when the layers of the skin become detached from each other, the gap being filled with a watery fluid from the damaged cell. They are usually due to ill-fitting shoes. Treatment should consist of releasing the fluid with a sterilised needle, snipping away the dead skin and applying tincture of iodine and a dry dressing. Repeated blistering can be prevented by using foot powder, soft insoles and two pairs of socks to prevent friction.

Athletes foot is a common fungus infection and is usually easily diagnosed. It is favoured by a moist, warm environment and is particularly common between the toes. Prevention by frequent changes of socks — preferably cotton, avoidance of plastic or sweaty training shoes, and the liberal application of foot powder is often more effective than treatment. Tolnaftate and Clotrimazole creams are both obtainable without prescription, but recurrences are common and it may be necesscary to paint the affected areas with Castellani's Paint.

Tinea cruris is a similar fungal infection of the groin often found when the underwear is not washed sufficiently frequently. Most of the remarks about athletes foot also apply. However, treatment may require an anti-fungal cream combined with a mild steroid — available only on prescription — *never* a steroid cream alone.

Ingrowing toe nails are usually accompanied by an infection of the nail fold. They are associated with tight training shoes and badly cut nails. First aid is by trying to 'jack-up' the affected nail using thin slivers of silver paper. The nail should be cut square rather than in a semi-circular fashion and a small V-shaped nick in the middle may encourage the nail to grow inwards. Treatment may require antibiotics to be prescribed, but it can prove necessary to have a small operation removing part of the toe-nail or to insert a small plastic guard along the side of the toe nail for two to three months.

Joggers nipple is characterised by tenderness, chafiing or even bleeding. Prevention is by covering the nipples with petroleum jelly or a plaster before the event, whereas treatment relies on an antiseptic cream or, if severe, a corn pad-type of protection.

Summary

Treatment and prevention of running injuries are usually based on conservative measures. Almost invariably a reduction in training mileage or rest is called for, depending on the type of injury, but this may also be helped by a change of shoes, running surface and the type of training carried out.

When pain is relatively mild, after injury, the application of ice for 10 minutes, the elevation of the injured part and stretching exercises may help. This should be followed later in the day by warmth and more stretching. If this fails to settle the injury after a few days, then the advice of a doctor or a qualified physiotherapist should be sought.

Prevention of injuries is all about flexibility of the joints and it is almost impossible to do too many loosening and stretching exercises both before and after running. Many exercises done against resistance will prevent imbalance injuries, whereas heel wedging or the rather more expensive orthotic devices will compensate for many of the congenital and bio-

Tip: Stretching

Never skimp on your warm-up and stretching exercises — even though *you* might feel ready to start running, your body does not. It needs some gentle preparation for action before you leap out of the front door. So make warming-up part of your running routine. Scientific studies have shown that it will help increase your maximum oxygen capacity and heart rate and reduce lactic acid in your muscles. It releases tension and relaxes and stretches tight muscles. Spend 10-15 minutes warming-up and perform all the exercises slowly and smoothly — jerky, quick movements will do more harm than good and may even tighten already tense muscles. You will feel more flexible too and help eliminate muscle soreness and stiffness which sometimes occur after a hard run. Be sure to repeat the exercises after your run to 'warm-down; This is often neglected by beginners and more experienced runners. It will prevent muscle tightness and help slow your heart rate back down to its normal level. Self-massage in the bath or shower can relax muscles. Just lie back in the bath and massage your calves and hamstring areas with fingers and thumbs. This will break up lactic acid and alleviate stiffness.

mechanical causes of injury.

When an injury is severe it may prove necessary for a doctor to prescribe oral non-steroidal anti-inflammatory medication. This should be taken as prescribed and not as and how the runner feels. If a steroid (cortisone) injection is required, the benefits may be almost magical, but it must be administered by a doctor familiar with sports injuries. Although mentioned above as the ultimate treatment for many injuries, surgery is rarely required, and the general fitness brought about by running usually ensures that the experienced runner has less need of a doctor than his flab-fighting contemporaries.

Running profile: Libby Pfeiffer
by Andy Etchells

When the then National Marathon Coach Don Shelley arrived at a training weekend for beginner runners in the autumn of 1981, he wasn't quite sure what to expect. His experience was with the *élite*- the men and women to whom racing is deadly serious and running long distances a way of life they have cultivated since adolescence.

He came away surprised at the enthusiasm, the thirst for knowledge and the willingness to work hard displayed by his novice charges. And in one particular case his surprise was at the talent already clearly showing. The story of one of the people on that course — 36 year old Libby Pfeiffer — reminded him that the stars he knew so much about did not have a monopoly of talent. They were the tip of the iceberg that was allowed to show; down below the surface, there was a lot more where that came from.

It is perhaps significant that Libby Pfeiffer was not a total newcomer to athletics: as a girl, she had been a member of Middlesex Ladies AC where she had concentrated on the shorter track events. "They weren't into road running in those days," she says. But then, who was? The athletics set-up then did not provide a real challenge for an active girl like Libby and like so many others of her age, she drifted away from all forms of sport after her marriage.

She only started doing a bit of gentle running in 1980 after the birth of her third child, sparked off in particular by being dragged around as tracksuit holder and spectator at meetings her teenage children Bjorn and Britt were competing in.

Bjorn especially, did not realise what he had let himself in for and his experience mirrors that of many perplexed men who find themselves well and truly beaten by 'mere women'. He and Mum ran the People's Marathon in Solihull in 1981. "Bjorn's ambition was to break three hours — or me," says Libby. On target most of the way for a 2:52, he 'hit the wall' at 24 miles, which was just when canny Mum sailed past to a 2:57 clocking while Bjorn had to be content with 3:05.

But that was not Libby's first time under the magical three hours barrier. In her very first outing over the distance — London 1981 — she recorded an astonishing 2:58:31, just nine months after her first serious week's running since her teens. That first week she clocked up 10 miles whereas now, when preparing for a race, she's on a steady 70 plus miles per week — on top of looking after the family and helping run the family restaurant in Wembley.

For a time, it seemed that she was recording a personal best (or PB as it's known to runners of all standards) every time she put on her kit. By the end of 1981 she had run four marathons and reduced her time to 2:53:53. Early in 1982, in the second London race, she ran 2:45:52 which placed her twelfth on the all-time British women's rankings.

The 37-year-old mother of three was now in the big time; before long she was receiving invitations to foreign races, including representing Britain in the Avon International Marathon in San Francisco later that year. How does she do it? For anyone over 35 who thinks that it's too late to start running, she says the key word is — consistency. "If you are consistent and disciplined in your training you get stronger without realising."

Her weekly schedule is based on a long weekend run and semi-long midweek jaunt with several other days of doubles — a morning and afternoon run giving her a total for the day of around 12 miles. She also trains with some of the best in the country as she's now a member of Barnet AC.

There are no other special secrets. She eats pretty much what she wants — perhaps rather more carbohydrates than before she started running seriously — and dislikes specialised training like track work. Having, as she puts it, "a sympathetic other half" is essential and although there are the usual moans if tea is late onto the table, the family are solidly behind her and revel in her success.

That includes Bjorn — but he still harbours hopes of outrunning Mum some day soon.

CHAPTER FIFTEEN

The role of physiotherapy

by Sandra Dyson

Physiotherapy is the use of physical, mechanical and electrical methods to restore the body to its original state after injury. The body will usually heal quite well without any outside help, but unfortunately most athletes cannot wait for this to happen naturally, as they would be missing important training time or a vital race. Very often a doctor will prescribe physiotherapy for an injury becuase he would rather it were treated by more natural methods than using drugs, especially in young people.

Physiotherapy is a very old method of treatment and has its beginnings in the age-old practice of massage. Although many physiotherapists today use very little massage, it has a big part to play in the treatment of sporting injuries, and all physiotherapists who treat sports people must be highly proficient in its use. As well as the treatment value of massage, it is very important in the assessment of an injury as will be discussed later.

Usually the first sign of an injury is that the runner suffers pain. Very often there will also be subsequent swelling at the site of the damage, particularly if it involves a joint. If the swelling were allowed to go unattended, then apart from increased pain, there would be a very definite danger of the swelling becoming permanent. One of the most important factors that an athlete should remember, as a first aid after injury, are the vital letters, I.C.E.

'I' stands for ice. This means that following injury, the patient should apply either an ice pack or cold water to the painful area. Ice cubes from the refrigerator can be broken up with a hammer or other suitable object and then put into either a polythene bag or a piece of cloth which has been wrung out in cold water. The ice shoud be left in place for 10 minutes and then removed, but may be reapplied several times subsequently, with at least one hour between applications. It is important that the correct time be adhered to when applying an ice pack. Do not think that if 10 minutes is good for the injury, then half an hour must be better! There are physiological reasons why 10 minutes is the optimum time, and putting an ice pack on for longer than this will actually hinder the condition rather than help.

'C' stands for compression. After an injury , apart from a certain amount of bleeding of the damaged part, which usually takes place, a watery fluid is often produced surrounding the injured part. The principal object of this fluid is to stop more bleeding and prevent any infection; it also provides a very useful, immediate and natural 'splinting' of the injured part, so that it is kept fairly immobile and prevents any further damage.

To aid the body's natural resources, when it is suspected that swelling might take place following an injury, the runner should apply a bandage as soon as possible. It is a very good idea for every sportsman to carry a crépe bandage in his sports bag as a matter of routine, either for his own use or for a colleague who might be injured. The bandage should be applied so that it is reasonably tight and will not slip off, but not uncomfortable. If it is too tight, the circulation of the blood will be restricted and the injury made worse. It is a good idea, at the first opportunity, to buy a Tubigrip bandage. This is a tube-shaped bandage, as the name implies, and comes in different sizes, according to the location of the injury. The chemist will help with the sizing. Tubigrip

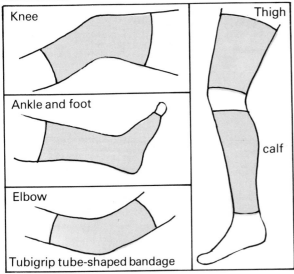

Knee

Ankle and foot

Elbow

Tubigrip tube-shaped bandage

Thigh

calf

allows the injury to heal more quickly, and will be much less painful.

It is quite simple to apply all three aspects of I.C.E. at the same time. Put on a bandage, lie on the floor (if it is a leg injury) with the leg resting on a chair or settee, and put on an ice pack for 10 minutes. According to the severity of the swelling, leave the leg elevated for between 30 minutes and one hour — but remove the ice pack after 10 minutes.

If these first aid procedures are adhered to, the job of the physiotherapist is made much easier and the runner will be back in training more quickly. The physiotherapist is then able to make an assessment of the injury and to select the most appropriate form of treatment.

By using first aid, the runner himself has taken care of the first two of the five aspects concerned with treating an injury — namely, relief of pain and reduction of swelling, which means that dysfunction will be kept to a minimum. The three other aspects are to regain mobility, increase strength and, finally, be rehabilitated back to running.

With the decrease in swelling brought about by first aid, the job of mobilising the injured joint or muscle is made much easier. In the early stages the patient will be helped by the physiotherapist and shown exactly how to stretch the injured part. He will then be given exercises to perform at home to speed up recovery. Only when the part is fully mobile will the runner be encouraged to restrengthen this area. It cannot be stressed too highly that if muscles are strengthened before they are fully mobile, then that mobility will never be regained later. This can be demonstrated quite easily when one thinks of a body builder with his superbly muscular body. He may be extremely strong, but it is impossible to envisage his performing Olga Korbut-type exercises on the asymmetrical bars because he has *sacrificed mobility to strength*

Finally, and often underrated, is the task of putting the injured runner back into competition. This must

is usually better than a crêpe bandage because it supports the injury site with a uniform pressure and does not tighten or slacken as the patient moves about. It is also much easier and quicker to apply, especially with young people or to an area such as an arm, which would be impossible to bandage by the person himself. By putting pressure on an injury site, the bandage is supporting it and preventing further damage by tearing. An ice pack may be applied without removing the bandage, although in this case it would be advisable to allow an extra five minutes for the cold to penetrate.

'E' means elevation, or raising the injured part. Swelling occurs after an injury, which must be removed somehow, and it will be absorbed gradually into the blood vessels and lymph vessels. If the injury is in the leg and swelling is allowed to go unchecked, it will descend to the foot and make that swell also. If, however, the patient sits or lies with the injured leg raised, the effect of gravity will be to draw the blood away from the injury site and allow it to be carried away in the circulatory system. This be done by someone who understands the sport. Often one finds that advisers err on the side of caution, which may be an excellent idea for the average man but could lose an athlete a chance of a race. However, runners left to their own devices usually go straight back to running with too little preparation, and consequently re-injure themselves. The key to a successful return to both training and competition is graduated exercise and the advice of a knowledgeable person.

As many young or new runners have never needed physiotherapy, they will be unsure of exactly what to expect from a therapist, should they sustain an injury. The following explains the various modalities at the disposal of such a therapist

Superficial thermotherapy

This refers to the use of heat at a level near the surface of the skin — it does not penetrate to the deeper tissues. Application of heat to the site of an injury causes vasodilation (opening of blood vessels) in the area. This helps to relieve pain and reduce muscle spasm by inhibiting nerve activity to those muscles. The increase of blood flow and subsequent rise in temperature, speeds up the metabolism of the area and thus any waste products are carried away more quickly.

Superficial tissue is a poor thermal conductor, which means heat is not readily passed on, so that the effects do not extend to the underlying structures, and muscle and joint circulation show little increase. However, this form of treatment does bring about relief of pain and so has a place in the treatment of injuries. The principal methods of applying superficial heat are by the use of an infra-red lamp to the injured part, or by hot packs filled with a chemical. Relief may even be found from immersing the injury in a hot water bath.

Cryotherapy

This method treatment, although it appears to contradict heat therapy, actually works mainly on the neurological aspect, ie. on the nerve supply, and also on the circulatory system. Initially, applying cold to the injury causes superficial vasoconstriction, followed by deep vasodilation (McMaster W.C. 1978), which means constriction of a vein near the surface of the body, followed by dilation deeper in the tissues. Current research suggests that cold penetrates the deep tissues with greater effect than heat (Abrahams W. 1974). Cold can be applied to any injury site by the use of cold packs, immersion in cold water and also by massaging with an ice cube. In fact, it is usually easier to apply cold than heat. Benefits can also be derived from exercising after icy therapy, because the application of ice serves to deaden pain, relieve muscle spasm and aid relaxation.

Contrast baths

This is a very effective way of reducing swelling. The affected part is immersed alternately in hot (120°C) and then cold (60°C) water. Another method would be to use hot water bottles followed by ice packs. The repeated vasodilation followed by vasoconstriction encourages drainage, but should not be introduced until 36 hours after injury.

A typical treatment would consist of one minute's applicaton of heat followed by three minutes' application of cold. The process is repeated five times and is very useful since it can be carried out at home several times a day without supervision.

Massage

As mentioned earlier, massage was the original form of treatment used by physical therapists, but unfortunately it is rather neglected these days because it is too time-consuming. It is a vital form of treatment, however, for any physiotherapist concerned with treating sports injuries, for when an athlete is incapacitated and his injury restricts activity, massage is an excellent way to improve the blood circulation

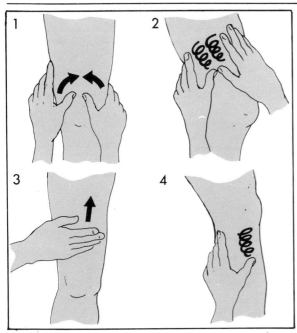

Some of the most common massage techniques are shown: petrissage, or kneading (1); friction (2 and 4), using regular circular movements, effleurage, or stroking (3). All these methods are useful in treating leg injuries, helping to break down adhesions and improve circulation.

endings are affected with a graze and only a very few with a cut. If, however, the object of the massage is to decrease oedema (ie. swelling), then the injured part would be raised to aid gravity, and a gentle but very firm stroke would be used down the limb, towards the heart. This is known as effleurage. The stroke must be firm to push the fluid along the blood and lymph vessels.

A completely different form of massage is to give deep frictions. This is employed in an area that is not very swollen but has thickening due to a muscle tear which has healed but left a swelling. If the area is large enough, circular movements are made with the fingers deep into the affected part. This can be quite painful at first but soon eases, and the patient usually finds great relief and increased mobility of the part. If the injury site is a tendon or ligament, then deep transverse frictions are used. This involves moving one or two fingers in short, deep excursions across the tendon, at right angles to it. This can also be rather painful at first, but the pain soon wears off and then the injured part feels numb. The object of using frictions is the same as with other forms of massage: to improve circulation and to break down adhesions which may have formed with surrounding tissues. However, it is a very specific form of treatment and used principally because the flow of blood through tendons and ligaments is less than that through the muscles and so requires greater stimulation. Overall, massage is one of the most important methods of treating running injuries and is an adjunct to all the other methods at the physiotherapist's disposal.

Faradism

A faradic machine is used to stimulate muscles electronically. It has been used on some sportsmen, mainly footballers, to try to maintain muscle bulk and strength whilst they are out of training. I prefer to use it, however, as another means, apart from massage, of reducing oedema. The method in this

and, through this, the nutrition to the muscles is maintained so that less atrophy, or wasting, results. This is obviously very important to a runner who may be out of action for quite a while.

Different methods of massage are used, depending on what results are required. A very gentle massage is an excellent way of relieving pain and is what most of us use when we hurt ourselves, without realising why we do it. There are nerve endings all over the surface of the skin, and if the skin is gently rubbed, the nerve endings are sedated and pain is relieved. This is why a graze on the knees is always more painful than a single cut, because far more nerve instance is to put two electrodes on top of pieces of wet lint and apply them to the injured area. If the damaged part is, say, a quadriceps muscle on the front of the thigh, one electrode would be placed just above the knee and the other about eight inches above that. The wet lint just makes the treatment feel more comfortable and thus a better contraction is obtained. The electrodes are held in place by a thick bandage which has a piece of waterproof material spread under it. This prevents water from the lint being absorbed by the bandage and hence some of the electrical current being lost and not travelling through the leg. The firm strapping is again to aid dispersal of fluid in the limb and the part is elevated to help further.

When the machine is switched on, a tingling sensation is felt at first, like pins and needles, and then a contraction of the muscle will occur, quite involuntarily on the part of the patient. It is a completely painless procedure and the current is increased until movement may occur at a nearby joint. The object is to simulate normal working of the muscles and bring about what is known as the 'muscle pump' action. Muscles surround blood vessels in the body, and during exertion, as the muscles contract and relax, they squeeze the blood vessels rhythmically, thus aiding circulation. This action is obviously greatly reduced while a runner is injured, and the faradic machine is a very useful aid to clearing excess fluid in the area. This method is called 'Faradism under pressure'. The patient should try to contract his muscles voluntarily whilst the machine is working to accustom him to using them strongly again.

If any injury is really severe or painful and the patient feels he cannot tense the muscles himself, then faradism is an excellent method of re-educating muscles. The machine is used as before to give a contraction involuntarily, and the patient is asked to try to contract the muscle himself. The machine is then slowly turned down in intensity, with the patient still working hard. Eventually, the machine is turned down to zero, while the patient is still able to bring about the contraction — this time completed unaided. This method gives the patient confidence in the early stages of his injury.

Ultrasound

This is probably the best known of the electrical treatments used by physiotherapists, apart from heat, and is widely used in the treatment of sporting injuries. Ultrasound, as its name suggests, consists of sound waves which are produced by a disc of quartz crystal in the head of the machine, which looks rather like a microphone. When an alternating current is applied to the crystal, it is deformed and changes shape by thickening and then contracting rhythmically. This has the effect of producing sound waves. The sound waves act on the walls of the blood vessels. Normally, blood and lymph vessels contain their fluid but when there is swelling in the tissues as a result of injury, the only way the fluid can be absorbed is through these vessels. The walls of blood and lymph vessels are selectively permeable, which means they are capable of allowing fluids to pass in or out, like a filter. The effect of the sound waves on the walls of the vessels is to alter their permeability so that they absorb the extra fluid more readily and swelling of the injured part is thereby reduced more rapidly than would otherwise be the case.

Ultrasound is also used in very stubborn cases and for harder swellings. The action of the sound waves on the tissues is that of very fine vibrations, which can help to break up thicker structures such as scar tissue and large areas like haematomas, or bruises. It may also be used for a few minutes at the end of a treatment as ultrasound has very good analgesic properties and will help to reduce pain.

Deep heat — short wave diathermy

This treatment is used after the initial stages of injury, when first aid has been dispensed with. It involves the application of high frequency (over 10 megacycles) oscillating electrical current through the deep tissues of the body, which results in a form of induction heating. The heating effect is very deep, occurring from the bone outwards. There is evidence that the temperature rise in the deep tissue can be as great as 9°F. Though physiologists have shown that the most effective way to increase joint and deep muscle temperature is by exercise, often when injury has been sustained, full range activity is not desirable. It is then that this form of treatment is most useful.

Short wave is applied by fixing two electrodes, covered in rubber, on either side of the injured part. When the machine is switched on, the alternating current flows backwards and forwards between the two plates, although not through the patient. The effect of this is to cause disturbance of electrons in the dielectric — which is the athlete's limb — in turn producing heat in the injury site. Heating the tissues causes an increase in blood flow and so the beneficial effects are once again produced — those of removing waste products from the site of the injury and returning it more quickly to its original state. The machine can also be used in a pulsed form which means that instead of continuous heat, the current is switched on and off at regular intervals of a few seconds. This is particularly useful with a recent injury as the heating effect is lower and therefore will not cause renewed bleeding, but will still have therapeutic advantages.

In addition to the heating effect of short wave diathermy, a strong electro-magnetic field produced. This is known as magnetic flux and works on the individual cells of the body. Each cell carries an electrical charge, which should be at neutral, but with an injury this charge may be upset and the effect of the short wave is to return the cells to equilibrium. So important is the magnetic field believed to be that some machines now on the market have no heating effect at all, just electro-magnetic waves, so that injuries can be treated immediately

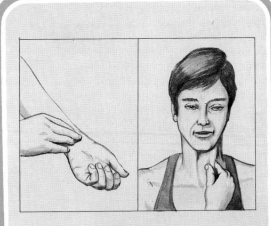

Running Tip

Taking your pulse
It is sometimes a good idea to take your pulse while you are out running to check the effect of exercise on your heart. Although people's resting rates vary considerably, it is common to have a resting pulse of between 60 and 80 beats per minute. This will increase, of course, when you run. Take it at the wrist or at the neck. To find out your maximum and minimum permissible pulse rates turn to page 18.

instead of having to wait until it is safe to give heat to the injury site.

Microwave diathermy

This treatment employs a much higher frequency electrical current than short wave diathermy — around 2,400 megacycles per second as compared with around 10 megacycles in short wave.

The effect is similar to that of short wave — generating an increase in temperature of those body tissues that are positioned within their electric fields. Whereas short wave treats a widely spread area, microwave diathermy can be directed to a much more specific area.

Microwave differs very little from short wave diathermy in the type of conditions that it treats. Both are very successful with joints, bursae, tendon sheaths and muscle injuries.

Interferential

This is a medium frequency electrical machine used largely in the treatment of acute injuries to produce an analgesic effect. Care must be taken, therefore, that after receiving such treatment the temptation is avoided to go back immediately to running, with its risk of worsening the condition.

Interferential can also be used, by the appropriate adjustment of the currents, for treating subacute lesions since it gives an increase in circulation. In addition it can be used to stimulate muscle which makes it suitable for certain kinds of chronic conditions.

The value of the deep heat producing machines over the superficial ones such as infra-red, is that they have more than one treatment head. Infra-red bombards a single area with heat, thus bringing more blood to an area which is already inflamed. The deeper modalities produce a heating effect which flows from one electrode to another. In this way, the circulation is increased, with all its beneficial effects, but blood is not drawn to one area. This is a very important point to remember with any injury — *never put heat on an area which is already inflamed* — that is, hot and painful.

Mobilisation

As soon as an injury is less painful and swollen, and usually whilst still undergoing treatment, the vital task of mobilising the injured part can begin. Most conditions respond better to active exercise

---

Tip: Winter running

Running in winter can be a risky business if you are not properly dressed and prepared for bitter winds, icy roads and frozen plough. Roads that are covered in snow and very slippery can be very dangerous indeed, especially in the twilight of late afternoon or early morning, and after dark. So try to fit your training in during daylight hours and choose running shoes with a good gripping sole. It will be hard when you start out of your warm house into the cold, but running produces eight to 10 times as much body heat as when you are at rest and you will soon warm up if you wear the right clothing.

The important thing is to avoid over-dressing or you will soon be sweating uncomfortably. Dress up warmly in a or tracksuit and a light-weight nylon windbreaker to keep out icy winds. Go for the lightest nylon which will least constrict movement but will effectively keep the cold out and the heat in. If it is really cold you can wear thermal underwear. Gloves or mittens will keep hands warm and a hood or woollen hat will prevent heat loss through your head and stop ears getting cold.

---

when the patient himself puts joints and muscles on the stretch. It should be possible for an athlete, given a specific injury, to work out for himself a way of stretching the injured part. For example, if he has torn the front of the thigh, then kneeling and sitting back on his heels, eventually leaning backwards, would stretch this muscle group. If the injury were to the calf or Achilles tendon then standing in a lunge position with the injured leg at the back, would put this muscle on the stretch. If you are in doubt, however, as to which stretching exercises are best for you, see Chapter 4 on stretching.

Traction

An increasing number of runners are training over high mileages on the roads and occasionally the repeated pounding is causing some impacting of the vertebrae in the lumbar region of the spine. This can result in a variety of symptoms including back pain, hip pain, knee pain, and sciatica, and often the only effective treatment is to reverse the impacting process by stretching the spine. This can best be achieved with a traction plinth onto which the patient is attached by harnesses, whereupon an electric motor applies a predetermined separating force — a modern equivalent of the rack!

Reconditioning

This is perhaps the most neglected area of treatment, many runners believing that as soon as they are symptom-free they are able to return immediately to full training or competition. Such action usually ensures a speedy return to the treatment plinth.

Even during the time that injury stops you running, it is important to find other ways of taking exercise — some of it prolonged such as swimming or cycling and some of it strengthening such as weights and/or circuits. There are very few injuries that make it impossible to find some alternative ways of taking exercise and the more work that can be done during this period, the fewer the problems and the shorter the time needed to recondition in preparation for full training or competition. The earliest stages of reconditioning are concerned with achieving a full, pain-free range of movement so that the joint or muscle is not going to 'react' if it is inadvertently taken to its extreme. For this purpose a progressive exercise programme needs to be drawn up.

Whenever muscles are rested they start to waste away and rapidly lose strength, so that even when all other injury symptoms have gone this legacy is left. It is ill-advised to attempt competition or exhaustive training until the strength has been built up to within 15 per cent of its original value. Since most people have no idea of the degree of original strength, a useful rule of thumb to remember is that when comparing with the uninjured side, the dominant

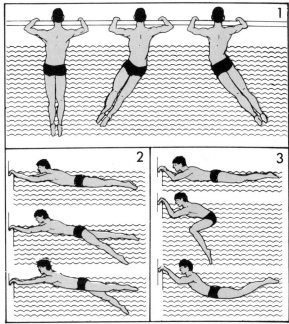

These water exercises help to strengthen muscles:
1 *Holding the rail and with toes pointed and legs straight, swing sideways from the waist, keeping torso rigid.*
2 *Holding ladder, float horizontally, kicking legs fast with knees straight five times, two minutes each.*
3 *Holding rail floating horizontally, bend knees upwards towards chest and then swing out legs behind you.*

side is usually 10 per cent stronger.

Hopefully, most runners will need very little time off from their running because of injuries, but if an injury does occur, then it is advisable to seek a good diagnosis and treatment as soon as possible. Often more time is lost than is necessary because a runner is fearful of doing too much too soon and exacerbating the condition, when controlled exercise is really what is needed. Of course, the reverse is also true and a runner may go back to his running too quickly and hinder his recovery. So, when in doubt, seek knowledgeable advice.

United Kingdom Club Directory

The addresses given below are correct, as far as we know at the time of going to press. Apart from the specialist women's only clubs, which are listed separately for England, many clubs have a women's section. If you have any queries you should notify the AAA.

England and Wales

Aberdare Valley AC,
C. Stanfield,
19 The Triangle,
Caegarw, Mountain Ash,
Mid Glamorgan

Abertillery AC,
N. Whitehouse,
1 Brynhyfryd Terrace,
Carn Road, Nantyglo,
Gwent

Aberystwyth AAC,
H.M. Roberts,
8 Brynglas Road
Llanbadarn Fawr,
Aberystwyth, Dyfed

Airedale & Spen Valley AC,
Miss Ann James,
3 Jesmond Avenue,
Bradford BD9 5DP

Aldershot Farnham District AC,
J. W. Lofts,
46 Perring Avenue,
Farnborough,
Hants GU14 9DB

Alton Joggers,
H.J.N. Bethell,
Hill House
Farringdon, Alton, Hants

Altrincham & District AC,
J.B. Saunders,
The Grange, Grange Road,
Bowdon, Altrincham,
Gtr Manchester

Amesbury AC,
P. Monk,
5 Edwards Road,
Amesbury, Wiltshire

Andover & District AC,
Mrs S. Perren,
Bryher, Evingar Road,
Whitchurch, Hants

Anglia Striders Club,
Mrs H. Sheppard,
No 3 Ainger Road,
Dover Court, Essex

Anglo Scottish AC,
G. Darroch,
117 Canterbury Grove,
London SE27 0NZ

Aquila AC,
H. Webb, Room 3F27, Proc Exec
MOD, Elect Qu Ass Direct,
Aquila, Golf Road, Bromley,
Kent BR1 2JB

Arena 80 AC,
Ms C. Wilson,
59 Telscombe Cliffs Way,
Telscombe Cliffs,
E. Sussex

Ashford AC (Kent),
D. Fox,
The Blades,
Maidstone Road,
Headcorn, Kent TN27 9RS

Ashington Joint Welfare AC,
T. Douglas,
4 Rosalind Street,
Ashington, Northumberland

Ashton Young Athletes Club,
Mrs M. Doyle,
25 Sunnyside Grove,
Ashton under Lyne,
Gtr Manchester

Assoc of Joggers & Runners,
Surrey Club, R.F.Smith,
14 Amberwood Rise,
New Malden, Surrey

Athletic Club of Tring,
Mrs A. James,
59 Buckingham Road,
Tring, Herts HP23 4HF

Avon AAA,
Mr H. Beswick,
19 Chestnut Grove,
Clevedon, Avon BS21 7LA

Banbury Harriers,
J. Rolland,
7 Wolseley Close,
Banbury, Oxon

Bankfield House AC,
J.B. Barker,
Bankfield House,
Banks Road,
Liverpool L19 8JZ

Barnet & District AC,
E. A. Kimber,
78 Dale Avenue,
Edgeware, Middx

Barnsley Road Runners Club,
D.H. Bennett,
40 Newhill Road,
Monk Bretton, Barsley S71 1HX

Barrow AC,
D.W.Rawlings,
18 Lord Robert Street,
Barrow in Furness, Cumbria

Barry Harriers AC,
Mrs G.M. Ellward,
6 Mendip View,
Cadoxton, Barry,
South Glamorgan

Barton Athletic Club,
M.B. Shacklady,
12 Adamson Road,
Eccles, Manchester M30 7AQ

Barton & District AC,
E.S.Bellamy,
17 Parkdale,
Barton upon Humber
DN18 5EQ

Basingstoke AC,
I.S. Byett,
21 Bardwell Close,
Basingstoke, Hants

Basildon AC,
G.J. Hawthorne,
30 Maplestead,
Basildon, Essex.

Bath & Percy AC,
Mr Blanchard,
78 Entry Hill,
Bath, Avon BA2 5NA

Beddau AC,
J. Turnbull,
16 St. Helens Court,
St. Martins Est, Caerphilly,
Mid Glamorgan

Bedford & County AC,
F.E. Wooding,
54 Carlisle Road,
Bedford MK40 4HU

Bedfordshire County AAA,
G. Woodham,
20 Spencer Road, Luton, Beds

Belgrave Harriers,
D.R. Crookes,
209 Lynmouth Avenue,
Morden, Surrey

Berkhamsted & District AC,
B. Devereux,
3 New Villas, Station Road,
Tring, Herts

Berkshire County AAA,
A. Ive,
179 Yorktown Road,
Sandhurst, Surrey

Berry Hill-Mansfield AC,
Mr J. Higginbottom,
5 Gordondale Road,
Mansfield, Notts

Berwick Harriers,
Ms Norma Campbell,
19 Ladywell Road
Tweedmouth, Berwick on Tweed

Bexhill AAC,
Mrs P. Shoesmith,
C/O Bexhill Sports Centre,
Little Common Road, Bexhill,
Sussex

Bexhill Youth Centre Harriers,
M. Gibby,
46 St. Leonard's Road,
Bexhill on Sea E. Sussex

Bexley Borough AC,
R. Sawyer, 34 Park Crescent
Erith, Kent

Biggleswade AC,
D. Ball,
16 Saffron Road,
Biggleswade, Beds

Bildeston Bounders,
Ms D. Bayliss,
6 Canterbury Gardens,
Hadleigh, Ipswich,
Suffolk

Billingham Synthonia AC,
I. Nurk,
17 Oaklea Close,
Northon, Cleveland

Bingley Harriers & AC,
G.W. Garrett,
15 Park Avenue,
Thackley, Bradford,
W. Yorks

Birchfield Harriers,
Mr M. Millincton,
19 Limetree Road,
Streetly, W. Midlands

Birmingham Prison AC,
Mr Ward,
Winson Green Prison,
Winson Green,
Birmingham

Bishop Thomas Grant AC,
M.J. Dunphy,
7 Everest Court,
South Norwood Hill,
London SE25 6D

Blackburn Harriers & AC,
Mrs. J. Hale,
31 Coleridge Drive,
Accrington BB5 2PU

Black Combe Runners Club,
S. Barnard, 35 Bankhead,
Millom LA18 4LZ

Blackheath Harriers,
W.F. Lake,
No 4, Sutherland Avenue,
Petts Wood, Orpington,
Kent BR5 1QZ

Blackpool & Fylde AC,
L. Rogerson,
34 Sharon Grove,
Blackpool, Lancs

Blaydon Harriers & AC,
P.J. Waters,
2 Lake Approach,
Axwell Park,
Blaydon-under-Tyne NW21 5PE

Body Program Runners Club,
P. Neall,
128 Maynard Road,
Walthamstow, London E17 9JF

Bognor Regis AC,
Mrs C. Bilham,
18 Cleveland Road,
Chichester, Sussex PO19 2HF

Bolehall Swifts Walking Club,
Mr A. Stokes,
96 Tamworth Road,
Amington, Tamworth, Staffs

Bolton Evening News AC,
D. Magilton,
33 Lower Drake Fold,
Westhoughton, Bolton

Bolton Postal Running Club,
P. Chapman,
6 Tavistock Road,
Bolton BL1 4SG

Border Harriers & AC,
P.A. Nash
87 Petterill Street,
Carlisle, Cumbria

Boreham Wood AC,
Miss P.A. Poole,
1 Chauney Avenue,
Potters Bar, Herts EN6 5LE

Borough of Enfield Harriers,
R. Stratton,
263 Larks Hall Road,
Chingford, London E4 9HY

Borough of Hounslow AC,
Mrs I. Woods,
512 Staines Road,
Bedfont,
Feltham, Middlesex

Boundary Harriers (I.O.M.),
R. Lambie,
22 Brisbane Street,
Douglas, I.O.M.

Bournemouth AC,
B.P. Joyce,
141 Southern Avenue,
Wimborne, Dorset BH22 OBJ

Bracknell AC,
J. Wright,
24 Vandyke, Great Hollands,
Bracknell, Berks RG12 4UP

Braintree & District AC,
D. Gilder,
31 Francis Way,
Silver End, Witham, Essex

Brecon AC,
Mr L. Davies,
Highmead, 10 Cradoc Road,
Brecon, Powys

Bridgend YMCA AC,
Mrs P. Williamson,
56 Longfellow Drive,
Bridgend, Mid Glamorgan

Bridgnorth AC,
Mr S. Williams,
2 Richmond Gardens,
Bridgnorth,
Shropshire

Brighton Concord AC,
A.J. Tilbury,
48 Fairway Crescent,
Portslade, Sussex BN4 2FL

Brighton Hash Harriers,
C.C. Hughes,
Carrs Cotts, Wellgreen Lane,
Kingston, Lewes,
East Sussex

Brighton & Hove AC,
K. Dale,
5 Birling Close,
Brighton BN2 4DH

Bristol AC,
Mr M. Douglas,
Pentire, Brinsea Road,
Congresbury, Bristol

British Marathon Runners Club,
Mr T. Lewins,
13 Albany Road,
Old Windsor, Berks

Brixham AC,
Mrs P. Reeves,
17 Wall Park Road,
Brixham, Devon

Bromsgrove & Redditch AC,
Mrs R. Brownlie,
21 The Spinney,
Wythall, Birmingham B47 6HB

Buckinghamshire County AAA,
P.J. Craft,
57 Lynton Road,
Chesham, Bucks HP5 2BT

Bude & Stratton AAC,
R. Gouch, 4 Elm Drive,
Bude, Cornwall EX23 8EZ

Bungay Black Dog Running Club,
Ms J. Green,
Waywards, Church Road,
Thurlton, Norfolk NR14 6RJ

Burnham Joggers,
R. Brown,
19 Green Lane,
Burnham, Bucks

Burnley AC,
Mrs E. Stephens,
14 Stonyhurst Avenue,
Burnley, Lancs

Burton AC,
Mrs J.M. Bowgen,
13 Rosliston Road,
Walton on Trent, Staffs DE12 8NC

Bury Athletic Club,
S. Jones,
102 Castelhill Road,
Bury, Gtr. Manchester

Bushfield Campus Joggers,
M.G. Cross,
68 Bringhurst,
Orion Goldhay
Peterborough PE2 ORT

Buxton & District AC,
C. Bent,
85 Corbar Road,
Buxton, Derbys

CAB Running Club,
L. Plumb,
11 Brodewater Road,
Borehamwood, Herts

Camberley & District AC,
Mrs. M. Paterson,
Meadow Close,
Camberley, Surrey

Cambridge & Coleridge AC,
R. Smith,
7 Marshall Road,
Cambridge, Cambs

Cambridge County AAA,
E. Mortlock,
50 Maids Causeway,
Cambridge, Cambs

Cambridge Harriers,
E.C. Nash,
12 Margaret Road,
Bexley, Kent

Cannock AC,
N.J. Bailey,
15 Chaseley Avenue,
Cannock, Staffs

Cantec Road Runners Club,
M. Shortland, PE Dept.,
Canterbury College of Technology,
New Dover Road, Canterbury

Canvey Island AC,
Ms. R. Holloway,
49 Lappmark Road,
Canvey Island, Essex SS8 7SZ

Cardiff AAC,
C. Webb,
18 Cleveland Drive, Risca, Gwent

Carlisle AC,
A. Heap,
80 Crossways, Harraby,Carlisle

Carmarthen Harriers Club,
D.S. Jones,
10 Manor Crescent,
Llanllwch, Carmarthen

Chalfont AC,
R. Ward,
70 Lovell Road,
Chalfont St. Peter, Bucks SL9 9NX

Charnwood AC,
Mr. Harper,
5 Eden Close, Gorse Covert,
Loughborough LE11 ORT

Chase AC,
M. O'Neill,
37 Hardinge Road, London NW10

Chelmsford AC,
R.J.H Woolgar,
4 Landisdale Dandury,
Chelmsford, Essex

Cheltenham & County Harriers,
Mr. S. Colvin,
18 Lichfield Drive,
Warden Hill, Cheltenham,Glos

Cheshire County AAA,
H. Goode,
24 Hall Lane, Stockport SK6 1PP

Cheshire Track and Field League,
A.G. Bunner,
3 Borrowdale Close,
Frodsham WA6 7LN

Chester & Ellesmere Port AC,
J.M. Gledhill,
7 Brook Lane, Chester

Chesterfield & District AC,
Mrs J. Weaver,
82 Brearley Avenue,
Chesterfield S43 2DY

Chester le Street & District Ac,
R. Tinkler,
27 Wardridge Road,
Chester Le Street,
Co. Durham DH2 3AF

Chiltern Striders,
J. Havard,
Heathlands, 7 Weedon Lane,
Amersham, Bucks

Chorley AC,
Mrs,B.J. Houghton,
3 Hampton Close,
Chorley, Lancs

City of Stoke on Trent AC,
Mrs Johnson,
Greywinds, 237 Crewe Road,
Sandbach, Cheshire

City of Plymouth AC,
Miss J. Trood,
28 Hermitage Road,
Mannamead, Plymouth PL3 4RU

Clayton Le Moors Harriers,
R. Lawson,
55 Highfield Avenue,
Burnley, Lancs

Cleddau AC,
T.B. Rees,
Bro Dawel, Tiers Cross,
Haverfordwest, Dyfed

Cleethorpes & District AC,
D.J. Roberts,
19 Taylors Avenue,
Cleethorps DN35 0LQ

Clevedon AC,
Mr N. Manners,
43 Beach Road,
West Portishead, Avon

Cleveland Schools AA,
R.A.Ward,
St Georges School,
Cowley Road, Middlesbrough

Colchester AC,
A.L.Thomas,
18 The Dale, Wivenhoe,
Colchester, Essex CO7 9NL

Collingwood AC,
Mrs. W.M. Knight,
32 Grosvenor Avenue,
Carshalton,Surrey

Colwyn Bay AC,
Mrs C. Bebbington,
12 Morlais,
Pensarn, Abergele,Clwyd

Congleton AAC,
T. Squires,
39 Blythe Avenue,
Congleton, Cheshire

Copeland Athletic Club,
C. Stainton,
36 Royal Drive,
Egremont, Cumbria CA22 2LG

Corby AC,
Mr J. Tomlinson,
20 Ashurst Crescent,
Corby, Northants

Cornwall County AAA,
Mrs C. Fisher,
Hillcrest,
Lanivet, Bodmin Cornwall

Coventry Godiva Harriers,
Mr. G. Paul,
707 Kenilworth Road,
Balsall Common, Coventry

Crawley AC,
R.J.W. Clarke,
179 Woodfield Road,
Northgate, Crawley,
West Sussex

Crewe and Nantwich AC,
T. Stone,
8 Moreton Close,
Sandbach, Cheshire

Crook & District Sports & AC,
Mrs E.F. Chesters,
Palmfield, Church Hill,
Crook, Co.Durham

Crowborough AC,
Mrs M. Rogers,
8 Eridge Gardens,
Crowborough, E. Sussex

Croydon AAA,
K. Burchell,
26 Norfolk Avenue,
Sanderstead, Surrey CR2 8BN

Croydon Harriers,
M. Fleet,
101 Blenheim Gardens,
Wallington, Surrey

Cumberland Fell Runners Association,
D. Hughes,
Hallsteads,
Gosforth, Cumbria

Cumbria County AAA,
J.R. Cameron,
Klondike,
Barngates, Ambleside,
Cumbria

Dartford Harriers,
R.H. Drew,
23 Claremont Crescent,
Crayford, Kent DA1 4RJ

Basil Heatley of Coventry Godiva Harriers won a silver medal in the Marathon at the 1964 Olympics. He is seen here winning the 1960 National cross-country event.

Daventry AC,
Mr A.W. Haycock,
19 Fisher Close, Kilsby,
Rugby, Warks CV23 8XH

Deeside AC,
A. Williams,
Rohais, Wepre Lane,
Northophall, Mold, Clwyd

Derbyshire County AAA,
C. Robinson,
27 Field Rise, Derby DE3 7DF

Derby & County AC,
G. Edwards,
3 Tressilian Close,
Darley Abbey, Derby

Derwentside AC,
A.B. Peveller,
2 Standish Street,
South Moor, Stanley, Co.Durham

Derwent/West Cumbria AC,
A.S. Miller,
32 St. Helens Street, Cockermouth

Devon County AAA,
Mrs J. Myers,
26 Trumlands Road,
St. Marychurch,
Torquay, Devon

Didcot & District AC,
M. Neave,
71 Green Close,
Didcot, Oxfordshire

Diss & District AC,
R.A. Wright,
Kenmore, 17 Roydon Close,
Diss, Norfolk

Docking Striders T/F Club,
R.F. Charnock,
September Cottage, Stanhoe Road,
Docking, Kings Lynn,Norfolk

Doncaster Plant Works AC,
E. Pogmore,
206 Westminster Crescent,
Doncaster, S. Yorks

Dorchester AC,
M. Gurd,
Stoneacre, 148A Westbay Road,
Bridport, Dorset

Dorking St. Pauls AC,
G.J. Manning,
17 Smithy Lane,
Lower Kingswood, Surrey

Dorothy Hyman Track Club,
Mrs K. Buckley,
363 New Road,Staincross,
Barnsley

Dorset County AAA,
E.H. Sutters,
Islay, 31 Avon Avenue,
Avon Castle, Ringwood,
Hants BH24 2BQ

Dorset Doddlers Jogging,
J. Shepard,
Little Plymton,
Sturminster Newton,Dorset

Dover Road Runners,
A. Greaves,
23 Valley Road,
River, Dover, Kent

Droitwich AC,
Mrs D. Slater,
17 Bainbrigge Avenue,
Droitwich, Worcs

Duchy of Cornwall AC,
M.A. Rawling,
Southernhay, 5 Pentalek Road,
Camborne, Cornwall TR14 7RQ

Dudley & District AC,
C. Gibbison,
18 Ethel Street,
Cramlington,
Northumberland NE23 7LU

Dudley & Stourbridge Harriersm
Mr J. Deaton,
8 Dovedale Road,
Kingswinford, Brierley Hill,
West Mids

Dunstable Titans Running Club,
N. Appleford,
31 Easthill Road, Houghton Regis,
Dunstable LU5 5EH

Durham City Harriers,
J. McMahon,
28 Burnigill, Meadowfield,
Co.Durham DH7 8SA

Dursley & District AC,
Mr R.K. Wild,
Charnwood, Coombe,
Wotton-under-Edge,
Glos GL12 7ND

Ealing & Southall AC,
C. Canton,
6 North Avenue,
Ealing, London W13 8AP

Eastbourne Rovers C & AC,
Miss J. Long,
6 Queens Road,
Eastbourne, Sussex

East Cheshire Harriers & AC,
E.J. Murphy,
6 Warley Grove,
Dukinfield, Cheshire

East Grinstead & District AC,
R.F. Mitchell,
Gorse Cottage, Vicarage Road,
Crawley Down, Sussex

East Hull Harriers & AC,
P. Dearing,
1 Collynson Close,
The Parkway, Willerby,
Hull HU10 6AS

East Kent AC,
Mrs J. Bourne,
Homelands,Pye Alley Lane,
Whitstable, Kent

East Lancs Cross Country Assoc,
C.E. Haslam,
10 Higher Dunscar, Egerton,Bolton

Eastern Counties AAA,
D. Goodwin,
8 Riverside Close, Bedford

Eastern Vets AC,
E.C. Butcher,
26 Rycroft Avenue,
Deeping St. James,
Peterborough PE6 8NT

Ellenborough AC,
M. Thompson,
12 Marsh Terrace,
Ellenborough, Maryport, Cumbria

Ellesmere Port AC,
J. Orford,
1 Dunkirk Drive, Whitby,
Ellesmere Port, South Wirral,
Cheshire

Elliott AC,
L. Murphy,
6 Exeter Walk, Rochester, Kent

Elmbridge Road Runners,
D. Gleed,
5 Walpole House, Approach Road,
West Molesey, Surrey KT8 0LP

Elswick Harriers,
I.S. Pillar,
28 Redewater Road,
Newcastle upon Tyne NE4 9UD

Epsom & Ewell Harriers,
Mrs R. Barwell,
33 Curtis Road,
West Ewell, Epsom, Surrey

Erme & Yealm Valley Harriers,
W. Shaw,
22 Crescent Gardens,
Ivybridge, Devon

Erycinus Club,
F.J.Russell, Athletic Section,
C.E. Heath & Co Ltd,
61 Victoria Avenue,
Southend, Essex

Eryri Harriers,
H. Davis,
Rhiwen Deiniolen, Gwynedd

Escafield Veterans AC,
J.A. McKenna,
32 Cotswold Drive,
Leeds LS25 2DD

Essex Beagles,
S.C. Robins,
2 Harrison Drive,
North Weald, Epping, Essex

Essex County AAA,
H. Williams,
84 Tyelands,
Billericay, Essex CM12 9PB

Eton Manor AC,
D. Kell,
129 Colworth Road,
Leytonstone, London E11

Exeter Harriers,
Mrs Miles,
Flat 5, Escot House,
Ottery St. Mary, Devon

Fareham AC,
A.J. Newell,
19 Clee Avenue, Fareham, Hants

Faversham Cycling & AC,
G.C. Ely,
19 Court Street,
Faversham, Kent ME13 7AT

Featherstone & District AC,
Mrs. D. Townend,
34 Castlegate Drive,
Pontefract, W.Yorks

Fen All Stars Jogging & AC,
A. Hurlin,
32 Cambridge Road, Ely, Cambs

Fleet & Crookham AC,
P. Beacham,
36 George Road,
Fleet, Hants

Fletibox AC,
P. Ray,
9 Norwick Close, Bolton BL3 4UL

Forbanks AC,
R. Wigley,
21 Newlyn Road, Welling, Kent

Forbanks S & S Club,
J. Kemp,
43 Beechcroft Avenue,
Barnehurst, Kent

Folkestone AC,
W.A. Figgins,
5 Palmarsh Crescent,
Hythe, Kent

Ford AC,
J. Rodwell,
HM Prison,
Ford, Arundel, West Sussex

Frodsham Harriers,
C.L. Proudfoot,
3 Trenance Close,
Sutton Park, Runcorn, Cheshire

Frome Running Club,
K.A. McLeod,
26 Nightingale Avenue,
Frome, Somerset

Furness Track & Field Club,
Mrs S. Hall,
10 Clifford Street,
Barrow in Furness, Cumbria

Gateshead Harriers & AC,
G.W. Sivell,
581 Westgate Road,
Newcastle upon Tyne NE4 9PR

Gilwern & District AC,
Miss P. Bevans,
5 Clarence Street,
Brynmawr, Gwent

Gloucester AC,
P. Hoddy,
43 Nine Elms Road,
Longlevens, Glos

Gloucester County AAA,
N. Thomas,
77 Estcourt Road,
Gloucester GL1 3LX

Golden Vale AC,
M.J. Barber,
66 Framfield Road,
Hanwell, London W7

Goole and District AC,
C. Glasby,
60 Jefferson Street,
Goole DN14 3SJ

Gosforth Harriers & AC,
D.F. Mullen,
12 Reynolds Avenue,
Newcastle upon Tyne NE12 0ET

Grantham & District Athletic Club,
R. Tristram,
19 Rushcliffe Road,
Grantham, Lincs

Gtr. Manchester Schools AA,
J. Harris,
4 Pasturefield Road,
Manchester M22

Great Yarmouth & District AC,
Mrs M. Olley,
Highland House, Beach Road,
Hemsby, Great Yarmouth, Norfolk

Green Man AC,
C. Lizieri AC, (Acting Hon. Sec.)
75 Railway Road,
Teddington, Middlesex TW11 8RZ

Grimsby Harriers & AC,
Mrs M. Leeming,
83 Highthorpe Crescent,
Cleethorpes,
South Humberside

Guildford & Godalming AC,
Mrs M.A. Nelson,
Orchardleigh, Beech Road,
Frimley Green, Camberley,
Surrey GU16

Gwent County Youth AAA,
C.J. Morgan, Leisure Officer,
C/O Director of Education,
County Hall, Cwmbran,
Gwent

Guernsey Island AAC,
Mrs J.M. Legg,
Rivendell, Bray Park Estate,
Bray Road, Vale,
Guernsey C.I.

Hailsham AC,
R.A. Hind,
1 Paul Close,
Lansdowne, Hailsham,
Sussex

Halesowen Athletic & Cycling Club,
Mr M. Cardew,
35 Brook Road,
Fairfield, Bromgrove B61 9GZ

Halifax Harriers & AC,
Mrs H. Windsor,
125 Huddersfield Road,
Halifax, W. Yorks

Hallamshire Harriers & AC,
G. Pickstone,
202 Rural Lane,
Sheffield S6

Haltemprice Road Runners Club,
D.R. MacDonald,
8 Cockpit Close,
Anlaby, Hull

Halton Athletic Club,
J. Smither,
2 Farndale,
Farnworth, Widness,
Cheshire

Hampshire County AAA,
J. Guilmant,
24 Whitworth Road,
Bitterne Park, Southampton SO24GF

Handforth AC,
A. Thomas,
15 Hallwood Road,
Handforth, Cheshire

Handy Cross Joggers (Running Sect),
1 Greenlands, Flackwell Heath,
High Wycombe, Bucks HP10 9PL

Harborne Harriers,
R. Care,
14 Kenilworth Road,
Oldbury, West Mids B68 0ND

Haringey AC,
Mrs D. Marney,
38 Grange Road,
Tottenham, London N17

Harlow AC,
D.C. Sharp,
214 Waterhouse Moor,
Harlow, Essex

Harrogate Academicals Running Club,
J.D. Gilliver,
3 Brooksfield Close,
Hampsthwaite, Harrogate, N. Yorks

Harrogate Athletic Club,
D. Welch,
14 Brewerton Street,
Knaresborough, N. Yorks

Hartlepool-Burn Road Harriers,
H. Rowland,
21 Salcombe Drive,
Hartlepool TS25 2PT

Haslemere Border AC,
B.J. Whitwell,
Misty Pines, The Glade,
Bucks Horn Oak, Farnham, Surrey

Hastings AC,
P. Emerson,
84 St. Helens Park Road,
Hastings, Sussex

Hatfield AC,
Admin Officer,
H.M. Borstal,
Thorne Road, Doncaster DN7 6EL

Havant AC,
R.J. Bradley,
14 Juniper Square,
Havant, Hants PO9 1JAG

Havering AC,
J.W. Naylor,
34 Newmarket Way,
Hornchurch Way,
Hornchurch, Essex RM12 6DS

Haywards Heath Harriers,
E.J. Honey,
7 Bruce Close,
Haywards Heath,
West Sussex RH16 4QE

Heaton Harriers,
C. Marshall,
4 Tynemouth Terrace,
North Shields NE30 4BH

Henley & District AC,
Mrs D. Seal,
2 Berkshire Road,
Henley-on-Thames,
Oxfordshire

Hercules Wimbledon AC,
R. Holt,
147 Leathwaite Road,
London SW11

Hereford & County AC,
H.L. Samuels,
The Barton,
Abbeydore, Hereford

Herefordshire County AAA,
H.L. Samuels,
The Barton,
Abbeydore, Hereford

Hermes AC (LTRASA),
P.J. Hunt,
British Telecom, Westel House,
32-38 Uxbridge Road, London W5

Herne Hill Harriers,
K. Kelly,
71 Penwortham Road,
Streatham, London SW16

Hertford & Ware AC,
Mrs S. Wright,
21 Barleycroft,
Waterford, Hertford,

Highgate Harriers,
M. Howard,
193 Jersey Road,
Osterley, Middx TW7 4QJ

Hillingdon AC,
R. Cressy,
45 Denham Lane,
Chalfont St. Peter, Bucks

Holbeach Athletic Club,
R.E.S. Clay,
82 Spalding Road,
Holbeach, Lincs PE12 7HH

Holmfirth Harriers & AC,
G. Hall,
18 Meltham Mills Road,
Huddersfield HD7 3AT

Horsham Blue Star Harriers,
J. Linfield,
23 Penfold Way,
Steyning, West Sussex BN4 3PG

Hornwich R.M.I. Harriers,
P. Schofield,
18 Stanley Grove,
Hornwich, Bolton

Houghton Harriers,
M.P.Page,
19 Balfour Street,
Houngton le Spring,
Tyne and Wear

City of Hull AC,
K.R. Bartlam,
103 Grove Park,
Beverley HU17 9JU

Hull Spartan AC,
E. Taylor,
455 Marfleet Lane, Hull

Humberside County AAA,
E.S. Bellamy,
17 Parkdale,
Barton upon Humber DN18 5EQ

Huntingdon AC,
Mrs S.M. Flint,
65 Layton Crescent, Brampton,
Huntingdon, Cambs PE18 8TT

Hyndburn AC,
Mrs V. Aldred,
219 Whalley Road,
Accrington, Lancs

Ilford AC,
M.I. Etchell,
178 Mortlake Road,
Ilford, Essex

Ipswich Harriers,
A.W.J. Milton,
Cherry Trees, Capel Road,
Bentley, Ipswich IP9 2BL

Invicta AC,
M. Knapp,
37 Norman Road,
Canterbury, Kent CT1 3LX

Jarrow & Hebburn AC,
C. Henzell,
277 Mowbray Road,
South Shields NE33 3NP

Jersey Spartan AC,
D. Wagstaffe,
Ballinturley Mont La Brune,
St. Brelade, Jersey, C.I.

Kettering Town Harriers,
E.W. Boyfield,
12 Wellington Road,
Raunds, Wellingborough,
Northants

Knowsley Athletic Club,
R. Trenholme,
18 Dover Road,
Maghull, Merseyside

Lakeland AAC,
J.R. Cameron,
Klondike, Barngates,
Ambleside, Cumbria

Lancaster & Morecambe AC,
C.W. Gemson,
20 Vale Road, Lancaster

Launceston AC,
Miss J. Kimberlee,
1 Western Road,
Launceston, Cornwall

Lauriston Runners Club
D. Beard,
17A Westleigh Avenue,
Putney, London SW15

Leamington C & AC,
Mrs V. Grant,
10 Normandy Close,
Hampton Magna, Warwick CV35 8UB

Leeds City Athletic Club,
J. Lunn,
654 Whitehall Road,
Leeds LS12 5KL

Leicester Coritanian AC,
E. Toft, 14 Croft Road,
Cosby, Leics

Steve Cram of Jarrow and Hebburn AC won gold medals in the 1500m events at the 1982 European and Commonwealth Games held in Athens and Brisbane respectively.

Leicestershire County AAA,
C. Angove MBE,
63 Buckminster Road,
Leicester

Leicester Walking Club,
J Shields,
73 Pembroke Avenue,
Syston, Leicester

Leigh Harriers & AC,
C.F. Madely,
3 North Brown Street,
Leigh, Gt. Manchester

Leighton Buzzard AC,
R.J. Arnold, 34 East Street,
Leighton Buzzard,
Beds. LU6 8HU

Les Croupiers AC,
Jeff Ward,
37 Africa Gardens,
Gabalfa, Cardiff

Lincoln City & Colleges Athletic Club,
Mrs F.A. Benson,
77 Hunt Lea Avenue, Lincoln

Lincolnshire Athletics,
Mrs J. Barnsdale,
15 Westfield Avenue,
Lincoln LN2 4RD

Lincoln Wellington Athletic Club,
Mrs J. King, 31 Larkin Avenue,
Cherry Willingham, Lincoln

Liverpool Boundary Harriers,
W. D. Dalton,
12 Grimshaw Green,
Parbold, Wigan,
Gtr. Manchester

Liverpool Harriers and AC,
T.J. O'Mahoney,
12 Kirkmore Road,
Liverpool L18 4QN

Liverpool Pembroke AC,
J. Lowry, 4 Poplar Drive,
Liverpool L32 0RU

Llanelli AC,
R.P. Oram,
36 Heol Innes, Felinfoel, Llanelli

Loddon AC,
R.A. Cunningham,
62 High Bungay Road,
Loddon, Norwich NR14 6RN

London AC,
T. Catchpole,
56 Gilpin Avenue, London SW14

London Irish AC,
J. Dorgan,
16 Haydon Road,
Oxhey, Watford, Herts

London RoadRunners Club,
Mrs P. Jackson,
15 St. Ursula Grove,
Pinner, Middlesex HA5 1LN

Longwood Harriers and AC,
J. G. Beckett,
32 Ingfield Avenue,
Huddersfield HD5 9HF

Loughton AC,
L.R. Smith,
11 Southview Road,
Loughton, Essex

Lowestoft AC,
F.T. Farmer,
12 Loxley Road,
Lowestoft NR33 9PG

Lozells Harriers,
L.J. Rooney,
521 Hob Moor Road,
Birmingham B25 8TH

Luton United AC,
T.S. Watson,
19 Wickmere Close,
Warden Hill, Luton, Beds

Macclesfield Harriers and AC,
G. Corr,
18 Kennedy Avenue,
Macclesfield, Cheshire

Maidenhead AC,
P. Krause,
3 Arundel Close,
Maidenhead, Berks

Manchester Harriers and AC,
W.G. Smith,
21 Almond Tree Road,
Cheadle Hulme SK8 6HW

Manchester YMCA Harriers Club,
Athletics Sec,
YMCA Peter Street,
Manchester M2

Mandale AC,
M.J. Starford,
2 Farley Drive,
Acklam, Middlesborough

Manx AAC,
R. Birchall, 31 Ballaughton,
Manor Hill, Braddon, I.O.M

March AC,
H.C. Bryant,
18 Laburnum Grove,
March, Cambs

Matlock Athletic Club,
C.D. Rosling,
23 Yokecliffe Drive,
Wicksworth, Derbyshire

Maylands AC,
M.L Ruffy,
181A West Avenue, Maylandsea,
Chelmsford, Essex

Medina Valley AC,
A.C. Stone,
47 College Road,
Newport, Isle of Wight,

Medway AC,
A. Howell,
13 Brambletree Crescent,
Borstal, Rochester,Kent

Melbourn AC,
G. Will,
56 The Moor,
Melbourn, Royston, Herts

Melksham Road Runners Club,
K. Jackson,
9 Meadow Road,
Melksham, Wilts

Mersey Harriers and AC,
D. J Hoare,
7 Clapham Road,
Liverpool L4 2TG

Metropolitan Walking Club,
A.W. Gutteridge,
23 Repton Way, Croxley Green,
Rickmansworth, Herts WD3 3PN

Mid-Cheshire AC,
G.R.Harvey,
87 Chester Road,
Castle, Northwich, Cheshire

Middlesbrough & Cleveland Harriers,
E. Murtagh,
140 Corporation Road,
Redcar, Cleveland

Middlesex County AAA,
E. Whitehead, Pen-Gwyn,
Kings College Road,
Ruislip, Middlesex

**Midland Counties Cross
Country Association,**
E.J. Skidmore, Trelawney,
The Green, Wordsley,
W. Mids DY8 5BN

Midland Veterans,
D. McWhirter,
24 Fugelmee Close,
Harborne, Birmingham B17 8SE

Middleton Fitness & Athletic Club,
T.R. Colson,5 Hollins Drive,
Middleton, Manchester

Milton Keynes AC,
B.R.Graves,
156 Shenley Road, Bletchley,
Milton Keynes, MK3 7AN

Mitcham AC,
J. Van Frederici,
129 Dorset Road,
Merton Park, London SW19

Mold Runners,
C. Johnson,
Derron, Penyfron Road,
Pentymwyn, Mold, Clwyd

Monmouth AC,
Peter Hopkins,
Beech Road, Monmouth, Gwent

Morpeth Harriers & AC,
M.J. Bateman,
12 Hareside, Cramlington,
Northumberland, NE23 6BH

Mynyddwyr de Cymru Fell Running,
L.R. Williams,
5 Rhyddlan Court,
Hendredenny, Caerphilly

Muswell Hill Runners,
H. Taylor,
32 Coldfall Avenue, London N10

Neath Harriers,
A. Currie,
7 Fothergill Road,
Cymgwrach, Neath

Nene Valley Harriers,
R. Church,14 Benland,
Bretton, Peterborough

Newbury AC,
D.W. Jagoe,
20 Cheviot Close,
Wash Common, Newbury, Berks

New Forest Runners Club,
Mrs M.J. Ford,
9 Buldowne Walk, Sway,
Lymington, Hants SO4 0DU

Newham AC,
Mrs K. Mawson,
8 Gosford Gardens,
Redbridge, Ilford, Essex

Newport Harriers,
I.T. Adams,
Shilton, 5 Camelot Court,
Caerleon, Newport, Gwent

Newton Abbot AC,
R.G. Evans,
C/O 1 Town Hall Place,
Bovey Tracey, Devon TQ13 9EQ

Newtown AC,
J. Bennett, Godre'r Coed,
Bryn Gardens, Newtown,
Powys

Newquay AC,
Mrs S. Harris-Jenkin,
Riverside, Treggunnel Hill,
Newquay, Cornwall

Norfolk Olympiads,
Miss C. Easter,
13 Howell Road,
Drayton, Norwich, Norfolk

Normanby Park AC,
W. Hind,
38 Cliff Closes Road,
Scunthorpe, South Humberside

Northampton County AAA,
R. Fenn,
21 St. Augustine Way,
Daventry, Northants

Northampton Pheonix AC,
R. Johnson,
67 Woodland Avenue,
Overstone, Northampton

N. Devon Track & Field Club,
Miss S.M. Gould,
151 New Street,
Torrington, North Devon EX38 8BU

Northern Veterans AC,
C.E. Haslam,
10 Higher Dunscar,
Egerton,Bolton

North London AC,
P.F. Vaughan,
58 Friern Mount Drive,
Whetstone, London N20 9DL

North Park Avenue AC,
W. Hesketh,
26 Carnforth Road,
Stockport

North Staffs Road Runners,
G. Kay, 5 Beech Road,
Eccleshall, Staffs ST21 6EA

**N/Yorks & S/Durham Harriers
League,**
R.F. Gamble,
10 Chelsea Gardens,
Norton, Stockton, TS20 1RZ

Norwich & Norfolk AC,
A.C. Huggins,
24 Fir Tree Road,
Thorpe, Norwich, Norfolk

Nottinghamshire AAA,
Mr. E. Onions,
12 Haddon Road, Retford,Notts

Notts AC,
F. Lowes,
61 Selby Road,
West Bridgford, Notts

Nuneaton Harriers,
E.J.Ewington,
16 Hemsworth Drive,
Bulkington, Nuneaton,Warks

Oldham & Royton Harriers & AC,
F. Hodson,
34 Alva Road,
Oldham, Gt. Manchester

Old Gaytonians AC,
Mrs B.E. Bush,
11 Woodland Drive, Watford, Herts

Omega Running Club,
C.R. Beauvais,
15 Clarence Drive,
Englefield Green, Surrey

Orion Harriers (Cr. Country only),
H.B. Lee,
7 Warren Hill,
Loughton, Essex

Oswestry Olympians,
Mrs Greenwood,
1 Moorside Cottage,
Woolston, Oswestry,
Shropshire

Overton Harriers & AC,
M.G. Gregory,2 Lambs Close,
Station Road, Overton,
Basingstoke, Hants RG25 3DX

Oxford City AC,
Mrs W. Pullen,
5 Beech Road,
Headington,Oxford OX3 7RT

Oxfordshire County AAA,
D. Talbot,
11 Edmunds Court,
Didcot, Oxon

Par AC,
Mrs C.C. Fisher,
Hillcrest, Lanivet,
Bodmin, Cornwall

Paxmans AC,
Hon. Secretary, Paxmans AC,
Edward Paxman Memorial Club,
Hythe Hill, Colchester,
Essex

Pendle Athletic Club,
Patricia A. Morris,
10 Higham Road,
Padiham, Lancs

Peterborough AC,
Mrs P. Reeson,
20 Sherborne Road,
Peterborough, Cambs

Peterlee & District AC,
P. Welsh,
24 Arthur Street,
Ersington Colliery, Co. Durham

Petersfield AC,
R. Noble, Pyramids,
South Harting West Sussex

Phoenix AC,
M. Paterson (Membership Sec),
21 Harrington Villas,
Brighton, Sussex

Pilkingtons Harriers & AC,
K. Glover,
58 Daresbury Road, Eccleston,
St. Helens, Merseyside

Players AC,
Mr Muxlow,
18 Homefield Road,
Aspley Lane, Nottingham

Plessey Harriers,
R.M. Montrose,
21 Bishop Drive,
Whiston, Merseyside L35 3SY

Polytechnic Harriers,
D. Barrington,
1 Fairburn Court,
St Johns Ave. London SW15

Pontypridd Roadents Running Club,
C. Gownes, 35 King Street,
Treforest, Pontypridd,
Mid Glam

Poole AC,
Mrs Higson,
92 Foxholes Road,
Parkstone, Poole, Dorset

Poole Runners,
G. Brown,
25 Egdon Drive; Merley,
Wimborne, Dorset BH21 1TY

Portsmouth AC,
A. Gibb,
8 Madgalan Court,
355 London Road,
Portsmouth PO2 9HH

Portsmouth Joggers,
G.R. Moffat,
24 Durham Gardens,
Waterlooville,Hants

Port Talbot Harriers AC,
D. Tayler,
184 Western Avenue,
Sandfields,Port Talbot

Preston Athletic Club,
B. Duckworth,
39 Regent Drive,
Preston PR2 3JB

Preston Harriers & AC,
D. Baisbrown,
22 Great Avenham Street,
Preston, Lancs

Pudsey & Bramley AC,
R.G. Loker,
Flat 2, 2 Tofts Road,
Pudsey LS28 7SQ

Purbeck AC,
P. Gibbs,
4 Moretone Lane,
Wareham, Dorset BH20 4HN

Queens Park Harriers,
P. Hunt,
9 Hill Road,
Harrow, Middlesex HA1 2PN

Ranelagh Harriers (Cr.country only),
Ian Milne,
26 Caen Wood Road,
Ashtead, Surrey

Reading AC,
B. Hinton, 32 Hill Street,
Reading, Berks

Redhill & Reigate AC,
Mrs M. Hunt,
2 Southall, Furze Hill,
Kingswood, Tadworth, Surrey

Reigate Priory, (sovereign) AC
Mrs J. Abell,
3 Carlton Green,
Redhill, Surrey RH1 2DB

Rhondda AC,
Mrs. C Davies,
241 Rhys Street,
Trealaw, Tonypandy,
Mid Glam

Rhymney Valley AC,
L. Jenkins, Dawn Cottage,
Aeron Place, Bargoed,
Mid Glam

Ribble Valley Harriers,
P.A. Wrathall,
16 Langshaw Drive,
Clitheroe, Lancs, BB7 1EY

Riccall & Selby Athletic Club,
Mrs K. D. McGuire,
31 Armoury Road, Selby, N. Yorks

Richard Lees AC,
M.W. Topliss,
3 Breydon Close,
Shelton Lock, Derby

Road Runners Club,
B. Baldwin,
9 Campbell Terrace,
Mountain Ash,Mid Glam

Road Runners Club,
D. Turner, 40 Rosedale Road,
Stoneleigh, Surrey

Rochdale Harriers & AC,
D.M Tomlinson,
18 Norwich Avenue,
Rochdale OL11 5JZ

Ron Hill Sports AC,
M. Deegan,
2 Tower Street,
Hyde, Gt. Manchester

Rossendale Harriers & AC,
I. Partington,
16 Woodcroft Avenue,
Rawtenstall,
Rossendale, Lancs

Rotherham Harriers & AC,
R.G. Rawbotham,
68 Wickersley Road,
Rotherham, S.Yorks

Royal Sutton Coldfield AC,
Mrs Butler, 41 Marlpit Lane,
Four Oaks,
Sutton Coldfield, B75 5PH

Royal Sutton Coldfield Race Walking Club/Birmingham W CL,
D. James, 112 Jordan Road,
Four Oaks, Sutton Coldfield,
West Mids

Rowheath Harriers,
Mrs C. Baker,
40 Marbury Close,
Kings Norton, Birmingham B38

Rowntrees Athletic Club,
G. Gregory,
54 Sixth Avenue,
Heworth, York YO3 0US

Ruddington & District AC,
Mrs Booth,
43 Clifton Road,
Ruddington, Notts

Rugby & District AC,
Mrs J. Alabaster,
4 David Road, Rugby, Warks

Runneymede Runners,
Mrs C. Brown,
51 Lynwood Avenue,
Egham, Surrey TW20 9RE

Rushmore & Hart AC,
R. Hamilton,
5 Larkspur Close,
Aldershot, Hants

Rutland AC,
J Tyley,
10 New Street, Oakham, Leics

Ryde Harriers,
The Secretary, Club HQ,
31 High Street, Oakfield,
Ryde, Isle of Wight PO33 1FJ

Saddleworth Runners Club,
I. Brierley,
Grove Farm Harrop Court,
Diggle, Oldham,
Gt. Manchester

Saffrons AC,
T. Wright, 26 Elm Grove,
Hampden Park, Eastbourne,
East Sussex

St Edmund Pacers Club,
T.J. Tasker,
29 Pemberton Walk,
Bury St Edmunds, Suffolk

St Helens Athletic Club,
E. Forshaw,
93 Knowles House Avenue,
Eccleston, St. Helens,
Merseyside

Sale Harriers,
H. Wilson,
3 Marley Drive,
Sale, Gt. Manchester

Salford Diocesan AA,
J. Thorpe,
11 Farley Close,
Radcliffe, Gt. Manchester

Salford Harriers & AC,
G. Doggett,
9 Athlone Avenue,
Moston, Manchester

Salford Metropolitan AC,
H.S. Brown,
8 Beechfield Road,
Swinton M27 1RE

Salisbury & District AC,
Mrs J. Parr,
42 Downview Road, Laverstock,
Salisbury, Wilts

Saltwell Harriers,
M. Armitage,
1 Thirlemere,
Birtley, Co. Durham DH3 2JY

San Domenico RR Club,
J. Kerry,
36 Plantagenet Street,
Riverside, Cardiff

Sandwell Valley Running Club,
3 Newmn Road,
Ocker Hill,
Tipton, DY4 DEN

Sarnia Walking Club,
R. Wright,
Friquet Villa, Hache Road,
Vale, Guernsey, Ch Islands

Scarborough Harriers, & AC,
R. Tribick
92 Hackness Road,
Newbury, Scarborough YO12 3SG

Scunthorpe Harriers & AC,
J. Fielding,
44 Canterbury Close,
Scunthorpe, South Humberside

Seaton Athletic Club,
N.D Lloyd,
32 Seaton Park, Seaton,
Workington, Cumbria

Sefton Harriers,
S. O'Keefe,
60 Elgar Road,
Liverpool L14

Serpentine Running Club,
Secretary, 38 Elmsdale Road,
Walthamstow, London E17 6PW

Sevenoaks AC,
N.C.P.Smith,
35 Lambarde Drive,
Sevenoaks,, Kent

Shaftesbury Harriers,
D. Bradley,
Flat 8, The Conifers,
Devonshire Road, Hatchend,
Middlesex

Dave Bedford of Shaftesbury, ex-10,000m world record holder, is unique in having won the Junior and Senior cross-country Southern Counties championships at Parliament Hill Fields, London, in the same afternoon in 1970.

Sheffield Athletic Club,
J. Sherwood,
59 Milden Road, Sheffield S6

Sheffield United Walking Club,
F. Clay, 50 Harris Road,
Sheffield, S6 1WA

Shirebrook Athletic Club,
T. Morley,
58 Park Road,
Shirebrook, Mansfield, Notts

Shrewsbury AC,
G. Minshall,
96 Coton Mount,
Shrewsbury SY1 2NH

Shropshire AAA,
Mrs J. Tudor,
The Plattins, Mytton Road,
Montford Bridge,
Shrewsbury SY4 1EU

Silson Joggers,
Dr. F. Newton,
Grafton Leys, Cattle End,
Silverstone, Towcester,
Northants

Sittingbourne & District AC,
W.H. Salmon,
The Tweeds, Highstead Valley,
Sittingbourne, Kent

Skipton & District AC,
S. Mallinson,
11 Victoria Street,
Sutton in Craven,
Keighley BD20 7HY

Skyrack Athletic Club,
M. Hardisty,
44 Skipton Road,
Ilkley, LS29 7EP

Slough & District Young Harriers,
C.G. White,
66 Lancaster Avenue,
Slough, Berks

Solent AC (Isle of Wight)
A.R. Mellor,
Lamb Cottage, Newtown,
Newport, Isle of Wight PO30 4PA

Solihull/Small Heath AC,
C. Simpson,
87 Willow Road,
Solihull, West Mids

Solway Athletic Club,
Mrs C. Taylor,
1 Brayton Street,
Workington CA14

Somer AC,
R.W. James,
12 Hillside Avenue,
Midsomer Norton, Bath, RA3 5LZ

Somer AC,
Mr James,
10 Hillside Avenue,
Midsomer Norton,
Bath, Avon

Somerset County AAA,
D.M.M. Shorrocks,
White House,
222 Staplegrove Road,
Taunton, Somerset

Somersham AC,
H.M. Wignall,
23 The Paddock,
Somersham, Huntingdon, Cambs

Southampton & Eastleigh AC,
N. Tabor,
43 St. Margarets Road,
Bishopstoke, Eastleigh, Hants

Southend-on-Sea AC,
Mrs. J. Dods,
93 Victoria Avenue,
Southend on Sea, Essex SS2 6EL

Southern AC (I.O.M.),
J. Comaish,
28 Crossag Close, Ballasalla, I.O.M.

Southern Counties Veterans AAA,
J. Heywood,
14 Darling Road,
London SE4 1YQ

South Liverpool AC,
D. Crumpton,
66 Lumley Street, Liverpool L19 1QP

South London Harriers,
M.J. Giddey,
20 Drake Road,
Chessington, Surrey KT9 1LW

Southport Waterloo AC,
R.J. Bishop,
24 Knowle Avenue,
Ainsdale, Southport PR8 2PB

South Shields Harriers & AC,
B. Kirkley,
2 Lanchester Street,
South Shields NE34 0AZ

South Western Counties AAA,
E.H. Sutters,
Islay, 31 Avon Avenue,
Avon Castle, Ringwood,
Hants BH24 2BQ

Sparkhill Harriers,
A. Hill,
Sparkhill Harriers HQ,
188 Stratford Road, Shirley,
West Mids

Spenborough & District AC,
B. Henderson,
22 New Street,
Cleckheaton BD19 5LL

Springfields Athletic Club,
P.E. Vickery,
21 Westby Road,
St Annes on Sea, Lancs

Sri Chinmoy Ac,
Sec T. Smith,
17 Cardigan Road,
London SW13

Stadium AC,
B. White,
H.M. Borstal,
Portland, Dorset

Stafford AC,
D. Cowley,
6 Riverway, Stafford

Staffordshire AAA,
M. Kelsall,
188 City Road, Tenton,
Stoke on Trent, Staffs

Staffordshire Moorlands AC,
T. Evans, Bryn Teg,
14 Ladydale Close,
Leek, Staffs ST13 5SE

Stamford & Dist Athletic Club,
J.T. Hardy,
5 Aberdeen Close,
Stamford, Lincs PE9 2TN

Stansfield AC,
P. Ould,
131 Pinto Way, Ferrier Estate,
Kidbrooke, London SE3

Star Road Runners,
L. Scanlon,
C/O Royal Star Garter Home,
Richmond Hill, Richmond,
Surrey

Stevenage & N. Herts AC,
S. Endean,
114 Marymead Drive,
Stevenage, Herts

Steyning AC,
D.J. Stevens,
26 Breach Close,
Steyning, Sussex BN4 3RZ

Stockport Harriers & AC,
G. Tivey,
38 Bean Leach Drive,
Offerton, Stockport

Stone Masters Marathons,
A. Murray,
25 The Avenue,
Stone, Staffs ST15 8DG

Stourport AC,
A Moreton,
59 Windermere Way,
Stourport-on-Severn, Worcs

Stratford on Avon AC,
C. Morris,
49 Kendal Avenue,
Stratford on Avon CV37 6SG

Stretford AC,
W. Murphy,
30 Gaydon Road,
Sale, Gt. Manchester

Stroud & District AC,
Mrs J. Taylor,
1 Hope Villas,
Up Springfield Road,
Uplands, Stroud, Glos

Sudbury Park Athletic Club,
B. Jackson, P.E. Dept,
H.M. Prison,
Sudbury, Derby

Suffolk Country AAA,
J. Mower,
188 Hadleigh Road,
Ipswich, Suffolk

Sunderland Harriers & AC,
K. Carr,
46 Ainthorpe Close,
Burdon Park, Tunstall,
Sunderland

Surrey AC,
K. Raymond,
35 King Charles Road,
Surbiton, Surrey

Surrey Beagles Ac,
A. Alden,
4 Barnfield Close,
Old Coulsden, Surrey

Surrey Walking Club,
P.W. Selby,
10 Millwood Close,
Maresfield, East Sussex

Sussex County AAA,
W.P. Robertson,
111 Orchard Road,
Burgess Hill, Sussex

Sutton & Cheam Harriers,
Mrs K. Avila,
76 Marlow Drive,
North Cheam, Surrey

Sutton Harriers,
W.R. McCall,
99 Pole Lane Court,
Pole Lane, Bury BL9 8QD

Sutton in Ashfield Harriers,
J. Ball,
44 Rannoch Drive,
Mansfield, Notts NG19 6QX

Swansea Harriers AC,
T.I Griffiths,
46 Lon Masarn,
Ty Coch, Swansea

Swindon AC,
G. Danswan,
13 Croft Road,
Swindon, Wilts SN1 4DG

Tadworth AC,
D.R.M. Sexton,
59A Kingswood Road,
Tadworth, Surrey

Tamworth AC,
Mrs S. Hodgkinson,
48 Claremont Road,
Tamworth, Staffs

Taunton & West Somerset AC,
Mrs G.B. Hall,
48 South Road,
Taunton, Somerset

Telford AC,
P. Sanderson,
41 Bridle Terrace,
Madeley, Telford, Shropshire

Tendring AC,
B. Williamson,
The Pavilion, Sea Lane,
Dulwich Road,
Clacton-on-Sea, Essex

Thames Hare & Hounds (CR. C & RD only),
F.J.W. Carpenter,
50 Flanders Mansions,
Flanders Road, London W4 1NF

Thames Valley Harriers,
P. Vivian,
4 Catherines Close,
West Drayton, Middlesex

Thetford AC,
A. Clarke, 16 Brecklands,
Mundford, Thetford, Norfolk

Thirsk & Sowerby Harriers,
Mrs M.A. Collier,
5A Saxty Way,
Sowerby, Thirsk, N. Yorks

Thurrock Harriers,
Mrs Harrison,
16 Mayfields,
Grays, Essex

Tipton Harriers,
T. Talbot,
100 Aston Street,
Toll End, Tipton, Staffs

Tiverton Harriers & AC,
A. Chave,
7 Stafford Place,
Tiverton, Devon

Todmorden Harriers & AC,
H. Clayton,
2 The Mount,
Todmorden, Lancs

Tonbridge AC,
D. Walsh,
2 Hopgarden Road,
Tonbridge, Kent TN10 4QS

Torbay AAC,
Mrs D. Massey,
18 Redburn Road,
Paignton, Torquay, Devon

Torfaen AC,
D. Huntbach,
1 Llyswen Walk,
Llanyrafon, Cwmbran, Gwent

Tower Hamlets AC,
H.H. Payne,
82 Old Church Road,
Tower Hamlets, London E1

Trigg Harriers,
A. Harvey, Cottage Retreat,
Gonvena Hill, Wadebridge, Cornwall

Trowbridge & District AC,
V. Cox,
4 Pikesfield,
Coulston, Westbury, Wilts

**Twenty Six Point Two Road
Runners Club,**
M.G. Lill,
99 Wickham Avenue,
Cheam, Surrey

Twickenham AC,
Mrs J. Neal,
4 Blandford Avenue,
Whitton, Twickenham, Middx

Tynedale Harriers & AC,
D.D. Smith,
6 Tyneview Terrace,
Fellside, Hexham NE46 1RG

Vale of Aylesbury AC,
J. Binks,
11 Wooton Path,
Stoke Mandeville, Bucks HP22 5YH

Vale of Glamorgan RRC,
K. Brown,
Clwyd Y Geiliog, Broadway,
Cowbridge, South Glamorgan

Verlea AC,
G.S. Brown,
3 Marley Road,
Welwyn Garden City, Herts

Veterans AC,
A. Shepherd,
38 Bromley Road,
Beckenham, Kent BR3 2JD

Victoria Park Harriers,
T. Gill, 6 Sandilands House,
Balcorne Street, London E9

Waingel's Copse Marathon Club,
C.T. Boulter,
16 Orchard Avenue,
Sonning Common, Reading,
Berks RG4 9LT

Wakefield Harriers & AC,
D.A. Atkinson,
37 Newton Close,
Wakefield, W. Yorks

Wallasey Athletic Club,
D. Hanna,
9 St. Elmo Road,
Wallasey, Merseyside

Wallsend Harriers & AC,
D.D. Bramley,
18 St. Aidens Road,
Wallsend NE28 8QG

Walthamstow AC,
B.W.Hart,
134 Forest Glade, London E4 9RS

Walton AC,
D. Gleed,
5 Warpole House, Approach Road,
West Molesey, Surrey

Warley AC,
B.C. Thorpe,
10 Battenhall Road,
Harborne, Birmingham B32

Warrington Athletic Club,
G.T. Edwards,
10 Honister Avenue,
Warrington, Cheshire

Warwickshire County AAA,
P. Milton,
49 Rodborough Road,
Dorridge, Solihull, West Mids

Watford Harriers,
J. Harris,
30 Springfield Close,
Croxley Green,
Rickmansworth, Herts

Waverley Harriers,
E. Holley,
Halfway, Hawkesford Lane,
Fernhurst, Haslemere, Surrey

Wellingborough AC,
Mrs J. Tropman,
7 Brooke Close,
Wellingborough WN8 7LJ

Wenlock Olympian Society,
N. Wood,
5 Slade Lane, Homer,
Much Wenlock, Shropshire TF13 6ND

West Bromwich Harriers,
J. Buckley,
26 Hall Green Road,
Stone Cross, West Bromwich, Staffs

Westbury Harriers,
P. George,
222 Bloomfield Road,
Brislington, Bristol

West Cornwall AC,
Mrs A. Gwynne,
119 Pendrea Park, North Roskear,
Camborne, Cornwall TR14 8PQ

West Norfolk AC,
Miss H. Matheson,
Whirlow, Wheatley Drive,
North Wootton, Kings Lynn

West Suff
G. Moyes,
43 Westgarth Gardens,
Bury St Edmunds, Suffolk

West Wight AC,
J. Rush,
Lamont House, Norton Green,
Freshwater, Isle of Wight PO40 9RY

**West Yorkshire Track and
Field League,**
F. Midgley, 57 Rein Road,
West Ardsley, Wakefield, W. Yorks

Weymouth St. Paul's Harriers & AC,
Mrs. M. Abery, 41 Buxton Road,
Weymouth, Dorset DT4 9PH

White Horse Harriers,
G.D.Martin,
9 Hardwell Close,
Grove, Wantage, Oxon

Whitworths AC,
M.T. Hall,
170 Kilnway, Queensway Est,
Wellingborough, Northants

Wigan Harriers & AC,
B. Darbyshire,
13 Mendip Avenue,
Winstanley, Wigan,
Gt.Manchester

Wiltshire County AAA,
N. Grist,
17 Churchlands,
North Bradley, Trowbridge,
Wilts BA14 0TD

Winchester & District AC,
Mrs V. Miller,
3 Wessex Drive,
Winchester, Hants SO22 6DQ

Windsor, Slouth & Eton AC,
D. Daly, 11 Carter Close,
Windsor, Berks

Winsford Athletic Club,
B. Hall, 13 Conway Avenue,
Winsford, Cheshire, CW7 1LJ

Winterslow AC,
P.R. Carmen,
19/21 Saxon Leas, Winterslow,
Salisbury, Wilts SP5 1RN

Wirral AC,
P.F. Humphreys,
15 Mount Park,
Bebington, Wirral, Merseyside

Woking AC,
Mrs B. Hourham,
2 Willow Way,
Dartnell Park, West Byfleet, Surrey

Wolverhampton & Bilston AC,
K.J. Evans, 27 Langley Road,
Merry Hill, Wolverhampton, Staffs

Wombwell Sporting Association AC,
Miss V. Tomlins,
144 Aldham House Lane,
Wombwell S73 8RZ

Woodbridge Shufflers Running Club,
J.J. Johnson,
21 Naverne Meadows,
Woodbridge, Suffolk IP12 1HJ

Woodford Green AC,
A.J. Maxwell,
165 Old Church Road,
Chingford, London E4

Woodstock Harriers,
F. Funley, 116 St. Aldates,
Oxford, OX1 1HA

Worcester AC,
Mr Tingle, Greenhill Cottage,
114 Newton Road, Malvern Worcs

World Runners Club,
P. Lloyd, 41 Trinity Square,
London EC3

Worksop Harriers,
P. Randall,
14 Cobwell Road, Retford, Notts

Worthing & District Harriers,
Mrs P. Leeves, Downside,
Stable Lane, Findon, Sussex

Wrexham AC,
R.D. Frost,
The Mount, Sychdyn, Mold, Clwyd

Wycombe Phoenix Harriers,
Phoenix Harriers Club House,
Keep Hill Road,
High Wycombe, Bucks

Wyeside AC,
A. Davies, 8 Kings Drive,
Talgarth, Brecon

Yeovil Olympiads AC,
Mrs E. Adams,
Badgers Wood, East Street,
West Coker, Yoevil, Somerset

Women's Clubs (England)

Barnet LAC,
Mrs L. Elmore,
9 Milton Ave, Barnet, Herts

Bromley Ladies AC,
Mrs D. Reed,
116 Woodland Way, West Wickham,
Kent BR4 9LU

Essex Ladies AC,
Mrs O. Megit,
41 Elmsdale Road,
London E17 6PN f005

Hayes Phoenix LAC,
Mrs P. Valentine,
33 Nicholls Ave,
Hillingdon, Middlesex

Hounslow AC,
Mrs I. Woods,
512 Staines Road,
Bedfont, Feltham, Middlesex

London Olympiades AC,
Mrs E. Nolder,
16 Melrose Close,
Greenford, Middlesex

Merton LAC,
Mrs M. O'Sullivan,
148 Hamilton Ave,
Sutton, Surrey SM3 9DT

Middlesex Ladies AC,
Miss E. Matthews,
91 Abbotts Drive,
Wembley, Middlesex

Parkside LAC,
Mr J. Purnell,
34 Rowlands Ave,
Hatch End, Middlesex

Portsmouth Atalanta AC,
Mrs V. Tubb,
46 Oliver Road,
Southsea, Hants PO4 9BY

Radley AC,
Mrs C. Gale,
Manor Farm, Appleford,
Nr. Abingdon, Oxon

Spartan Ladies AC,
Mr P. Price,
60 Pembroke Road,
London E17

Uxbridge and District AC,
Mr M. Bishop,
47 Stowe Crescent,
Ruislip, Middlesex

Women's Veterans AC,
Miss B. Cushen,
156 Mitcham Road,
West Croydon, Surrey

Northern Ireland

Albertville AC,
J. McCormick,
58 Bray Street, Belfast

Annadale Striders,
J.A. McKnight, 105 Manse Road,
Newtownabbey

Ballydrain AC,
K. Dines, 32 Thornleigh,
Ballydrain, Comber

Ballymena and Antrim AC,
B. Downing, 7 Springway,
Neillbrook, Randalstown

Belfast Ladies AC,
M. Brennan, 40 Deramore Drive,
Malone Road, Belfast 9

Castlederg AC,
D. Loughlin, 109 Strabane Road,
Castlederg, Co. Tyrone

Co. Antrim AC,
D. McAuley, 125 Malone Ave,
Belfast 9

Duncairn Harriers
C. McCullough
16 Lowood Park,
Belfast 15

Duncairn Nomads,
J. Morrow, 11 Carnview Park,
Ballymena, Co. Antrim

East Antrim AC,
K. McAdam, 21 Beech Green,
Doagh, Newtownabbey

Hillville AC,
J. Bradbury, 166 Linne Road,
Larne, Co. Antrim

Laurelhill AC,
Mrs E. McGibbon, 21 Clonevin Park,
Lisburn

Lisnagavrvey AC,
R.J. Wallace, 218 River Road,
Dunmurry, Belfast

Magherafelt and District AC,
B. Holmes, 20 Lissadell Drive,
Magherafelt, Co. Down

Newcastle AC,
R. Rodgers, 155 Central Promenade,
Newcastle, Co. Down

North Belfast AC,
E. McAvoy, 71A Colinward Ave,
Newtownabbey

North Down AC,
Mrs H. O'Neill, Rosemount,
26 Bryansburn Road,
Bangor, Co. Down

Omega AC,
C. Boylan, 68 Craigowan Road,
Carrickfergus

Pyramid AC,
G. McCabe, 4 Wanstead Drive,
Dundonald, Belfast

Shorts AC,
G. Montgomery, 66 Orkney Street,
Belfast

Shorts Ladies AC,
Mrs White,
19 Belmont Church Road,
Belfast 4

Silverwood Cheetahs,
Mrs B. Gourley, 12 Meadowbank,
Craigavon

Sparta AC,
Mrs K. Crilly, 55 Messines Park,
Londonderry

Tailte AC,
Miss R. Atkinson,
17 Willowbank Park, Belfast 6

Ulsterville AC,
G. Wilson, 43 Ainsworth Ave,
Belfast

Veterans AC,
J. Sheridan, 3 Elmfield Crescent,
Glengormley

Willowfield AC,
J. Allen, 87 Cherryhill Road,
Dundonald, Belfast

Scotland

Aberdeen AC,
W.H. Watson,
14 Burnieboozle Place,
Aberdeen AB1 8NL

Annan and District AC,
R. Morgan, 5 Three Trees Road,
Newbie, Annan

Ayr Seaforth AC,
T.G. Harrower,
4 Blackburn Drive, Ayr KA7 2XW

Ayrshire AC,
Mrs C. Gisbey,
2 Berriedale Road,
Barrasie, Troon

Badenoch AC,
R.G. Ritchie Jnr,
Clune Terrace, Newtonmore

Banchory AC,
Mrs J. Thom,
Ennockie,
Finzean, Banchory

Bellahouston Harriers,
C.O. Joss, 76 Hillend Crescent,
Clarkson, Glasgow

Blackhill Harriers,
Mrs A. Thomson,
6 Gun Road, Earlston,
Berwickshire

Bo'ness Harriers AAC,
A. McGregor,
15 Grahamsdyke Road,
Bo'ness, West Lothian

Bute Shinty and AAC,
J.W. Duncan, 11 Barone Road,
Rothesay

Caithness AAC,
J. Cassells,
12 Lythmore Road,
Thurso, Caithness

Cambuslang Harriers
D.W. Yuill, 5 Stanhope Drive,
Burnside, Glasgow G73 5AQ

Central Region AC,
A.R. Booth, 67 Argyle Way,
Dunblane, FK15 9DY

Clyde Valley AAC,
William Marshall, Ross Crescent,
Greenacres, Motherwell, Strathclyde

Clydebank AC,
J. Tonner, 28 Kirkwood Ave,
Clydebank

Clydesdale Harriers
P. Dolan, 16/3 Windsor Crescent,
Radnor Park, Clydebank G81 3AE

Colzium AC,
T. Bolan, 3 Gateside Ave,
Kilsyth

Cowal AC,
Mrs W. Addison,
Dhailling Lodge Villa,
153 Alexandra Parade,
Dunoon PA23 8AW

Dumbarton AAC,
P. Hamill, 61 Whiteford Ave,
Dumbarton G82 3JH

Dunbartonshire AAC,
Dr D.P. Gilmore,
7 Marchmont Terrace,
Glasgow G12 9LS

Dundee Hawkhill Harriers,
A.T. Barrie,
44 Albany Terrace, Dundee

Duns AA and CC,
Mrs M. Cartwright, The Manse,
Swinton, Duns, Berwickshire

East Kilbride AAC,
D.B. Dickson, 1 Deveron Road,
East Kilbride

Edinburgh AC,
R.L. Morris, 33 Morningside Road,
Edinburgh EH10 4DR

**Edinburgh and District
Athletic League,**
P. Brown, 14 Gala Park,
Galashiels TD1 1EX

Edinburgh Southern Harriers,
J.H. Robertson, 49 Ferniehill Drive,
Edinburgh EH17 7AX

Edinburgh Western Harriers AC,
I.E. MacGregor, 36 Drum Brae Drive,
Edinburgh EH4 7BZ

Elgin AAC,
Mrs M.A. Cooke, Ommaroo,
James Street, Lossiemouth IV31 6QZ

Falkirk Victoria Harriers,
D. Markie, 10 Woodhill Court,
Grangemouth

Fife AC,
D.J. Cowieson, 9 Osnaburgh Court,
Cairsie, Cupar, Fife KY15 4SU

Fife Southern Harriers,
R. McGill, 14 Southerton Crescent,
Kirkcaldy

Forres and District AAA,
S. Brander, Kerrera,
Forres IV36 0SX

Forres Harriers,
N. Martin, Divie Lodge,
Logie Estate,
Dunphail, Forres, Morayshire

Gala Harriers,
G. Meikle, 11 Forest Place,
Galashiels, TD1 1JT

Galloway Harriers AAC,
W.B. Hume, Barraer Cottage,
Newton Stewart, Wigtownshire

Garscube Harriers
S. Cullen, 25 Croan Ave,
Glasgow G15 60B

Giruan AAC,
Mrs M. Wallace,
2 Ailsa View, Kirkwood Place,
Giruan

Giffnock North AC,
E.L. Logue, 36 Etive Drive,
Giffnock, Glasgow

Greenock Glenpark Harriers,
W.H. Elder, 60 Belville Street,
Greenock

Greenock Wellpark Harriers,
G.M.Newman, 1 St John's Road,
Gourock, Renfrewshire

Hamilton Harriers,
I. Duffy, 6 Sycamore Grove,
Blantyre

Harmeny AAC,
K.W. Jack, 21 Corslet Crescent,
Currie, Edinburgh

Inverness Harriers AAC,
C.G.F. Bannerman, 6 Dores Ave,
Inverness

Irvine AC,
G. Hannan, 6 Barra Crescent,
Broomlands, Irvine

Kilbarchan AAC,
A.M. Smith, 12 Langside Drive,
Kilbarchan PA10 2EL

Kinlochleven AAC,
J. Anderson, 27 Lovat Road,
Kinlochleven

Kirkintilloch Olympians,
H. Docherty, 22 Applecross Road,
Langmuir Estate, Kirkintilloch

Lanarkshire AAA,
A. Riddell, 15 Wylie Street,
Hamilton

Lasswade AC,
D.L. Goodall, 15 Pendriech View,
Bonnyrigg, Midlothian

Law and District AAC,
Mrs M. Ramage,
238 Wilton Road, Carluke

Linlithgow AAC,
J.D. Fairgrieve, 42 Bellsburn Ave,
Linlithgow, West Lothian

Livingston and District AC,
Mrs E.A. Brody, 18 Corston Park,
Almond West, Livingston

Lochaber AC,
E. Lee, Leesholme,
Cameron Road, Fort William

Longbar AC,
Mrs J. Balmer, 22 Smith Ave,
Glengarnock, Ayrshire

Lothian AC,
A. Cullen, 190C New Street,
Musselburgh, Midlothian

Maryhill Harriers,
T. Harrison, 9 Kirkoswald Drive,
North Drumry, Clydebank

Melrose AAC,
Mrs E. Crawford, Dunkeld,
Fordel Gardens, Melrose

Nairn District AAC,
D.J. Brown, 7A Society Street,
Nairn

Nith Valley AC,
Mrs E. MacClymont,
47 Deerpark Ave, Sanquhar,
Dumfries-shire

North Merchiston AC,
A. Robinson, 2 Braberton Mains,
Bank, Edinburgh EH14 3ED

Orkney Islands AAA,
I.M. Robertson, 94 Victoria Street,
Stromness, Orkney

Paisley Harriers AC,
K.J. Stevenson, 25 Hunterhill Road,
Paisley

Penicuik Harriers,
G. McEwan, 14 West Cairn Crescent
Penicuik

Pentastar AC,
P.C. McAtier, 8B West Court,
Paisley PA1 2XG

Perth Strathtay Harriers,
G. Duncan, 22 Wilson Street,
Perth

Peterhead AAC,
R. Kitchen,
71 Sprinbank Terrace,
Peterhead

Pitreavie AAC,
Miss B. Buchanan, 28 Whitelaw Road,
Dunfermline, Fife

Renfrewshire AAA,
D. McKellar, 7 Palmerston Place,
Johnstone

Ross-shire AAA,
T. Coleman, 19 Clyde Street,
Invergordon

Scottish Marathon Club,
G. McKirdy, 55 Dunedin Drive,
Hairmyres, East Kilbride

Scottish Veteran Harriers Club,
H. Muchamore, 5 Templedean Park,
Haddington EH41 3ND

Shetland AAA,
I.S. Carrick, 14A Commercial Road,
Lerwick, Shetland

Shettleston Harriers,
M. Finbow, 4 Fairholm Street,
Glasgow G32 7QB

Shettleston Harriers (Ladies),
Mrs D. Stephen,
162 Brownside Road, Burnside

Spango Valley AC,
G. Spence, 13 Garve Ave,
Gourock

Springburn Harriers,
W.M.Callan, 9 Heatherbrae,
Bishopbriggs G64 2TA

Sri Chinmoy AC,
B.J. Grassom, 72 Loch Awe Street,
St Leonards, East Kilbride, Glasgow

Stewartry Athletic Club,
Mrs N. Ritchie, 46 Victoria Street,
Kirkpatrick Durham, Castle Douglas,
Kirkcudbright

Stonehouse AAC,
Mrs L. Morrow, 58 Muirhead,
Stonehouse

Strathkelvin Ladies AC,
Mrs L. Gorman,
36 Pinewood Ave, Kirkintilloch

Tayside AAC,
J.L. Ewing, 43 Hill Street,
Monifieth, Dundee

Teviotdale Harriers,
A.C. Douglas, 2 Princess Street,
Hawick

Tweeside AC,
R.J. Wardhaugh,
2 Abbotsford Terrace,
Darnick, Melrose

Vale of Leven AAC,
B. Morrison, 71 McColl Ave,
Alexandria G83 OHQ

Victoria Park AAC,
J. Wallace Crawford,
60 Annan Drive, Bearsden

Westerlands Cross Country Club,
A.S. Brown, 15 Cardowan Road,
Carntyne, Glasgow

National addresses

Men

AAA (England and Wales)
Francis House,
Francis Street,
London SW1P 1DL

Scottish AAA
16 Royal Crescent,
Glasgow, G3 7SL

Northern Ireland AAA
20 Kernan Park,
Portadown,
Co. Armagh

Women

WAAA (England and Wales)
Francis House,
Francis Street,
London SW1P 1DL

Scottish WAAA
16 Royal Crescent,
Glasgow, G3 7SL

Northern Ireland WAAA
Tir na Nog,
Old Calgorm Road,
Ballymena

Regional Associations (men only)

Northern Counties AAA
Studio 44,
Bluecoat Chambers,
School Lane Liverpool L1 3BX

Southern Counties AAA
Francis House,
Francis Street,
London SW1P 1DL

Midland Counties AAA
Devonshire House,
High Street, Deritend,
Birmingham B21 OLP

Welsh AAA
Winterbourne, Greenway Close,
Llandough, Penarth,
South Glamorgan

Specialist Associations

The Road Runners Club
40 Rosedale Road, Stoneleigh,
Epsom, Surrey

The British Marathon Runners Club
5 Priory Close,
Deeping St James,
Peterborough

The Potteries Marathon Club
51-67 Bryan Street, Hanley,
Stoke on Trent ST1 5AF

The Scottish Marathon Club
55 Dunedin Drive, Hairmyres,
East Kilbride G75 8QF

The Fell Runners Association
25 Meadowcroft Cottages,
Bowness-on-Windermere,
Cumbria LA23 3JE

Bibliography and suggested reading

Books:
Aerobics: Dr Kenneth Cooper
(Bantam Books)
The Challenge of the Marathon: Cliff
Temple (Stanley Paul & Co Ltd)
The Complete Book of Running:
James Fixx (Random House and
Penguin Books)
Cross Country and Road Running:
Cliff Temple (Stanley Paul & Co Ltd)
Fitness after Forty: Hal Higdon (World
Publications)
*Guinness Book of Athletic Facts and
Feats:* Peter Matthews (Guinness
Superlatives)
The Marathon Book: Neil Wilson,
Andy Etchells, Bruce Tulloh (Virgin)
The Marathon Guide (annual): 51-67
Bryan St, Hanley, Stoke on Trent
The Road Racer's Guide (annual): 225
Tufnell Park Road, London N19
Run the Lydiard Way: Arthur Lydiard
and Garth Gilmour (Hodder and
Stoughton)
The Runner's Handbook: Bob Glover
and Jack Shepherd (Penguin Books)
The Runner's Repair Manual: Dr
Murray Weisenfeld and Barbara Burr
(W.H. Allen)
Van Aaken Method: Ernst Van Aaken
(World Publications)

Magazines:
Athlete's World: Peterson House,
Northbank, Berryhill Industrial,
Estate, Droitwich, Worcs
Athletics Weekly: 344 High St,
Rochester, Kent ME1 1DT
Marathon and Distance Runner:
Peterson House etc as above
Runner's World: 1400 Stierlin Rd,
Mountain View, California 94043
Running: PO Box 10990, 1508 Oak
St, Eugene, Oregon, 97440
Running Magazine: 57-61 Mortimer
St, London W1N 7TD

How to compare performances over different distances by Rolf Clayton

"Is a marathon in 3 hours better or worse than 10 miles in 1 hour or 20,000m in 1 hour 25 mins?" Most runners are naturally competitive and sooner or later ask these questions. It may be just a desire to know which of your personal best performances is 'the best', or you may want to find out if your best 10,000m time is 'worth' more or less than a friend's best marathon time. The principle of considering times for running different distances to be of 'equivalent merit' or 'equal worth' is well established in the scoring tables used for the Decathlon in which running 100m, 400m and 1500m, are compared directly with each other. Such comparisons are not simple; if you run 100m in 11.0 sec (world record: 9.95 sec) the equivalent 400m time is *not* 44.0 sec, and the equivalent 10,000 time is *not* 11.0 x 100 = 1100 sec, or 18 min 20 sec, since the world record for the distance is 27:22:4!

When comparing men's and women's times, obviously a woman's marathon time of 3 hours is superior to a man's time of 3 hours; but is a man's time of 3:00:00 better or worse than a woman's 3:30:00?

By analysing the performances of men and women runners in 1981 and world records as of 31st January 1982, one can answer these questions. (A marathon in 3:00:00 is slightly worse than 10 miles in 1 hour but better than 20km in 1 hour 25 mins; a woman's time of 3:30:00 for a marathon is superior to a man's 3:00:00.)

The table shows times of equivalent merit (or equivalent worth) for 20 distances. For example, column 20 gives the times of equivalent merit for a 3 hour marathon and is valid for comparing men with men or women with women (but *not* women with men). Thus a 3 hour marathon by a man or a woman is equivalent to 10 miles run in 63 min 45 sec or 5,000m in 18 min 5 sec (by a runner of the same sex).

If you wish to compare a man's time with a woman's time then the following formulae should be used:

	1	2	3	4	5	6	7	8	9	10	11	12	13	14	15	16	17	18	19	20
800m	1:47	1:50	1:52	1:54	1:56	1:57	2:00	2:02	2:04	2:06	2:07	2:08	2:11	2:13	2:14	2:15	2:17	2:20	2:23	2:2…
1500m	3:42	3:46	3:50	3:55	4:00	4:02	4:07	4:11	4:16	4:21	4:23	4:25	4:30	4:34	4:37	4:40	4:44	4:49	4:55	5:…
1 mile	4:00	4:04	4:08	4:13	4:18	4:22	4:26	4:31	4:36	4:42	4:44	4:46	4:52	4:56	4:58	5:02	5:06	5:12	5:20	5:…
3000m	7:50	7:58	8:07	8:16	8:25	8:32	8:40	8:50	9:00	9:11	9:15	9:20	9:31	9:39	9:44	9:50	10:00	10:10	10:25	10:…
2 miles	8:26	8:35	8:45	8:55	9:05	9:12	9:22	9:32	9:42	9:55	10:00	10:04	10:16	10:25	10:30	10:37	10:47	10:58	11:15	11:…
3 miles	13:04	13:18	13:33	13:48	14:02	14:15	14:30	14:45	15:02	15:21	15:30	15:35	15:54	16:07	16:15	16:27	16:40	17:00	17:25	17:…
5000m	13:34	13:49	14:04	14:20	14:35	14:48	15:04	15:20	15:36	15:56	16:05	16:10	16:30	16:45	16:53	17:05	17:20	17:40	18:05	18:…
5 miles	22:40	23:04	23:30	23:56	24:20	24:43	25:10	25:35	26:04	26:37	26:50	27:00	27:34	27:58	28:11	28:30	28:54	29:28	30:12	30:4…
10000m	28:37	29:10	29:40	30:15	30:45	31:15	31:48	32:20	32:56	33:38	33:56	34:08	34:50	35:20	35:37	36:03	36:32	37:14	38:10	38:5…
7½ miles	35:03	35:42	36:20	37:02	37:40	38:16	38:57	39:36	40:20	41:12	41:33	41:48	42:40	43:16	43:38	44:10	44:44	45:36	46:45	47:…
10 miles	47:48	48:40	49:35	50:30	51:20	52:10	53:06	54:00	55:00	56:10	56:40	57:00	58:10	59:00	59:30	60:10	61:00	62:10	63:45	64:…
20000m	1:00:24	1:01:30	1:02:38	1:03:50	1:04:53	1:05:55	1:07:07	1:08:15	1:09:30	1:10:58	1:11:35	1:12:02	1:13:30	1:14:33	1:15:10	1:16:05	1:17:05	1:18:33	1:20:32	1:21:…
½marathon*	1:04:00	1:05:08	1:06:20	1:07:35	1:08:43	1:09:50	1:11:05	1:12:17	1:13:37	1:15:10	1:15:50	1:16:17	1:17:50	1:18:58	1:19:37	1:20:35	1:21:40	1:23:12	1:25:18	1:27…
15 miles	1:13:58	1:15:20	1:16:43	1:18:10	1:19:27	1:20:45	1:22:10	1:23:34	1:25:07	1:26:55	1:27:40	1:28:13	1:30:18	1:31:18	1:32:03	1:33:10	1:34:24	1:36:12	1:38:38	1:40…
30000m	1:33:30	1:35:10	1:36:57	1:38:46	1:40:25	1:42:00	1:43:52	1:45:36	1:47:34	1:49:50	1:50:48	1:51:30	1:53:45	1:55:23	1:56:20	1:57:43	1:59:18	2:01:35	2:04:40	2:06…
20 miles	1:40:50	1:42:40	1:44:35	1:46:32	1:48:20	1:50:03	1:52:03	1:53:55	1:56:02	1:58:30	1:59:30	2:00:15	2:02:43	2:04:28	2:05:30	2:07:00	2:08:40	2:11:10	2:14:27	2:16…
35000m	1:50:22	1:52:22	1:54:27	1:56:36	1:58:33	2:00:27	2:02:38	2:04:40	2:07:00	2:09:40	2:10:50	2:11:37	2:14:18	2:16:14	2:17:21	2:19:00	2:20:50	2:23:33	2:27:10	2:29…
25 miles	2:08:15	2:10:35	2:13:00	2:15:30	2:17:45	2:19:57	2:22:30	2:24:53	2:27:35	2:30:40	2:32:00	2:32:55	2:36:03	2:38:17	2:39:36	2:41:30	2:43:40	2:46:47	2:51:00	2:58…
marathon**	2:15:00	2:17:26	2:20:00	2:22:37	2:25:00	2:27:20	2:30:00	2:32:30	2:35:20	2:38:37	2:40:00	2:41:00	2:44:15	2:46:37	2:48:00	2:50:00	2:52:16	2:55:34	3:00:00	3:03…
30 miles	2:36:04	2:38:55	2:41:50	2:44:53	2:47:40	2:50:20	2:53:25	2:56:20	2:59:35	3:03:23	3:05:00	3:06:07	3:09:55	3:12:38	3:14:15	3:16:32	3:19:10	3:23:00	3:28:05	3:34…

*½marathon = 13 miles 193 yds   ** marathon = 26 miles 385 yds or 42195m or 26.22 miles

= 21 km 975 m

+ average/mile : 4'53"

6'/mile

(man's time) = (woman's time) x 1.2
or (woman's time) = (man's time) x 0.833
or (woman's time) = (man's time) ÷ 1.2

Thus a man's marathon in 4 hours is equivalent to a woman's in 4 x 1.2 = 4.8 hours or 4:48:00; a woman's marathon in 4 hours is equivalent to a man's in 4 ÷ 1.2 = 3.33 hours or 3:20:00.

To calculate equivalent time for a time not shown in the table, you can get an approximate answer by 'interpolating'. For example, if the time for which you wish to have comparisons is mid-way between two times given in the table, then all the equivalent times will be approximately mid-way between all the listed times; if the

available time for a particular distance is one-third of the way between two listed times for the same distance, then you should assume that all the equivalent times are roughly one-third of the way between all the other listed times. Suppose you wish to find out the equivalent times for a half-marathon in 1 hour 50 min. The table gives the following:

half-marathon..... 1:45:18   1:53:45
marathon.......... 3:42:10   4:00:00

The half-marathon time of 1 hour 50 min is found to lie 55.5% of the way between 1:45:18 and 1:53:45. If you add 55.5% of the time-difference between the two marathon times to the first time you get 3:52:04. (The time given by the computer

for a marathon equivalent to a half-marathon in 1:50:00 is also 3:52:04, so only relatively small errors arise by 'interpolating' provided the gap between the times in the table is also relatively small.)

Note: the comparisons cannot take account of such factors as weather, temperature, terrain etc. You must assume similar conditions when making a comparison of times. Also note that comparisons cannot be exact to the last second, especially for longer distances; generally, the figures given are true to within about 1 per cent.

2:28	2:30	2:33	2:36	2:38	2:39	2:41	2:43	2:44	2:46	2:47	2:49	2:52	2:55	2:57	3:11	3:23	3:35	3:47	3:59	4:23
5:05	5:09	5:16	5:22	5:26	5:30	5:33	5:36	5:40	5:43	5:45	5:50	5:56	6:02	6:06	6:35	7:00	7:25	7:49	8:14	9:04
5:29	5:34	5:41	5:47	5:52	5:55	6:00	6:03	6:06	6:09	6:13	6:16	6:24	6:30	6:35	7:06	7:33	8:00	8:26	8:53	9:46
10:45	10:53	11:08	11:19	11:28	11:35	11:43	11:50	11:57	12:03	12:10	12:16	12:31	12:45	12:53	13:55	14:47	15:39	16:31	17:23	19:08
11:35	11:44	12:00	12:12	12:22	12:30	12:38	12:46	12:53	13:00	13:07	13:14	13:30	13:45	13:53	15:00	15:56	16:53	17:49	18:45	20:38
17:57	18:10	18:35	18:54	19:10	19:20	19:32	19:46	19:57	20:08	20:20	20:30	20:54	21:17	21:30	23:14	24:41	26:08	27:35	29:00	31:56
18:38	18:52	19:18	19:38	19:54	20:05	20:18	20:32	20:43	20:54	21:05	21:37	21:43	22:05	22:20	24:07	25:38	27:08	28:39	30:10	33:10
31:07	31:31	32:13	32:47	33:13	33:35	33:53	34:17	34:36	34:54	35:15	35:33	36:15	36:55	37:17	40:16	42:47	45:18	47:50	50:20	55:23
39:20	39:50	40:43	41:25	42:00	42:25	42:50	43:20	43:43	44:06	44:32	44:55	45:50	46:40	47:07	50:54	54:05	57:15	60:26	63:37	70:00
48:10	48:44	49:52	50:44	51:25	51:55	52:26	53:03	53:33	54:00	54:32	55:00	56:07	57:08	57:42	62:20	66:14	70:07	74:00	77:55	85:42
65:40	66:30	68:00	69:10	70:05	70:48	71:30	72:20	73:00	73:38	74:20	75:00	76:30	77:53	78:40	84:58	1:30:17	1:35:36	1:40:54	1:46:13	1:56:50
1:23:00	1:24:02	1:25:56	1:27:24	1:28:36	1:29:30	1:30:21	1:31:24	1:32:15	1:33:04	1:33:58	1:34:46	1:36:40	1:38:25	1:39:25	1:47:23	1:54:06	2:00:50	2:07:30	2:14:14	2:27:40
1:27:54	1:29:00	1:31:00	1:32:35	1:33:50	1:34:47	1:35:42	1:36:50	1:37:43	1:38:35	1:39:32	1:40:23	1:42:24	1:44:15	1:45:18	1:53:45	2:00:50	2:08:00	2:15:04	2:22:10	2:34:24
1:41:37	1:42:55	1:45:14	1:47:02	1:48:30	1:49:35	1:50:40	1:51:56	1:53:00	1:53:58	1:55:05	1:56:04	1:58:23	2:00:33	2:01:44	2:11:30	2:19:44	2:27:57	2:36:10	2:44:23	3:00:50
2:08:26	2:10:03	2:13:00	2:15:16	2:17:07	2:18:30	2:19:50	2:21:28	2:22:46	2:24:02	2:25:25	2:26:40	2:29:37	2:32:20	2:33:51	2:44:12	2:56:35	3:06:58	3:17:22	3:27:45	3:48:32
2:18:32	2:20:18	2:23:32	2:25:55	2:27:54	2:29:25	2:30:50	2:32:36	2:34:00	2:35:22	2:36:52	2:38:14	2:41:23	2:44:20	2:45:58	2:59:17	3:10:30	3:21:40	3:32:54	3:44:06	4:06:31
2:31:37	2:33:33	2:37:00	2:39:42	2:41:53	2:43:30	2:45:06	2:47:00	2:48:33	2:50:03	2:51:40	2:53:10	2:56:38	2:59:52	3:01:40	3:16:13	3:28:30	3:40:45	3:53:00	4:05:17	4:29:48
2:56:10	2:58:25	3:02:26	3:05:34	3:08:06	3:10:00	3:11:50	3:14:04	3:15:50	3:17:36	3:19:30	3:21:13	3:25:15	3:29:00	3:31:03	3:48:00	4:02:15	4:16:30	4:30:45	4:45:00	5:13:30
3:05:27	3:07:48	3:12:02	3:15:20	3:18:00	3:20:00	3:21:55	3:24:17	3:26:10	3:28:00	3:30:00	3:31:50	3:36:03	3:40:00	3:42:10	4:00:00	4:15:00	4:30:00	4:45:00	5:00:00	5:30:00
3:34:25	3:37:08	3:42:02	3:45:50	3:48:55	3:51:13	3:53:27	3:56:10	3:58:20	4:00:30	4:02:21	4:04:53	4:09:47	4:14:20	4:16:50	4:37:28	4:54:50	5:12:16	5:29:30	5:46:50	6:21:31

For further information write to R. Clayton, Sackville Publishing, 32 Great Titchfield Street, London W1

average/mile: 7'18"

average per mile: 9'13"

8'mile

Maximum permitted racing distances — cross-country

Men Age group	Age on September 1 preceding competition	Must not exceed (miles)
Colts	11 & 12	2.5
Boys	13 & 14	3
Youths	15 & 16	4
Juniors	17, 18 & 19 (1)	6
Seniors	20 and over	no limit

Note (1) In open senior races, men aged 17 on the day of competition may race up to 15km (9½ miles); 18 up to 25km (15½ miles); and 19 up to 35km (21¾ miles)

Women		(km)
Girls	11 & 12 (1)	3
Juniors	13 & 14	3.5
Intermediates	15 & 16	5
Seniors	17 and over	17: 15
		18: no limit (2)

Notes

(1) Plus girls aged 11 on the day of competition

(2) 18 or over on the day of competition

Maximum permitted racing distances — road

Men Age group	Ages on April 1 for events April to August; on September 1 for events September to March	Must not exceed (miles)
Colts	12 & 13	2.5
Boys	14 & 15	3
Youths	16 & 17 (1)	4
Juniors	18 & 19 (1)	6
Seniors	20 and over	No limit

(1) In senior open races (ie. when there is not a specific youths or juniors race) the following rules apply for 16 and over:

16 and over on day of race — 15km maximum

17 and over on day of race — 25km maximum

18 and over on day of race — 50km maximum

To run more than 50km men must be 20 or over on the day.

Women	Ages on September 1 preceding event	Must not exceed (km)
Girls	11 & 12	3
Juniors	13 & 14	3.5
Intermediates	15 & 16	15: 10
		16: 15
Seniors	17 & 18	17: 25
		18: no limits (1)

(1) 18 or over on the day of competition.

Note that women's rules are different for road relays as opposed to road races. Finally, these are AAA/WAAA rulings. There are some differences in age groups in Scotland.

Index